The Swiss Equity Market

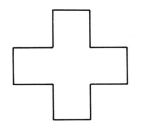

The Swiss
Equity Market

A guide for investors

Edited by
Dr Henri B. Meier

Q

Quorum Books
Westport, Connecticut

Published in the United States and Canada by
Quorum Books, Greenwood Press, a division of
Congressional Information Service, Inc.,
Westport, Connecticut

English language edition, except the United States and
Canada, published by Woodhead-Faulkner Ltd

First published 1985

Library of Congress Cataloging-in-Publication Data
Meier, Henri B.
  The Swiss equity market.

  Bibliography: p.
  Includes index.
  1. Stocks—Switzerland. 2. Stock-exchanges—
Switzerland. 3. Investments—Switzerland. I. Title.
HG5652.M45 1985   332.64'2494   85-12195
ISBN 0–89930–147–9 (lib. bdg.)

Library of Congress Catalog Card Number: 85–12195

ISBN: 0–89930–147–9

Printed in Great Britain

Editor's introduction

The performance of Swiss shares from 1970 to 1984 in real terms was better than that of US shares – despite the fact that the Swiss franc was undervalued in 1984. Nevertheless, the Swiss share is hardly known worldwide, although Switzerland's international capital market is among the largest in the world. Why is it so little known?

Rather than try to discover the reasons for this, we felt that we should do something about it – particularly at a time when shares are becoming attractive investments again, after a decade of non-performance. Trends which had made the share unattractive in the 1970s – such as the growing state bureaucracies, certain wasteful social security concepts and misguided salvage operations for outdated corporations – have been broken in the early 1980s. In mid-1982, a 12-year period when shares were in the doldrums ended. This was a period when productivity increases became smaller and smaller, but when people's claims, 'feathered' by 25 years of steady growth in income, continued to increase. Demands on government for more safety and more protection also continued to grow, but the means to finance them did not. To the extent possible, taxes were raised until hard work was taxed so heavily that it became unattractive to work, invest and produce – just when exceptional efforts were required to innovate and to face the new competition on the international market. One government after another began to practise 'deficit games' or inflation gimmicks. In addition to the tax and social security burden, interest rates increased. Since debt servicing had priority, the shareholder and his dividend took second place. The average share owner became poorer between 1970 and 1982 in real terms. More and more shareholders quit and too little risk capital was forthcoming.

But this has changed, and the share is 'in' again! The newly discovered wisdom that only innovations and new investments create jobs and wealth augurs well for the share of the 1980s, and Swiss shares should fully benefit from the economic reorientation that is taking place wherever market forces are again being allowed to determine the allocation of resources.

Furthermore, certain shares should benefit from the second industrial revolution that is taking place, indicated by the large shifts of labour from one economic sector to another. The shares of corporations whose new products or services cater to the rapidly growing new markets should benefit and show a premium for this innovation.

If an investment history is ever written, the 1980s will probably be characterised as the 'decade of securities', whereas the 1970s would probably be called the 'decade of raw materials' in view of their sharp increase in value, and the 1960s the 'decade of labour'. Today's determination of governments with leading currencies to maintain the value of money by keeping it scarce will again give paper investments a chance of satisfactory returns. And the Swiss share, which has traditionally ber.efited from a low-inflation currency, should be no exception to this.

But the Swiss stock market tends to react rather slowly to good as well as bad news. A study by Bank Vontobel (March 1985) estimates the profit increase of 102 Swiss corporations, whose shares are listed in the Zurich Stock Exchange and account for 99% of total stock exchange capitalisation, at 30% for the year 1984 and 15–20% for the year 1985. The same study calculates dividend increases at 11% in 1983 and 15% each for 1984 and 1985. The stock price index increase for 1983 (24%) and 1984 (2%) only reflects the dividend increase of 1983 and 1984, but does not anticipate the 1985 results. For the five-year period 1980–84, corporate profits increased by an estimated 120%, dividends by 62%, but stock prices by only 50%, pushing the p/e ratio down from 13 to 9.

The object of this book is to familiarise the English-speaking reader with the peculiarities of Switzerland's equity market. It first gives a short historical perspective, noting that the Swiss contribution to the development of the share as a finance instrument had been very small. But having observed the experience of other countries, Eugen Huber – the ingenious 'father' of the most important Swiss laws – produced a masterpiece of a civil law code which also deals with the share in a way that is unique in its clarity and conciseness. The historical review also points out that important trends detrimental to equity markets were broken in Switzerland in the mid-1970s and early 1980s, namely the increase of the share in gross national product (GNP) of the Swiss federal government's expenditures and the social security schemes. It also notes the changing role and influence of the shareholder in Switzerland and the issues currently being debated in connection with a proposed revision of the share law (Aktienrecht).

The second chapter reveals the surprising performance of the Swiss equity market, which never hits headlines but by continuous, gradual gains emerges with a rather impressive record. This chapter also investigates the main determinants of share price cycles, with money supply again in the cross-fire.

The following chapters (3–9) are organised in such a way that they can easily be used for reference purposes:
- Chapter 3 presents a brief description of all the stock exchanges of Switzerland, their history, organisation and significance.
- Chapter 4 describes the various types and forms of shares and share-like securities traded on the Swiss capital market. The description is not limited to

the legal nature of these securities and to Swiss peculiarities; it also examines their function and actual market significance.

- Chapter 5 concentrates on the procedures, problems and costs involved in the issue of new shares.
- Chapter 6 contains the information a dealer requires regarding procedures and costs, trading hours, and types of transactions, as well as quotation lists and samples of individual billings. It also describes actual dealing at a Swiss stock exchange.
- How to list a share on a Swiss stock exchange is the subject of Chapter 7.
- Chapter 8 is addressed to foreign investors, dealing with their tax situation, legal restrictions upon transfer of shares and the implications of Swiss banking secrecy.
- The following chapter and Appendix 1 are for the investor who is ready for business: a presentation of Swiss accounting principles and the interpretation of Swiss accounts (Chapter 9), and an analysis of the shares of leading Swiss companies. The most surprising aspect to most foreigners is the fact that Swiss law does not allow an overstatement of assets but tolerates understatements leading to the famous secret reserves of Swiss corporations.

The organisation of the book's chapters permits the reader to zero in on one issue or problem, guided by the table of contents; he or she is not forced to read everything to participate effectively in the benefits of the Swiss equity market. And whereas this market cannot be all things to all men, there are situations like today when an undervalued Swiss franc and a restructured full-employment economy offer above-average opportunities in the framework of a trustworthy legal and political system.

HandelsBank NW   Henri B. Meier
Zurich
September 1985

Contents

Notes on contributors

Dr Henri B. Meier (*Editor*), born 1936, member of HandelsBank's Management Committee, is also the author of the first book on the Swiss capital market, as well as of many publications and studies on international finance, marketing and development economics. He is one of a few prominent Swiss international bankers who writes from a broad base of experience outside the banking sector (General Accountant, Williams Brothers, South America; member of the management team of Motor Columbus Consulting Engineers). Writing – a hobby on flights and during holidays – was taken up while travelling extensively for the World Bank in Washington, which he joined as a young professional, leaving as a Division Chief in 1973.

Dr Urs W. Benz holds the academic titles of Dr jur. of the University of Zurich and MCL of the University of Chicago. An attorney-at-law, his professional practice includes work with the District Court of Zurich and the Federal Court in Lausanne, as well as with a large trust company in Zurich. Since 1981, he has headed the Legal Department of HandelsBank NW.

Theo Bütler, born 1956, studied economics and business administration at the University of Zurich, where he received his MBA. Since 1981, he has worked for HandelsBank NW in various functions, including foreign exchange and portfolio administration. He is now in charge of the Financial Futures and Options Department.

Heini P. Dubler, born and educated in Zurich (Swiss Commercial School, Zurich), has been active for more than 15 years in international investment banking. He has served in various capacities with major international banks in New York, London, Bermuda and Zurich. He is a Vice-President of HandelsBank NW, heading the Foreign Currencies New Issues Department. He is also responsible for Special Investment Transactions and venture capital business.

Jean-Pierre Frefel, born 1948 in Basle, holds a Swiss Commercial Association diploma. He spent more than a year and a half at different stock exchanges (Brussels, Chicago, New York) and started as a securities dealer at the Basle Stock Exchange in 1969. He joined HandelsBank NW, Zurich, in 1972. He is a Vice-President in charge of the Securities Trading Department.

Dr Alexander F. Galli, born 1945, has been chief economist and Senior Vice-President at HandelsBank NW, Zurich, since 1980. He previously spent eight years in economic research at the Swiss central bank (National Bank of Switzerland). He studied at the University of Basle (1966–71) and at Carnegie-Mellon University, Pittsburgh (1975–76); he obtained a doctorate in economics from the University of Basle in 1978. He is the author of several works on Swiss monetary affairs.

A. Pauchard, a financial analyst, studied a humanities programme at Sir George Williams College, University of Montreal. He undertook a four-month trainee programme with Dominick & Dominick, New York, and completed a course in securities analysis. He is a member of the Swiss Society of Financial Analysts and a member of the commission concerning information flow to shareholders, a leading commission of the SSFA.

Pier-Luigi Quattropani, born 1944, obtained his basic professional training at the Kantonale Handelsschule, Zurich, where he received his diploma. He has been in banking since 1963 and in the securities industry since 1965, where he has spent most of his professional life. He is Senior Vice-President of HandelsBank NW, in charge of securities dealing, securities placing and securities administration.

1 History of the Swiss equity market

Dr Henri B. Meier

In spite of the fact that Switzerland is the highest per capita share-trading country in the world, its historical contribution to the invention and evolution of the share as the decisive financial instrument in the economic development of the West has been close to nil. The principal reason for Switzerland's delay in developing and using the share was its absence from colonial adventures, when the main features of the share were created.

Because of the influence it had on certain legal structures in medieval Italy, such as the *montes*, the *maonae* and the *comenda*, historians argue that the share was created from a seed sown in Roman times when the Societas Vectigalium became part of Roman law. However, those elements in Roman law that are thought to show a resemblance to today's corporate share could have been found in almost any association created to perform economic activities.

The first clearly identifiable predecessor of today's share was recorded in the Netherlands in the seventeenth century. It was here that the name *Actien* (which later became *Aktie* in German and *Action* in French) was coined in connection with the formation of the Dutch East India Company on 27 February 1610. One year later another clearly identifiable root of today's share was created with the issuance of 'joint stock' by the British East India Co. The rough initial profile of the early share was structured, defined, redefined and polished in the following centuries, mainly by shipping and trading companies in the Netherlands, Britain, Denmark, Sweden and France. Its development was hastened, no doubt, by the discovery of South-east Asia and the Far East. In this era of colonisation by European powers, the share became an ideal instrument to raise risk capital for financing ventures in distant places. Once its usefulness in collecting large amounts of savings had been proved, this 'non-security' became the decisive instrument for financing industrialisation and for raising the huge sums needed to fund the construction of Europe's infrastructure.

Switzerland's first exposure to this revolutionary instrument, the 'share', was in the nineteenth century, during the period of industrialisation and construction of the first modern infrastructure – particularly railways. Before the nineteenth century, major funding efforts took place in the context of families, clans or communities. Switzerland's large capital exports at that time were mainly in the form of loans by Swiss cities. Major economic efforts, especially in the field of mutual exploitation of natural resources, were undertaken in the framework of co-operatives (rather than joint-stock corporations). It was only the construction of the first Swiss railways in the middle of the nineteenth century that made the share popular in Switzerland. So mammoth were the funding requirements of this project that neither the families nor the cities were sufficiently wealthy to meet them.

By the time of the Swiss railway construction boom, the share and the joint-stock corporation had been largely defined by many foreign laws and their revisions, and tempered by a long experience of misuse, scandals and bankruptcies. In addition, the main characteristics of the share and the corporation had been elaborated and refined in other European countries. The French Code de Commerce of 1807 and the German corporate codifications (e.g. the Prussian law on joint-stock companies of 1843) and Austrian laws were particularly advanced in this area. Switzerland also benefited from its long domestic experience with traditional co-operative societies.

All the main characteristics of this financial and investment instrument, the share, were present by the middle of the nineteenth century:
1.   Participation in the joint-stock share capital of a clearly identifiable legal entity.
2.   Limitation of an individual's liability to his contribution to the share capital.
3.   Transferability of the share.
4.   Marketability (bearer shares).
5.   Profit participation.
6.   Owner's rights, voting rights, etc.
7.   Separation of shareholders' rights from management functions.

The absorption and digestion of foreign thinking and experience in the legal systems of the Swiss cantons, each of which had its own laws and rules regarding shares, occurred in the decades before 1881 when the first national commercial law, the Obligationenrecht (OR), was promulgated. This legislation and its subsequent codification were masterpieces in terms of their clarity of concept and thought, their simplicity of wording and their high ethical standards. They were concise, understandable and, to this day, are unique and unchanged in their essence. The articles dealing specifically with the share and the joint-stock company remained largely unchanged until 1936, when the authentic *Swiss* share, growing out of Swiss conditions, needs and convictions, was created. This revised version has lasted for almost 50 years, and it was during this period that the joint-stock company (*Aktiengesellschaft, société anonyme*) became the most important legal entity in the Swiss economy; in 1980, it accounted for 43% of all registered companies. In spite of this success, changes in the rules governing joint-stock companies have always been debated.

In the course of Swiss equity market history, political attitudes towards shares and the corporations behind them have vacillated between a mood sympathetic to investors and a position favouring management, the board of directors or the interests of the national economy. As in most other countries, reforms of the respective laws have been requested at regular intervals to codify the prevailing and somewhat transient convictions of the day. Fortunately, the creation of new Swiss laws has usually taken so long that fashionable short-lived views have tended to be outdated by the time the new law was ready to be promulgated. (The work for the draft law on shares referred to in this book was begun by a commission in 1968 and had still not become law by mid-1985.) On the whole, a finely tuned long-term balance, reflecting all the various substantial interests, has resulted.

Over the past few decades, certain basic trends and beliefs which have negatively affected the attractiveness and effectiveness of the share have persisted – although they have been somewhat less pronounced in Switzerland than in comparably developed countries. All these trends could be summarised under the heading 'flight to protection'. If one can generalise, this is an inherent part of the growth pattern or life cycle of all developed nations' capital markets. Once a country reaches the stage where its financial markets are performing their basic function (i.e. channelling funds from ultimate savers to ultimate investors), and once it has passed the threshold of providing citizens with adequate living standards, its focus of concern changes. The creation of new wealth gradually, but unmistakably, loses ground to the protection of existing wealth. Consequently, legislation is passed to guarantee these safeguards. Bureaucracies are created to enforce the rules. Taxes are raised to support the bureaucracies and, in general, corporate and market efficiency suffer. It is this trade-off between growth and protection that has played and will continue to play a role in shaping Switzerland's capital market environment.

The most significant trend with the most drastic long-term consequences has been the belief that the 'state' can correct any evil. This idea still persists, long after the acceptable limits of bureaucracies' inefficiencies have been passed. The state, through new laws, has been overloaded with tasks and control functions. Quite often, these laws and regulations, particularly in the finance sector, were implemented at the request or pressure of other countries' excessive bureaucracies. Such bureaucratic zeal has inhibited not only the efficiency of corporations but also the efficient trading and issuing of shares.

Equally important, to cover the costs of performing these tasks, the state needed more and more taxes; corporations had to participate in funding these requirements, which affected their profitability. Fortunately, however, around the mid-1970s, the growth of the Swiss federal government's expenditure as a percentage of GNP came to a standstill, and with it an important factor that had prevented growth in share values.

The third basic trend has been the excessive desire for protection against all economic risks, as expressed, for instance, in the rapidly growing social security system in the period 1960–80. Since the cost increase for funding this system was faster than the productivity increase, it inhibited the possibilities of corporate earnings and helped keep share prices during the 1970s on about the same level. While it is very unlikely that the relative share of social security costs will increase further, few doubt that the sharp expansion of the social security system has had the double effect of absorbing savings that could otherwise have been used for productive investments and reducing the attraction for the remaining savings to go into such investments. Today there is a growing conviction that only productive investments in a healthy economy (rather than insurance schemes!) able to finance research and innovation can protect against the risk of economic decline. This new conviction regarding taxes and the 'relative security' of social security systems augurs well for the share of the 1980s.

The fourth basic trend, prevailing everywhere except perhaps Japan, is the tendency to protect existing money-losing corporations and help them to survive rather than to build new ones. Although originally conceived to safeguard employment, this attitude has had the opposite effect and is partly responsible for a lower-than-possible standard of living. To channel new money to old, established, loss-generating corporations with good-sounding names is usually more acceptable than to invest in new ventures. Politicians are inclined to acknowledge that the interests and influence of known employees and unions are always stronger than those of the unknown beneficiaries of future corporations. There seems to be an in-built psychological defence mechanism against accepting the obvious, i.e. that corporations should die when the services they provide cease to be demanded. Shares of such crippled corporations usually have been withdrawn too late from trading and have damaged the record of the share.

The complexities of modern-day technology, the sophistication of business practices and the host of bureaucratic interventions have given rise to a continuous shift in power away from shareholders to management. Switzerland has not escaped this movement and there seems to be no reverse trend in sight. Most investors are interested basically in the financial results and find no time to supervise or influence the management of companies from which they have bought shares.

The delegation of the power of attorney to custodian banks has not changed this basic trend. This lack of shareholder influence has had at least one drawback, especially with profitable companies in saturated markets. Rather than return surplus cash flows to the shareholders and give them the liberty to invest or consume, such corporations have used the surplus cash to buy other companies – often in different economic sectors – and to form conglomerates which have seldom shown above-average yields.

More important, a further trend has put into question the original concept of shareholder influence, whose function it should be to allocate financial resources optimally. After the Second World War, the broader distribution of income, the corresponding creation of wealth and the birth of a large number of investment-hungry pension funds caused the number of investors to increase dramatically. Parallel to this trend there has been an even faster growth of investment opportunities, both domestically and internationally. How can a shareholder possibly follow the record of a corporation in which he has invested? Does this diversification not preclude any serious company analysis?

After the Second World War – the period during which a true international financial market developed in Switzerland – legal concepts and systems of foreign countries, mainly the United States and the European Community countries, again began to exercise considerable influence on the thinking in Switzerland concerning legal aspects of the share. Partly because of this influence from abroad and partly because of the structural changes in the ownership of shares within Switzerland, reform movements arose. The purchasing spree of US corporations in Europe, encouraged by the overvalued dollar in the 1950s and 1960s, brought about as a protective reaction the introduction of the *vinkulierte Aktie*, a registered share that needed the approval of, for instance, the board of directors for its transfer to a new owner. The *Mehrstimmaktie* again had the purpose of maintaining a voting majority of Swiss shareholders but often also of the founding members or any other interest group.

In the 1960s and 1970s, most European countries reformed their respective joint-stock company laws, and the Council of the European Economic Community issued guidelines to co-ordinate national laws for the purpose of warranting the free establishment of corporations in all member countries. Furthermore, the ministers of the OECD countries issued a declaration in 1976 which, among other things, requested from multinational corporations specific information and publicity.

Beginning in the late 1950s and all through the 1960s and 1970s, reform proposals were also presented in the Swiss Parliament and study groups/ commissions were nominated to examine the defects of the 1936 norms, as well as the recent experience of other countries. On 23 February 1983, the Federal Council of Switzerland presented to the Federal Assembly the new draft law, which in mid-1985 was still being debated and studied. It will not surprise those familiar with the Swiss environment that no revolutionary changes are being proposed, but mainly adjustments which should have been made a long time ago – except perhaps for the treatment of the 'hidden reserves', which has become a rather controversial issue. There was, of course, no change proposed that did not find opposing voices, but the opposition's strength for each item is not sufficient to prevent passage. An eternal issue in any small country is the controversy over *disclosure versus secrecy*. Even in compiling national statistics this is a problem, because in certain sectors of a small economy there is just one large company whose performance can be inferred from consolidated figures. In such instances of controversial debates one is surprised again and again by the powerful voices of the 'nationalistic minority' in the middle of a highly internationalised economic community. A glance at Switzerland's most important shares shows that the underlying assets or income of corporations are abroad, and it would be difficult to argue that they should be reserved for the Swiss.

The most important changes of this draft law, while maintaining the traditional principles, are as follows:

1. Publication of better information about the financial position and the earning situation of a corporation, including accounting principles, minimum requirements regarding information, classification and presentation; publication of the balance sheet as well as the profit and loss statement, and the introduction of compulsory consolidation for conglomerates.

2. The famous 'hidden reserves' of Swiss companies continue to be permitted,

but to a more limited extent. Under the newly proposed rules, the liquidation of 'hidden reserves' must be made public.

3. Improved protection for the shareholder, not only through more and better information, but also by relaxing the restrictions in by-laws regarding the transfer of normal shares (*Vinkulierung*), by the protection of shareholders' rights to the acquisition of newly issued shares (*Bezugsrecht*) and by facilitating the execution of shareholders' rights to take legal action (*Klagerecht*).

4. Maintenance of the organisational structure of the joint-stock company (shareholders' meetings, board of directors, management, audit) and the functions of the various bodies as originally perceived. Recognising that shareholders are often unable to participate in general assembly meetings, the possibilities of expressing their will is improved (*Depot und Organvertretung*). The banks' voting on behalf of shareholders has been a political issue in Switzerland for quite some time. Therefore, the draft law requires that votes given by banks (*Depotstimmen*) be exactly stated in the protocol. Proxy voting is also to be regulated. The main duties of the board of directors are clearly defined, as well as preconditions and consequences of delegation of responsibility. Nobody can, for instance, accept more than ten mandates as a member of boards of publicly quoted corporations. The professional standards and requirements for auditors are also increased.

5. Misuse and criminal acts are to be prevented by specific norms regarding the founding of joint-stock companies and the increase in share capital. Specific regulations are to be introduced for: the purchase of a corporation's own shares; share exchanges between corporations; minimum capital (SFr 100,000) and minimum paid-in capital; and approved and conditional capital increase, the latter mainly for facilitating the issue of convertible bonds and notes.

6. First-time introduction of a draft law that includes the certificate of participation (*Partizipationsschein*), an instrument developed by the market (rather than through legislation) and representing only financial rights, but no voting and similar corporate rights. It is basically a non-voting share, which has a significant position in Switzerland's capital market.

Among the draft law's curiosities is one of interest to students in management sciences. It mentions certain duties of the board of directors which cannot be delegated. Among these are approval and arrangements referring to finance planning, accounting, and finance control. If interpreted too narrowly, Switzerland might soon have a shortage of board members.

Looking back, the history of the Swiss share has been a relatively short one – just over 100 years – due to Switzerland's abstention from colonisation and its tradition and experience with co-operative forms of economic organisations. Once the share became a necessary tool for raising the huge funds for railway building, Switzerland could benefit from other countries' experience with the share. Once a truly Swiss share had been created in the mid-1930s, the joint-stock company became the prevailing corporate organisation and the share the most important risk capital instrument. Following the post-Second World War growth period (early 1970s), it gradually lost its attraction for the investor due to rapidly increasing 'internal protectionism', including the tax and social security burden. Around the turn of the decade 1970–80, a worldwide recognition that it took profits and investments to further increase the standard of living also conquered Switzerland. And while the tax burden on the economy as a percentage of GNP had stopped growing in the second half of the 1970s, the recession of the early 1980s also tempered new claims for higher social security contributions. This worldwide trend to cut taxes and bureaucracies should make shares much more attractive in the 1980s than they were in the 1970s.

2 Influences on the Swiss equity market

Alexander F. Galli

The stock market's function in the economy

In Switzerland as well as in other countries, stock prices climbed dramatically from summer 1982 to spring 1984, with share price indexes rising in some countries by more than 50%. Stock prices, particularly in the United States, began rising while unemployment rates in many countries were still high and economic activity still low. This might appear paradoxical; however, for many people stock prices are a reliable leading indicator of economic activity. In the United States and to some extent also in Switzerland, the increase in stock prices has, indeed, been followed by a marked cyclical economic upswing.

Stock prices not only signal future changes in economic activity; they may also have a direct impact on spending and investment decisions. This impact is caused by the so-called wealth effect of stock price movements. Thus, for instance, the rise in US stock prices in 1982–83 increased household wealth by about $500 billion. Such an increase should induce consumers to increase their spending, with positive effects on the economy. This applies not only to consumer spending but also to investment spending on plant and equipment. In 1983, when the equity market soared, equity funding had a renaissance too – following a period when companies had relied mostly on debt financing. The renewed increase in corporate equity improved the stability as well as the credit rating of companies.

The stock exchange thus plays an important role in the economy. The key functions of this market are the valuing of securities and the provision of a well-run market-place where investors can buy and sell shares. The valuation of shares and bonds is important as it provides signals for the allocation of capital. Investment funds are thus channelled towards those companies that make the most profitable and expedient use of the capital. The allocation function of share prices is very important in a free market economy; therefore well-run market-places like Zurich's Stock Exchange are the *sine qua non* for dealing with shares. Only in such places can share prices be valued correctly.

If share prices are to be correctly valued and the stock exchange is to work, a perfect market is needed. The major requirements of such a market are: homogeneity of the goods; many buyers and sellers; the freedom of entry and exit; unlimited supplies of stocks; and finally, shares and perfect knowledge about the shares. In Zurich and in other major stock exchanges of the world, the first four requirements are met. In particular, there is homogeneity of goods: one ordinary share of Nestlé confers the same rights as any other share of Nestlé. The fifth condition, perfect knowledge, requires that all knowledge relating to the value of a company must be known by market participants and that this knowledge must be accurately reflected in share prices. Obviously, this requirement is not met. However, the major stock exchanges have managed to provide reasonable pricing. This chapter deals with the volume of the Swiss equity market, and the pricing and development of share prices on the Swiss stock exchanges.

Market volume

There are no exact statistics available on the Swiss equity market. The data published by the Swiss National Bank refer only to new public issues of shares and to some new private placings. A further source of information can be found in the publications of the stock exchanges. In their annual reports, the stock exchanges publish figures on trading volume, share prices, listed securities, etc. However, information on the trading of shares outside the stock exchanges is not available.

To demonstrate the importance of the Swiss financial market in an international comparison, the trading volume of the Zurich Stock Exchange is very often used. However, the calculation of this volume is not precise, so that the trading volume of shares at the Zurich Stock Exchange has been estimated.*

The estimated volume of the equity market (see Fig. 2.1) rose from SFr 1.5 billion in 1950 to SFr 92.5 billion in 1984, more than a sixtyfold increase. Noteworthy is the increase since 1970. In this period the volume climbed from about SFr 11 billion to SFr 92.5 billion. The considerable expansion in the volume of the equity market was possible because in the period under observation the total monetary sector was also growing rather quickly. Total assets of all banks in Switzerland rose from SFr 30 billion in 1950 to SFr 630 billion in 1983.

Of some interest is the annual growth of the equity market. As can be seen in Fig. 2.2, the annual growth rate of the equity market fluctuated quite heavily. However, this was more or less in line with the liquidity situation in Switzerland as well as with economic development. But Fig. 2.2 also shows that even during periods of liquidity squeeze and economic slowdown, the market grew at a high speed. This was mainly due to an expansion of the issue of new shares, which had a strong impact on the equity market.

On the Swiss equity market, a relatively large share of traded equities is of

* To eliminate double counting, the published trading volume is first divided by two. Secondly, it is assumed that only about 60% of the total trading volume involves transactions in shares. This assumption is based on the number of quoted domestic and foreign shares on the Zurich Stock Exchange.

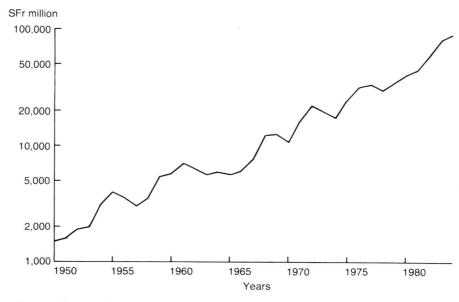

Fig. 2.1   Trading volume on the Zurich Stock Exchange
Source: Zurich Stock Exchange, Annual Report.

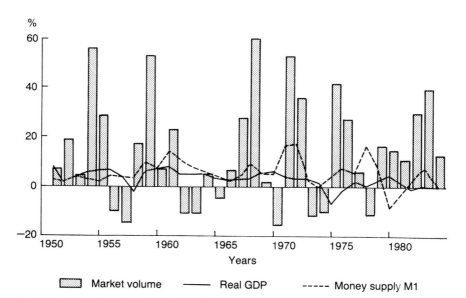

Fig. 2.2   Growth of the Swiss equity market: percentage changes
Sources: Zurich Stock Exchange, Annual Report; Swiss National Bank, Monthly Bulletin.

foreign origin. In recent years about 60% of total quoted shares at the Zurich Stock Exchange were foreign shares. In the 1960s and early 1970s this ratio of foreign shares was even higher. The most important countries in the Swiss equity market are the United States, Canada, West Germany and the Netherlands. Domestic shares traded on the Swiss equity market originate from different business sectors. However, most numerous are the shares of industrial and transportation companies (see Table 2.1).

Table 2.1 Number of quoted shares at the Zurich Stock Exchange

Sector and country	1981	1982	1983	1984	Percentage distribution average (1980–84)	
Domestic shares	66,193	66,484	96,437	87,312	40.8	
Banks	12,324	12,174	13,601	15,422	6.9	
Finance companies	17,766	19,396	34,395	26,224	12.6	
Insurance	6,648	6,358	7,320	7,348	3.6	
Industrial, transportation	25,564	24,633	37,200	34,129	15.7	
Trusts	3,891	3,923	4,049	4,189	2.1	
Foreign shares	101,072	95,031	129,472	132,882	59.2	
United States, Canada	72,374	70,475	91,111	93,930	42.3	
West Germany	7,090	7,481	13,608	11,864	5.2	
Other countries	21,608	17,075	24,753	27,088	11.7	
Total shares	167,265	161,515	225,909	220,194	100.0	55.0
Total bonds	129,110	165,055	170,132	169,689		45.0
Total securities	296,375	326,570	396,041	389,883		100.0

Source: Zurich Stock Exchange, Annual Reports 1981–84.

Factors affecting share prices

A discussion of variations in the share price index becomes more meaningful if we consider the reasons for stock prices being a leading indicator. There are of course several views as to why movements in stock prices generally precede changes in real economic activity. According to a traditional view, the price of some stock equals the present or discounted value of expected future dividends. Under this assumption stock prices rise because of higher expected corporate earnings. A lower required rate of return used by investors to discount future earnings may also cause higher share prices.

Stock prices, however, will fall immediately if market participants expect a deterioration of corporate profits because of a prospective economic downturn. In this case share prices would decline before the actual fall in corporate earnings and general economic activity. Because expectations of future corporate profits can be erroneous, however, the stock market could send false signals about future economic fluctuations.

Uncertainty about future profits of a company or expectations of higher returns on other assets may also lead to a reduction of stock prices. This fall in stock prices could be followed by an economic downturn too, because increased uncertainty about the future and/or higher real interest rates discourage investment plans and thus may depress the economy with some time lag. In both cases the share price index would act as a leading indicator of business cycles.

The stock markets also reflect in some way the confidence of investors in the economy and political institutions. This so-called psychological element is very often cited in connection with stock markets. Stock prices begin to rise when people decide the economy is improving and are thus willing to make new financial investments, even in rather risky assets. In this case, it is the state of confidence rather than a forecast of higher corporate earnings that moves share prices and finally the economy upwards.

Another view on stock prices as a leading indicator was developed by some monetary theorists. Following their argument, changes in the supply of money have strong impacts on the economy as well as on stock prices. Stock prices, however, react more quickly to expected changes in the economy than does the real economy. Therefore, the stock price index may play the role of a leading indicator.

Factors determining Swiss share prices since the Second World War

Selection of a share price index

In Switzerland the first share price index was established in 1910. This index was calculated by the Swiss Bank Corporation. In the 1920s the Swiss National Bank and the Swiss Bank Corporation agreed that only one index, calculated by the central bank, should be published. The share price index of the Swiss National Bank is printed in its monthly bulletin. This index includes the share prices of the Stock Exchanges of Zurich, Basle and Geneva, and is representative of the whole Swiss equity market.

In the period 1927–68, the share price index of the Swiss National Bank was never basically changed. However, this index lost some of its representative value during periods of equity capital increases by companies, because the index was showing strong share price rises only very moderately. As a result, in 1968 the Swiss National Bank decided to revise the old index.

The new index, available from 1966 onwards, is adjusted by taking out special factors causing unwanted index movements. Included in the index were about 100 companies which had issued 117 securities (registered and unregistered shares). The number of companies as well as the number of shares has changed from time to time in order to catch market variations. The total index comprises 11 different sub-indexes of the industrial and services sectors.

Although the Swiss National Bank index is very valuable for analytical purposes, it is not widely used in the market – the main reason being its unavailability. The index is calculated only once a week and published only on a monthly basis. Therefore, several other indexes for the Swiss equity market are calculated and published daily. The most important ones are those of Crédit Suisse and the Swiss Bank Corporation. The Crédit Suisse index is compiled in the same way as the Dow Jones Index, comprising only 25 unweighted equities. This index has been available since 1963. The index of the Swiss Bank Corporation (SBV-Index) is built on a much broader basis. It includes 90 shares on the Stock Exchanges of Zurich, Basle and Geneva. The index is published daily and is available in the afternoon of each trading day. This index is most widely used in securities trading. Apart from the aggregate index, the Swiss Bank Corporation also works out a share price index for the banking sector, the insurance companies, the engineering sector, the chemical industry, the consumer sector and utilities. In the following sections the Swiss National Bank index is used because it is available for the whole period after the Second World War.

Development of the share price index (1945–84)

The share price index of the Swiss National Bank is shown in Fig. 2.3. The index shows a strong cyclical pattern and an upward trend as well. The *lowest* turning points of the several cycles increased from about 35 index points (average 1966=100) in March 1945 to 140 in October 1981. Thus, an investor with exactly the same titles in his portfolio as are included in the index would have quadrupled his wealth in nominal terms over the period, at the worst. Even in real terms the portfolio's worth would have increased by 25%.

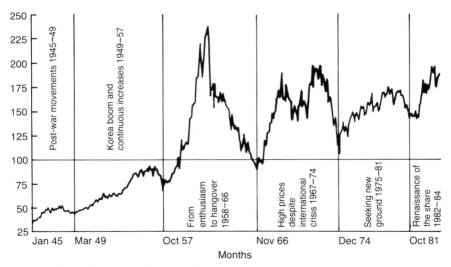

Fig. 2.3   Swiss share price index, 1945–84
Average 1966 = 100.
Source: Swiss National Bank, Monthly Bulletin.

The upward movement of the share price index since 1945 reflects two sides of the Swiss economy: on the one hand, it is obvious that inflation had a strong impact on the equity market; on the other hand, the upward trend in real terms may also give some indication that real wealth has expanded considerably in the past 40 years. On the following pages the development of share prices since the end of the Second World War will be discussed. In order to make the discussion somewhat easier, the 40 years are divided into several subperiods. The beginning and end of a subperiod are determined by troughs in the share price index. As can be seen in Fig. 2.3, there are six such subperiods, each characterised by a particular event which had a strong impact on the Swiss equity market.

The whole period starts with the post-war economic upswing (1945–49). The second cycle was the result of the Korean War boom, which induced a long period of increasing share prices (1949–57). The liberalisation of international capital flows as well as the first international monetary crisis characterise the third subperiod (1957–66). The fourth period is determined by the beginning of international economic instability and the breakdown of the Bretton Woods monetary system (1967–74). In the 1970s the world economic system was battered by two oil-price shocks and therefore was seeking new ground (1975–81). Finally, since 1982 share prices worldwide have climbed to new heights. The Swiss equity market was also influenced by foreign factors, which will be discussed in the final section of this chapter.

Share price movements immediately after the Second World War (1945–49)

Immediately after the Second World War, share prices started to move upwards and trading expanded considerably on all Swiss stock exchanges. From March 1945 to September 1947, share prices rose by about 50%. After this date the share price index began to fade out and reached its lowest turning point in March 1949, some 17% below the peak in 1947 (see Fig. 2.4).

The main forces of share price development originated in the business cycle, which showed a more or less coincident pattern. The repeal of the war laws and war restrictions in the course of 1945 induced a strong economic upswing as well as a run on the stock market. This was very much in contrast to the end of the First World War, which was followed by economic and political disaster. The new international organisations like the United Nations and IMF, and of course the financial aid from the United States (which became the Marshall Plan in 1948), had a positive impact on the world economy and world trade.

In Switzerland all demand components of GNP except government expenditure accelerated in growth. Capital and goods exports showed a strong recovery. Unemployment, which caused some problems during the war years, fell drastically. Unfortunately, the price level started to rise too, particularly after 1947, when import prices began to increase as a result of the abolition of price controls in the United States.

Economic policy and particularly monetary policy did not contribute much to share price behaviour and the economic recovery. However, fears about an overheating of the economy and about inflation urged the Swiss National Bank

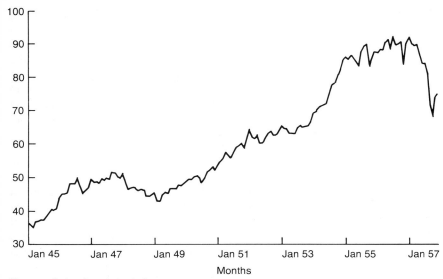

Fig. 2.4 Swiss share price index, 1945–57
Average 1966 = 100.
Source: Swiss National Bank, Monthly Bulletin.

and the government to take appropriate measures. With the help of several restrictions, the Swiss National Bank tried to limit the inflow of capital and the creation of credits. The tightening of monetary and economic policy in 1948–49 had a dampening effect on the economy and on the stock market.

During almost the whole of 1948 the stock market was more a buyer's than a seller's market. However, this was partly caused by the New York Stock Exchange, which also showed a rather weak performance in 1948. The main reason for this stagnation was the increased tension between West and East after the war. Interest rates were nearly stable in this period. The government bond yield fluctuated between 3% and 3½%. The official discount rate remained at 1½% during the whole period. Swiss interest rate moves and changes in money supply were not significant and therefore had no strong impact on the stock market.

The Korean War boom and continuous share price increases (1949–57)

The weakness of the stock market was brief, and in March 1949 the share price index started a very long upward movement. Indeed, between March 1949 and January 1957 the share price index rose rather steadily by about 10% per annum. From January to October 1957 share prices fell quite steeply, by about 30% (see Fig. 2.4).

Different factors influenced the stock market in 1949. Worth mentioning is the rather high liquidity, which had a positive impact on general securities trading. The depreciation of the pound sterling in September 1949 shocked the market for a short while only, and prices soon started to rebound. Also important was the economic development in Switzerland, which ended in a recession in 1949. However, the recession was short-lived, and because economic conditions were favourable in other countries, most market participants expected higher economic growth and particularly higher corporate profits.

The outbreak of the Korean War in June 1950 caused a strong worldwide economic upswing. The Swiss economy fully participated in this recovery. This can best be demonstrated by the development of imports in the period May 1950 to March 1951. In these ten months import value grew by 61%. However, the Korean War boom was brief, and in 1952 was followed by a new recession.

The stock market reacted only slightly to the deceleration in economic growth. From March 1949 to December 1952 the annual growth rate of the share price index was 11%, but fell to 4.7% in 1953. The main factors that prevented a setback of share prices in the aftermath of the Korean boom were, on the one hand, the expectation of investors and of the export industry that the measures taken by the government to dampen imports and exports were only temporary. On the other hand, the Swiss National Bank supplied enough liquidity to the market, and there was some excess supply and a lack of investment possibilities on the bond market. Despite the economic slowdown, trading volume at all stock exchanges in Switzerland grew rather rapidly.

In 1954 the share price index rose by 27%, indicating a strong economic recovery which started in the middle of 1953 and ended in June 1957. In the years 1954–56, real GNP rose by a rate of 5.5% annually. This favourable economic environment had a positive impact on the stock market. Also positive was the effect originating from monetary policy, which was rather easy at that time. Moreover, an important impulse came from the liberalisation of the foreign exchange markets. Although full convertibility was introduced only in 1958, capital inflows began to play an important role in the Swiss economy in the mid-1950s.

In 1954 the new Swiss National Bank law came into effect giving the central bank the right and the possibility to actively influence the money and capital markets. However, the fight against the capital inflow and its inflationary consequences was at that time possible only through credit controls. Open market operations under a fixed exchange rate regime were hardly feasible. In the mid-1950s the Swiss National Bank also introduced the so-called Gentlemen's Agreement with the banks in order to hold back capital imports. It is quite obvious that a large part of the foreign capital had been invested in the Swiss stock market, thus reinforcing the surge of stock prices.

In 1955–56 share prices rose at an annual rate of only 3.5%. In this period the government imposed a rather tight monetary control which caused some liquidity squeeze. But at the same time the upward pressure stemming from Wall Street had a strong influence on the Swiss stock market. Only the political situation and the nationalisation of the Suez Canal by Egypt in 1956 caused some minor setbacks.

In 1957 the business cycle reached its upper turning point. It was the end of a period of strong domestic demand and huge imports, particularly of investment goods. For the first time since the Second World War, the current account balance showed a deficit and caused a significant reduction in liquidity. And for the first time since 1936 the Swiss National Bank increased the official discount rate, from 1.5% to 2%. This measure, as well as the deficit in the current account, contributed to the liquidity squeeze and therefore also to the moderate recession in 1958. Share prices reacted strongly and fell by about 30% in the course of 1957. The drop in share prices was much stronger in Switzerland than in other countries.

Since 1950 the Swiss National Bank has published a complete set of monetary statistics. In Fig. 2.5 the growth of the adjusted monetary base and the share price index are compared for 1951–57. The impact of monetary policy on the stock market was usually not very strong in the 1950s. Only in 1953 did the increase of the monetary base by about 10% create a favourable situation, which led to the rocketing upward movement of share prices in 1954. The growth of money supply M_1 was rather modest in those years too, and did not increase share prices substantially. The rather strong economic growth was thus the major force behind the continuous increase in share prices from 1949 to 1957.

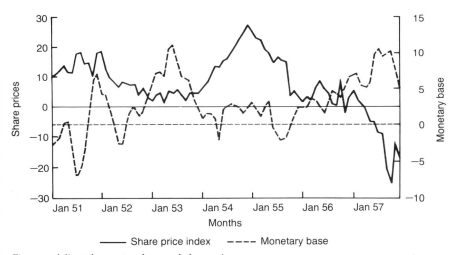

Fig. 2.5   Adjusted monetary base and share prices, 1951–57: year-over-year percentage change
Source: Swiss National Bank, Monthly Bulletin.

The 1960s: from enthusiasm to hangover (1957–66)

This steady increase in share prices came to a sudden end in 1957. However, by November of that year they surged up again and reached their all-time high in February 1962. During this period the share price index increased at an annual rate of 29%. After these four years of fast upward development, share prices fell continuously until November 1966. During that time the index decreased at a rate of 21% per annum. This development was unprecedented in the industrialised countries (Fig. 2.6).

The cause for the booming stock market between November 1957 and

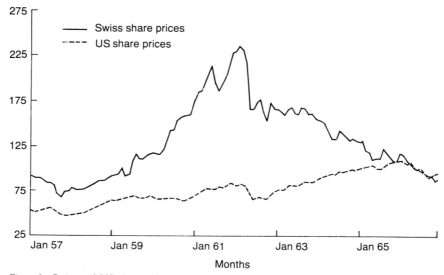

Fig. 2.6   Swiss and US share prices, 1957–66
Average 1966 = 100.
Sources: Swiss National Bank, Monthly Bulletin; OECD, Main Economic Indicators, 1984.

February 1962 was the rebound of the US economy and the US stock market. Although in Switzerland the recession continued until the middle of 1958, share prices already reached their pre-recession level towards the end of that year.

Apart from the developments in the United States, there were two main reasons for the price rise. On the one hand, the easy monetary policy and the reduction of interest rates on the capital market created a favourable environment for the stock market. On the other hand, capital inflow again became an important factor for the liquidity situation. In particular, the introduction of free convertibility of currencies in 1958 and the new economic co-operation in Europe (EEC, EFTA) led to positive expectations with respect to economic growth, not only in Switzerland but in all industrialised countries.

Whereas on foreign stock markets the upswing faded out in the course of 1959, in Switzerland it gained momentum towards the end of the year. Indeed, there were considerable structural shifts among the investors on the stock market. Worth mentioning are the investment trusts, which expanded their activities enormously towards the end of the 1950s in a still rather narrow stock market. Moreover, the economic expansion induced the establishment of new joint-stock companies in Switzerland as well as abroad. The number of quoted shares therefore increased on all Swiss market-places during those years. Heavy trading and high-flying prices for old and new shares were typical of the years 1961 and 1962, when all records were broken. From December 1960 to December 1961 the share price index soared by 42%, thus encouraging everyone to invest in shares.

Why was there such a bull market? Very important was the capital inflow in

1958 as well as in 1960–61. At the end of the 1950s capital mobility was guaranteed in most countries of the Western world. It was thus possible for the reduction in US interest rates, and the war and political unrest in the Middle East, to cause a huge capital inflow into Switzerland. The Gentlemen's Agreement between the Swiss National Bank and the private banks to stop such imports was repealed in March 1958. In addition, in 1958 foreign trade produced only a small deficit due to sluggish economic activity; thus the current account balance turned out to be in huge surplus.

In 1960–61 the easy US monetary policy caused interest rates to fall considerably and induced a capital outflow towards Europe, particularly into Switzerland. The expansionary US monetary policy put increasing pressure on the exchange rate of the dollar. That of course also led to speculative money flows into the Swiss capital market: as a consequence, the Swiss National Bank again imposed measures on banks against accepting foreign capital inflows. However, the speculation against the US dollar and the pound sterling was so strong that the Deutschmark and the Dutch guilder were revalued in 1961. Money also flew towards Switzerland because of the Berlin crisis. Since this capital import occurred in periods of fixed exchange rates, the Swiss National Bank was forced to increase the domestic money supply, thus providing the capital market with excess liquidity. The rather strong correlation between the growth of the money supply $M1$ and the share price index is shown in Fig. 2.7. In 1959–60 the expansion of liquidity stagnated because of interest rate increases abroad.

The spring of 1962 saw the start of a hangover which seemed never-ending in Switzerland. The primary cause of the setback in share prices was again a sudden fall in prices on Wall Street, which induced many investors to sell in order to

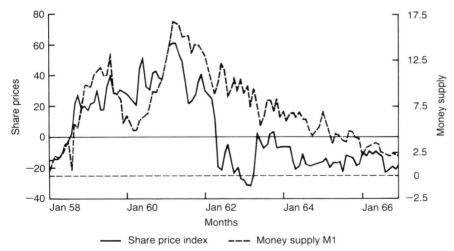

Fig. 2.7 Growth of money supply $M1$ and share price index, 1958–66: year-over-year percentage change
Source: Swiss National Bank, Monthly Bulletin.

rescue their profits. The downward movement was quite impressive. From February to May 1962 the Swiss share price index fell by 30%.

Starting at that date uncertainty was the dominant force on the stock market, thus holding price fluctuations to a very limited scale. From May 1962 to November 1963 share prices were practically stagnant, with a slight downward trend. This was in contrast to share price increases in New York, where prices started to soar again at the end of 1962 and continued to do so until the beginning of 1966. In Switzerland prices began to fall steadily in November 1963, soon after the assassination of US President Kennedy. This trend persisted until November 1966. During this period the index fell at an annual rate of nearly 20%.

The widespread uncertainty had political as well as economic causes. The Cuban crisis in October 1962 sustained the bear market. More important for the rather long downward trend was monetary policy (see Fig. 2.7). In April 1962 the Swiss National Bank imposed tight credit controls and stiffened the controls against capital inflow. As can be seen in Fig. 2.7, the growth rate of the money supply M1 fell steadily from about 16% in 1961 to around 2–4% in 1965–66. These measures were taken because inflation, which had already started to pick up in 1960, became more and more virulent as time went on.

The tight monetary policy not only caused a reduction of real GNP growth in the years 1962–66, but also had a negative impact on the stock market. Moreover, the fact that interest rates rose from around 3% in 1961–62 to about 4% or more in 1966 increased the attraction of alternative investments. Reduced economic activity lessened the expectation of higher corporate profits and therefore also contributed to the downward trend in share prices. Five years of sinking prices discouraged investors and kept more and more individuals out of the stock market. In addition, the financial return on equity was rather low in the 1960s. Therefore, after 1962, when there was only a low probability of making a profit with share price increases, investors were not at all stimulated to buy shares. The tax burden also made shares somewhat unattractive during those years.

High prices despite an international monetary crisis (1967–74)

During the period 1967–74, the world economy was shaken by several far-reaching political and monetary events. Nevertheless, the Swiss stock market reacted more favourably than stock markets in financial centres outside Switzerland. With the exception of the Tokyo Stock Exchange, Swiss share prices showed the best performance in the years 1967–74. However, this was very much the result of the low base caused by the bad performance in 1962–66.

The turning point of the share price index was November 1966, when share prices were at about the same level as in 1958. From 1966 to October 1969 prices nearly doubled, rising at an annual rate of 23%. Then in the next 12 months prices fell by 20% – but rebounded in 1971–72 and reached their highest level in January 1973. From November 1970 to January 1973 share prices increased by an annual 15%. In 1973 prices fell sharply and at the end of 1974 were half what they were at the beginning of 1973.

In 1966 a strong cyclical upswing of business activity began in the United States, which had positive effects on world trade as well as on the stock market. In

Switzerland all restrictive policy measures were abolished in spring 1966. Thus foreign money flew into the capital market and contributed to the fast rise in share prices during 1967. It also became more and more evident that the economic recovery was gaining ground in Switzerland, which of course stimulated potential investors to return to the stock market.

Despite the various restrictive measures previously in force, inflation peaked in 1966 at nearly 5%, which was the second highest level in the period under report. Interest rates at that time were rising too. However, the inflation rate was even higher, and thus the real interest rate was negative. Investors therefore became increasingly convinced that only shares would protect the capital value of a portfolio. Under these conditions, market participants found their way back to the stock market.

Monetary policy in 1967–68 was rather easy; thus the adjusted monetary base as well as the money supply M1 were expanding with high rates (see Fig. 2.8). As in former years, capital imports played a key role in the money supply process. There was series of events at the end of the 1960s which caused foreigners to invest their money in Swiss francs. Those worth mentioning include the fact that interest rates rose to a level to make 'Regulation Q' effective in the United States, which was one of the main reasons for creating the Eurodollar market and also the flow of funds into Switzerland. The speculation against the pound sterling in late 1966 had the same effects. Then there was the six-day Israeli–Egyptian War; the repeal of the gold pool in 1968, which led to the *de facto* abolition of the gold convertibility of the US dollar and which in 1971 was followed by the *de jure* suspension by the US President; and the change in the dollar parity of the French franc and the Deutschmark in 1969. It was rather quiet in 1970 but much less so in 1971.

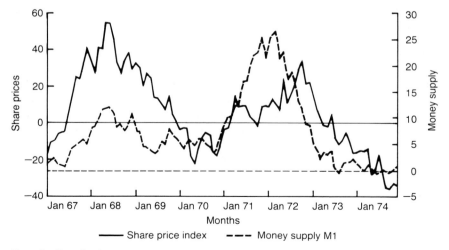

Fig. 2.8   Growth of money supply M1 and share price index, 1967–74: year-over-year percentage change
Source: Swiss National Bank, Monthly Bulletin.

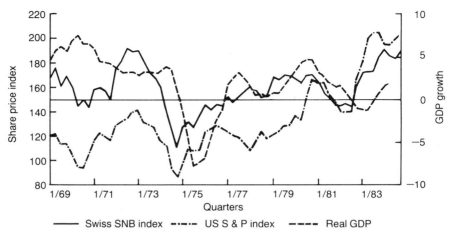

Fig. 2.9   Share prices and economic growth, 1969–84
Indexes: average 1966 = 100. Growth: year-over-year percentage change.
Sources: OECD, Main Economic Indicators, 1984; Swiss National Bank, Monthly Bulletin; Federal
Office of Statistics, Wirtschaftsspiegel, 1984.

The Swiss franc was revalued by 7% in 1971, which was, however, not at all enough. Therefore only a small portion of speculative capital left Switzerland in 1971. From August 1971 exchange rates floated until the introduction of the Smithsonian Agreement in December 1971. However, foreign exchange markets remained volatile, and in January 1973 the fixed exchange rate system of Bretton Woods broke down for good. Switzerland and most industrialised countries introduced a flexible exchange rate system. Finally, the oil price hike of 1973 (from 1972 to 1974 oil prices rose by more than 400%) ended a long period of rapid economic growth in the Western world.

In those years (1971–73), Switzerland suffered huge capital inflows; this led to an excessive money supply, especially in 1971, which stimulated the economy as well as the stock market. Particularly in the housing construction sector, it created excess demand leading to an acceleration of the rate of inflation. Together with increased oil prices this caused Switzerland's highest inflation rate, on the whole, after the Second World War.

The oil price shock of 1973, the high inflation rate and the very restrictive monetary policy caused one of the most severe recessions experienced in Switzerland. Workers had to be laid off and unemployment suddenly became a problem. In 1975 real GNP fell by 7.7%

During these years (1972–74) the stock market also suffered from precarious economic conditions. In the stock market comments on 1974, this year is referred to as a 'black year'. Indeed, share prices fell by more than 50% and were again down to the level of the 1960s (see Fig. 2.9).

Seeking new ground (1975–81)

Compared with the 1950s and the 1960s, economic growth was rather limited in the 1970s. The transition from a fixed to a flexible exchange rate system caused many more problems than previously envisaged. That magic power to solve economic difficulties had evaporated. Industrialised countries had to learn to live with higher energy prices, which brought many structural changes in all economic sectors. This also caused higher production costs and lower profits. In the OECD countries the growth rate of real GDP dropped from 5% in the 1960s to 2% in the 1970s. That of course had a negative impact on the stock market. On average, Swiss share prices increased by only about 4% annually.

As can be seen in Fig. 2.10, the growth of the money supply M1 again had a dominant influence on share prices. Only in 1975 and 1978 was there a significant divergence between the share price index and money supply growth. Whereas in 1975 share prices increased by about 30% and the money supply by only about 5%, in 1978 the money supply grew by more than 20% and share prices stagnated. In both years special factors were at work.

In 1975 some modifications of the Swiss stock market took place. The 'big three' banks issued new restricted transferable registered shares. Unlike most Swiss companies, these banks previously had only bearer shares outstanding. The Swiss federal government recommended that they issue registered shares in order to enable them to maintain ownership control.

The battle against inflation turned out to be successful in 1976. The inflation rate fell from 11% to 1.3%. Low interest rates stimulated the share market; thus trading at the Zurich Stock Exchange reached an unprecedented volume of more than SFr 100 billion. Stock prices were, however, not subject to extreme

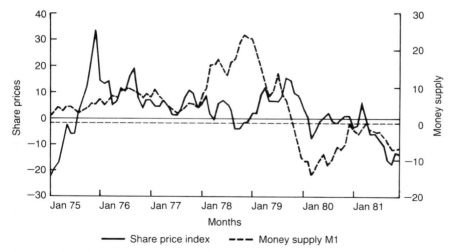

Fig. 2.10 Growth of money supply M1 and share price index, 1975–81: year-over-year percentage change
Source: Swiss National Bank, Monthly Bulletin.

fluctuations. At the end of the year, the stock price index was only 5% higher than 12 months earlier.

In 1977 money and capital markets were characterised by low interest rates and the increasing volatility of the Swiss franc exchange rate. Nevertheless, the relatively healthy condition of the Swiss economy had positive effects on the stock market. Trading volume again increased considerably and the stock price index rose once more by 5%.

By any standard 1978 was a bad year for the stock market. Not only did trading volume fall by 12% and stock prices decline slightly, but for the first time since the Second World War the number of securities listed on the Zurich Stock Exchange was reduced in the course of the year. The main reason for this development was the extreme revaluation of the Swiss franc. As the US dollar fell to SFr 1.80 late in February 1978, the Swiss National Bank, together with the federal government, imposed a ban on investment in Swiss securities by persons living outside the country.

Regulations were very stringent. Non-residents selling Swiss shares or bonds were not allowed to reinvest this capital in the stock market. Since they were also forced to pay a 40% commission charge on new deposits in banking accounts in Switzerland, the only reasonable alternative was to export the capital. The investment ban was relaxed on two occasions during 1978 and lifted in January 1979.

The investment ban had significant effects on the equity market but completely missed the main objective, namely the stabilisation of the Swiss franc exchange rate. Therefore, the Swiss National Bank had to intervene very heavily in the exchange market, which pushed the growth rate of the money supply M1 up to more than 20% instead of 5%, the target set for 1978. But despite the excessive liquidity supply, the stock market's performance was, due to the investment ban, rather discouraging.

After the price decline in 1978, share prices rebounded in 1979. Due to favourable economic conditions (see Fig. 2.9) as well as to optimistic forecasts, the excessive liquidity in the banking system, and the abolition of the investment ban in January, in 1979 the stock market was favourable for investors. The stock price index rose by 8% until the end of the year. However, the index reached its peak in early October, which was a six-year high. But the performance was not overwhelming, considering the high liquidity and fine economic prospects.

Switzerland's economy performed unexpectedly well during 1980. However, the inflation rate, which had picked up in 1979, rose to 7.5% in the course of 1981. The second oil price hike in 1979 and the excess supply of money in 1978 pushed the inflation rate up. As a consequence, the Swiss National Bank and the central banks in other countries introduced restrictive monetary policies (see Fig. 2.10). Thus both short-term and long-term interest rates began to climb to new heights. But not only did interest rates rise; they also became extremely volatile in 1980 and 1981. In the United States the prime rate was set at 21.5% at the beginning of 1981. Although Swiss interest rates also rose in those years, there was still a very large difference between Swiss and US interest rates – more than ten percentage points. During both years there was a substantial capital flow from Switzerland into dollar-denominated securities.

The increase in interest and inflation rates, the restrictive monetary policy, and the first signs of a worldwide economic recession had a negative impact on equity markets. Although security trading on the Zurich Stock Exchange reached a new peak in 1981, the performance of share prices was discouraging. After the small increase of 3.4% in 1980, share prices dropped by 15% in 1981. With the exception of Canada, Tokyo and Brussels, all leading stock exchanges suffered considerable price drops in 1981.

Renaissance of the share (1982–84)

As in most industrialised countries, the Swiss economy had a fairly bad start into the 1980s. Both 1982 and 1983 were disappointing from an economic point of view (see Fig 2.9). In 1982 real GNP fell by about 1.2%. In 1983 the growth rate was around zero, although a recovery started in the second half of 1983 and led to a growth of about 3% in 1984. The unexpectedly strong economic upswing in the United States, which had already started in 1983, had a positive impact on all countries and led to strong export growth. This was caused mainly by the foreign value of the US dollar, which began to move upwards in 1980.

In the first nine months of 1982 the stock market was still under the influence of the severe recession in the United States and the extremely high interest rates. In August 1982 share prices on Wall Street were at their lowest level since the silver crisis in spring 1980. But the US Federal Reserve then turned its monetary policy around and let the money supply grow at a very high rate. This induced a sudden fall in interest rates and stimulated the stock market – marking the beginning of the renaissance of the share.

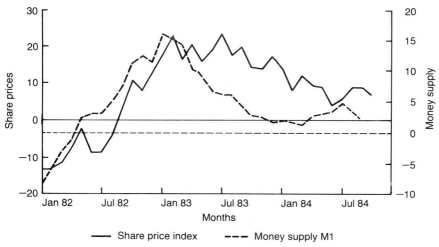

Fig. 2.11 Growth of money supply M1 and share price index, 1982–84: year-over-year percentage change
Source: Swiss National Bank, Monthly Bulletin.

Whereas from October 1981 to September 1982 share prices rose by only 2.4%, they shot up by 15% to the end of 1982 and soared another 17% in the course of 1983. This was the highest level since the early 1960s (see Fig. 2.3). In 1984 share prices did not show large movements but remained at the high level they had reached in 1983. The high-flying US dollar exchange rate, the relatively high interest rates and some fears of a renewed recession in the United States in 1985, were the main determinants of the flat price movement.

Monetary policy more or less supported the share price movements (see Fig. 2.11) in 1982. Subsequently the policy was more restrictive and therefore there was no excess liquidity on the money and capital markets. As a result, interest rates were not as low as some forecasters had expected. Thus alternative investments were successfully competing with shares.

An international comparison

In Fig. 2.12 the Swiss share price index is compared with share price indexes of some other financial centres. Up to the beginning of the 1970s all share price indexes showed a very similar pattern. However, in 1972 Tokyo, and in 1977 London, started a much steeper upward trend which has not yet come to an end. Swiss and US share prices did not diverge strongly from one another. It is therefore interesting to look somewhat more closely at these two indexes.

In Fig. 2.13 the Swiss share price index is compared with Standard and Poor's Composite share price index. Both indexes are inflation-adjusted and corrected for exchange rate effects. As the graph shows, in the long run it would have been only of slight importance whether a one-time investment had been made in the

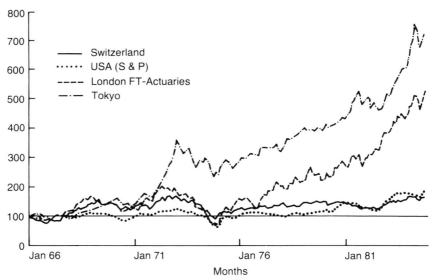

Fig. 2.12   International comparison of share prices, 1966–84.
Average 1966 = 100.
Source: OECD, Main Economic Indicators, 1984.

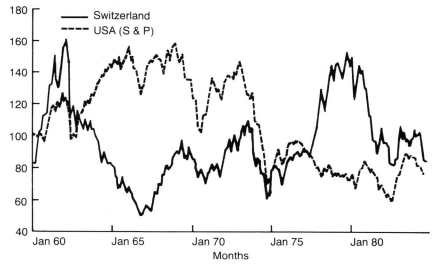

Fig. 2.13   Comparison of Swiss and US share prices, 1966–84
Inflation- and exchange-rate-adjusted 1960 = 100.
Sources: Swiss National Bank, Monthly Bulletin; OECD, Main Economic Indicators, 1984.

shares of one country or the other. However, for short-term investments, the differences would have been considerable. In the 1960s and at the beginning of the 1970s, share prices were significantly higher in the United States than in Switzerland. The contrary was true in 1977–82, the period of the strong revaluation of the Swiss franc. In 1984 the indexes moved together again.

Conclusion

In Switzerland as well as in several other countries, the equity market is to some extent a reflection of the economic situation. The share price index seems to be a particularly accurate indicator of future economic development. However, in periods of erratic economic and political movements, the signals from the share price index can be wrong. Most striking is the dominant influence of monetary policy since the beginning of the 1960s, with the increasing impact of foreign capital on the Swiss capital market. During the first 15 years after the Second World War, international capital flows were still strongly regulated and thus did not influence the Swiss capital market. Since the end of the 1950s, however, the correlation between money supply and share price movements has been surprisingly close.

In the 1970s the equity market appeared to lose ground as the leading financing instrument for companies. Investors preferred short-term time deposits to shares in periods of high and volatile interest rates. But developments in the 1980s have made it obvious that shares are still attractive if the economy progresses on a more or less stable path. Economies of the Western world are moving in this direction, which has contributed to the renaissance of the share.

3   The organisation of Swiss stock exchanges

Pier-Luigi Quattropani

The Association of Swiss Stock Exchanges

The Association of Swiss Stock Exchanges was founded in the late 1930s for the purpose of co-ordinating the co-operation among the stock exchanges in Switzerland. It also represents Switzerland within the Fédération Internationale des Bourses de Valeurs (International Federation of Stock Exchanges).

Members
The Association of Swiss Stock Exchanges is formed by the stock exchanges of:
– Basle
– Geneva
– Zurich
– Berne
– Lausanne
– Neuchâtel
– St Gall
(Lucerne, which has a very small stock exchange, is not a member.)

Organisation
The regulatory and supervisory bodies of the Association are:
(a)   the General Meeting (assembly of delegates),
(b)   the Executive Committee, and
(c)   the auditors.
   The *assembly of delegates* is composed of members of the boards of the various Swiss stock exchanges.
   The five *executive committee* members are elected by the assembly of delegates. Only one representative from any of the Swiss stock exchanges is eligible for membership of this committee. The stock exchanges of Basle, Geneva and Zurich are entitled to a seat on the executive committee.

Tasks and duties

Among the regular tasks of the Association are:

(a) acceptance of new stock exchanges as members, and

(b) decisions on rules and regulations changes, etc.

The Association's important duties are defined in its statutes as follows:

1. The Association must take all possible measures to promote and expand the securities business at the stock exchanges.

2. The Association takes an active role in establishing the rules which govern the admission of foreign securities for listing at the Swiss stock exchanges.

3. The Association may also safeguard the interests of the owners of securities, either alone or in co-operation with other organisations.

In order to carry out the second of the duties mentioned above, the executive committee nominates stock exchange representatives to sit on the Swiss Admission Board for Foreign Securities (Schweizerische Zulassungsstelle für die Kotierung ausländischer Wertpapiere).

The Association also establishes the commission structure (Agreement on Commission Rates or *Courtage-Konvention*), which stipulates the minimum commissions binding on all stock exchange member firms.

The Swiss stock exchanges

Although the individual Swiss stock exchanges are of differing natures, either governed by cantonal legislation or acting as private institutions, they have a number of things in common, as outlined below.

Rules

On all stock exchanges, essentially the same rules governing the conduct of business are adopted and applied.

Dealing system

In Switzerland the so-called *à la criée* system is used in stock exchange dealing. Prices are fixed and transactions concluded by open auction, establishing loudly and clearly the bid, asked and closing prices. To facilitate the dealers' job and the traders' actions, the vocabulary and special terms are tightly regulated and clearly defined.

Commissions

As already noted, the Swiss stock exchanges have agreed on a fixed commission structure (*Courtage-Konvention* – Agreement on Commission Rates). The minimum rates fixed in this agreement must in all cases be applied by all stock exchange member firms throughout Switzerland.

Settlements

All transactions effected through any of the Swiss stock exchanges are settled in the same way, mostly through SEGA (Schweizerische Effektengiro-AG), the

Swiss clearing system for securities transactions. It is also understood that the same value date is applied throughout the country.

The importance of the Swiss stock exchanges
Looking at the different stock exchanges in Switzerland it is easy to realise that their importance varies substantially. Taking into consideration the role they play, there are three distinct types, which are as follows:

1. *Stock exchanges with an international character.* These include the stock exchanges of Basle, Geneva and Zurich.
2. *Local stock exchanges with some international exposure.* Berne and Lausanne fall into this category.
3. *Local exchanges.* These comprise the stock exchanges of Neuchâtel, St Gall and, the smallest, Lucerne.

The Basle Stock Exchange

History of the Basle Stock Exchange

In Basle the existence of so-called *Sensale* or *Courtiers* can be traced back to the year 1683. Their business was to act as brokers or intermediaries for transactions in commodities or bills of exchange. Over the years the regulations governing the work of these *Sensale* were changed several times by governmental decree. On 12 March 1855, the first official regulations regarding dealing in securities were published (Sensalen-Ordnung vom 12. März 1855). By this legal act the groundwork for transactions in securities was laid, although broking in securities still represented a minor part of the *Sensale*'s functions.

A next step towards the foundation of a stock exchange was made in November 1866, when the Basler Börsenverein came into being. It was a merchants' association, meeting daily between 11.00 a.m. and 12.00 to exchange information, discuss trade matters and decide on rules. At the very beginning of this association no bankers or industrialists participated, but very soon the *Sensale* frequented the gatherings of the merchants regularly. The growth of the capital market in Basle, evidenced by a flow of new bond and equity issues, led to increasing interest in securities dealing. This resulted in the printing of an official quotations list starting 1 January 1870.

After the war between Germany and France in 1870–71, the demand for investment possibilities grew considerably, and dealing in securities became still more important. In view of these events, the need for an efficient market-place for securities transactions was accentuated. With the decision of the government of Basle that the *Sensale* regulations still in force were no longer up to date, and based on a change in the Constitution of the Canton of Basle regarding freedom of enterprise, private initiative taken by the *Sensale* on the one side and seconded by the bankers on the other side brought about the draft of statutes for a stock exchange using the *à la criée* system. Following this step it was only a matter of months until the organisation of the stock exchange was completed, with dealing beginning on 1 July 1876.

The success of the exchange was encouraging, and in 1880 Basle was already a leader in bond dealing. Soon the rising volume called for more space, and in September 1880 the market moved to new premises. By that time the Stock Exchange Association counted 44 members, of which 29 were allowed to have a seat on the exchange. The year 1891 marked the beginning of a transition period during which the voices for more government control became louder. It took all parties involved until 1897 to reach an agreement regarding the future of the Basle Stock Exchange, and in April of the same year a law was passed which put the stock exchange under the jurisdiction of the Canton of Basle. On 2 January 1898 the first trading session under the new law was held.

Another milestone was marked in January 1908, when the stock exchange moved into new premises because of rising business transactions. The securities market developed well during the following years, but its further evolution was halted by the First World War. The stock exchange was closed at the end of July 1914. At the end of 1916 trading resumed and the market returned more or less to normal. During the following years with their ups and downs, the stock exchange continued its positive course.

Nothing dramatic happened at the Basle Stock Exchange during the Second World War, except that the exchange had to be closed for a few weeks during May and June of 1940. In 1944 a revision of the stock exchange law decreed that all securities transactions, whether effected through the exchange or in the free market, needed a dealer's licence. During the next decades the Basle Stock Exchange continued to prosper. It was the first stock exchange officially to list closed-end investment funds, in 1960–61, followed by open-end funds in 1972. In 1973 a second *Ring*, or trading area, was inaugurated, on which trading in bonds took place. The changes in the securities business and the continuous internationalisation of the securities markets called for another revision of the stock exchange laws, which was effected in 1982. As a result of the ever-growing securities market and the increasing volume in securities transactions, the Basle Stock Exchange, as a next important step in its future development, will move into a new Stock Exchange building by 1986. This will inaugurate the next era in the 300-year history of Basle's financial traders.

The organisation of the Basle Stock Exchange

The Basle Stock Exchange is a public institution subject to the laws of the Canton of Basle. The legal basis is provided by the 'Law regarding dealing in securities and the stock exchange' (Börsengesetz) dated 14 January 1982. This law regulates:
(a) membership,
(b) purpose and organisation of the stock exchange, and
(c) the regulatory and supervisory bodies of the stock exchange.

Membership

Any private or legal person who intends to engage professionally in the trade or distribution of securities needs the permission of the Canton of Basle. Such permits are issued to:

(a)   traders in securities (having access to the stock exchange directly), and
(b)   off-the-floor securities traders (not represented at the stock exchange).
In order to obtain either of the above licences the following requirements must be met:
(a)   domicile in the Canton of Basle, and
(b)   registration in the register of commerce.

In addition, a fixed amount must be deposited in trust as collateral (either in cash or in bonds of the Confederation); and it must be proved that the applicant has a good reputation, that it is his aim to be active in the securities markets, and that finances, organisation and personnel are appropriate to carry out these activities.

Purpose of the stock exchange
The Basle Stock Exchange's purpose is to arrange regular meetings at a fixed time to allow its members to deal in securities under the supervision of the cantonal government. The necessary premises must be provided, at no cost to the members, by the canton. As a compensation, a cantonal tax is levied on all securities transactions and paid to the canton.

Regulatory and supervisory bodies of the stock exchange
The Securities Law of 1982 requires the following authorities:
(a)   the executive power of the government (Regierungsrat),
(b)   the Stock Exchange Commission,
(c)   the Stock Exchange 'Commissariat',
(d)   the Stock Exchange Chamber.

The *executive power* issues regulations based on the securities laws, approves the statutes of the Stock Exchange Chamber and elects the members of the Stock Exchange Commission and the Commissioner.

The *Stock Exchange Commission*'s duties, among others, are to make proposals to the executive power regarding the regulations mentioned above, the election of the Commissioner, his substitute and the other personnel of the 'Commissariat'. The Commission decides whether a dealer permit is to be granted or withdrawn. It has the power to ban a member from the exchange, to stop trading and to supervise the officials of the 'Commissariat'.

The *Stock Exchange 'Commissariat'* is headed by the Commissioner. It is the immediate supervisory body of the daily trading session. It is also responsible for publishing the daily quotations list.

The *Stock Exchange Chamber*, composed of the stock exchange members, assists in the supervision of the exchange's activities and represents the interests of its members.

The importance of the Basle Stock Exchange

Basle, situated at the border of France and Germany, is a very important centre for industry and trade. Not only are the big Swiss chemical corporations located here, but also some of the insurance companies and practically all of the forwarding agencies, as well as the headquarters of the Bank for International

Settlements. This in itself demonstrates how important the stock exchange is for the development of the region. It also underlines the fact that Basle has kept its tradition of being a financial centre extending far beyond the Swiss border. It is thus quite natural that the Basle Stock Exchange plays a role in the international securities markets and ranks third among the Swiss stock exchanges. Proof of this fact is found in the long list of foreign companies' shares actively traded at the exchange.

The Geneva Stock Exchange

History of the Geneva Stock Exchange

The cornerstones of the Geneva Stock Exchange can be found in the Protestant Reformation in the sixteenth century. The influx of refugees into Geneva brought the city a lot of new know-how and contacts with many other countries. At the same time there was a flow of money into the banks in Geneva from the European Protestants which was entrusted to the bankers for management.

As the financial activity became more and more important, in 1713 a new civil code was decreed in which a whole chapter regulated the business of the brokers. Although Geneva suffered heavily from the financial crisis which followed the fall of Louis-Philippe in 1848, the activities of the *Courtiers* continued to grow rapidly.

This development called for a professional organisation of the brokers' business. It was a minor incident that actually led to the foundation of the Société des Agents de Change, or more precisely some disputes over execution prices. Upon a proposal to meet regularly in order to establish common prices, a convention was signed by 24 brokers on 26 February 1850, which gave birth to this association. Since the government abstained from any interference, the Geneva Stock Exchange could be constituted according to the needs of its users and in complete freedom. In 1856 the government of the Canton or State of Geneva tried to create a cantonal stock exchange. Due to heavy resistance by the brokers and the banks, these plans failed and the agreement reached in 1857 paved the way for the system which is still fundamentally in existence today.

This cantonal law, which cemented the role of the Société des Agents de Change as the backbone of the Geneva Stock Exchange, was enacted on 30 December 1856 and, together with a supplement edited in 1860, is still in force. The statutes of the brokers' association remained in force until 1930, when the Chambre de la Bourse was founded. As reform was badly needed, this reorganisation allowed the banks, which had had no access to the stock exchange, to widen their activities in securities trading and to take over the brokers' business at the end of the Second World War. The ever-growing securities market brought with it the need for suitable premises, and in 1916 the stock exchange was able to acquire and move into its own building, still in use after renovations in 1952 and 1957. The continuing expansion and increasing volume resulted in the construction of a second *Ring* in 1973, so that trading in shares and bonds could take place simultaneously.

The Geneva Stock Exchange is the oldest in Switzerland and one of the oldest in Europe.

The organisation of the Geneva Stock Exchange

The Geneva Stock Exchange is a public institution governed by a law issued by the government of the Canton of Geneva in December 1856 and by a set of cantonal regulations in force since September 1930. These two documents give the general guidelines under which the Stock Exchange Chamber organises and administers the daily trading in securities.

Membership
Any person (private or legal) who intends to be professionally active as a broker must declare his intention to a government office (Chancellerie d'Etat). In order to be accepted as a member of the Geneva Stock Exchange, the applicant must:
(a)   be of Swiss nationality and domiciled in Geneva for at least one year, having worked during this time for a bank or a broker,
(b)   make a written request to the Board of Directors of the Geneva Stock Exchange,
(c)   participate in the capital of the stock exchange,
(d)   be listed in the Register of Commerce.

As a peculiarity, it should be noted that being a member of the Stock Exchange Chamber does not necessarily mean having a seat on the exchange.

An associate membership is also possible upon participation in the capital.

Purpose of the stock exchange
The law defines the stock exchange as the place where, under the auspices of the cantonal government, the brokers meet for dealing in all securities.

Regulatory and supervisory bodies of the stock exchange
The Geneva Stock Exchange is governed and administered by the following bodies:
(a)   the Stock Exchange Chamber (Chambre de la Bourse de Genève),
(b)   the Board of Directors of the Stock Exchange Chamber,
(c)   the Stock Exchange Commissioners, and
(d)   the Secretariat.

The *Stock Exchange Chamber* (i.e. the Stock Exchange Association) is responsible for the functioning of the stock exchange in accordance with its statutes and regulations as approved by the government of the Canton of Geneva (Conseil d'Etat). The Chamber must provide for the publication of the daily price list.

The *Board of Directors*, as the executive power of the Stock Exchange Chamber, organises and supervises the activities on the exchange. It nominates the Secretary and employs the personnel of the exchange. It represents the interests of the membership and elects the Stock Exchange Commission.

The *Stock Exchange Commissioners*, who are employed by the cantonal government, supervise the correct conduct of the securities business. They are responsible for keeping the official price list up to date. The Commissioners have the power to exclude any person from the trading session for misconduct.

The *Secretary*, besides being responsible for all the secretarial duties imposed by the Board, notes and registers the daily prices in co-operation with the Commissioners. The Secretary also edits the official stock exchange quotation list.

The importance of the Geneva Stock Exchange

At a very early stage, Geneva banks initiated and specialised in portfolio and fund management. But this is only one factor that helped the city to become a financial centre. The geographical location – Geneva being situated on the lake of Geneva (Lac Léman) and being one of the places where the river Rhône could be crossed – proved very beneficial to the city. Even the Romans, at the time of Julius Caesar, realised this, occupying Geneva and controlling the river bridges. In the early fourteenth century the Florentines, at that time the leading financiers of Europe, recognised its importance and established themselves as bankers in Geneva.

Historically, Geneva was the first financial centre of Switzerland, being orientated very much to the international scene. This international flavour is underlined by the fact that many international organisations have their seat in Geneva, and that a number of the largest multinational companies have located their European headquarters there.

Today, Geneva has the second largest stock exchange in Switzerland.

The Zurich Stock Exchange

History of the Zurich Stock Exchange

The history of Zurich's securities trading, similar to that of Basle, can be traced back to the middle of the seventeenth century. In 1650 the existence of a *Sensale* could already be found, and in 1663 the first *Sensale*'s Order was put in force. This order, issued by the Zurich Directory of Commerce, was copied by and large from a set of rules adopted in St Gall 20 years earlier. It contained the terms of acceptance as a broker and represented the code of conduct for their business.

These regulations were changed several times until September 1835, when the *Sensale*'s Law was enacted by the legislative body of the government of Zurich (Grosser Rat). This meant the liquidation of the City of Zurich Directory of Commerce; as a consequence the supervision of the *Sensale* passed to the Chamber of Commerce, a cantonal agency.

An important chapter in the history of the Zurich Stock Exchange began in 1843 when the *Neue Zürcher Zeitung* started to publish quotations from the Paris Bourse as well as currency prices. A few years later, shortly after the foundation of the Confederation of Switzerland in 1848, plans were made to create a meeting place for merchants. Three years later an association of exchange members was founded. As its participants had decided to meet every Friday, the Friday Exchange was institutionalised. After a search for suitable premises, the exchange moved into the Old City Symphonic Concert Building in 1869. In the same year the first official quotation sheet appeared, showing prices for some 40 stocks and 20 bonds.

The activities of the exchange expanded rapidly and soon the need for more space arose. Aided by a generous donation from Heinrich Bodmer-Pestalozzi (a descendant of the Bodmer-Escher family, which was considered to be among the wealthiest in Zurich and which played a dominant role in the Zurich silk industry), the construction of a stock exchange building was planned, and in August 1880 the new premises opened for business. Prior to this, in 1876, the Stock Exchange Association adopted its first by-laws.

Another milestone in the history of the Zurich Stock Exchange is the year 1883, when the first cantonal stock exchange law came into force. It made the profession of broker subject to the issuance of a licence by the authorities. At the same time a Stock Exchange Commissioner was appointed. In 1896 a new law was enacted, giving the banks the formal right of access to the exchange. It took almost 20 years before the law was completely revised, but in 1912 the voters approved the 'Law concerning the professional trade in securities', still essentially in force today.

The turn of the century brought many ups and downs to the exchange. On the one hand, the transaction volume rose by 50% in 1899. On the other hand, the Zurich Stock Exchange lost some of its most attractive stocks as a result of takeovers, and the membership of the exchange was decimated by the economic situation and depression.

In the late 1920s securities trading boomed and, as a result, the Stock Exchange Association pressed hard for the construction of a new building. Since the cantonal government fully supported this demand, a site near Zurich's Paradeplatz was acquired. Construction began immediately, and on 4 August 1930 the first trading session was held at the new exchange. The Stock Exchange building, still in use today, had two trading pits or *Rings* on the trading floor.

Although the Zurich Stock Exchange suffered setbacks, its development could not be halted and its international importance grew steadily. At a very early date it created an international quotations sheet and established close ties with other securities markets.

The 1960s were noteworthy for the new record volumes that were achieved in the trading of securities. Again, this meant that space was no longer sufficient, and a third *Ring* had to be built. Since then, the ever-growing turnover has made a new stock exchange building necessary. Plans for a new building are now ready and are to be realised by 1989. Until then the existing trading floor is being enlarged and modernised, with a fourth *Ring* in operation as of February 1985.

The organisation of the Zurich Stock Exchange

In contrast to the other stock exchanges in Switzerland, the Zurich Stock Exchange is a semi-public institution governed by the 'Cantonal Law concerning the professional trade in securities' of 22 December 1912. It is, therefore, not an independent legal entity.

This law defines the terms on which licences to deal in securities are granted. It stipulates that the firms operating on the exchange must constitute and be members of the Zurich Stock Exchange Association. The law stipulates the duties and tasks of the stock exchange members, the off-the-floor securities traders, the Stock Exchange Association and the Stock Exchange 'Commissariat'.

Membership
In order to engage professionally in the securities trade, a permit must be obtained from the cantonal government acting through the Department of Public Economy. Licences are granted for:
(a)   a seat on the exchange, and
(b)   off-the-floor trading in securities (without direct access to the stock exchange).
In both cases the applicant must:
(a)   be domiciled in the Canton of Zurich,
(b)   have a good moral reputation, and
(c)   have a sound knowledge of the securities business.

Purpose of the stock exchange
The stock exchange's purpose is to provide the necessary infrastructure to facilitate trading in securities. The cantonal government provides the premises needed to carry out this function.

Regulatory and supervisory bodies of the stock exchange
Besides the executive power of the government (Regierungsrat), which issues or accepts the necessary regulations, in Zurich these responsibilities are split between:
(a)   the Stock Exchange Commission,
(b)   the Stock Exchange 'Commissariat', and
(c)   the Stock Exchange Association (formed by the stock exchange members).
   The *Stock Exchange Commission* examines new or existing regulations and submits its recommendations to the executive governmental power. It gives its opinion regarding the admission of an applicant or the expulsion of a licence-holder and proposes suitable candidates for the office of the Commissioner and his assistants.
   The *Stock Exchange Commissariat* is the government's executive body, supervising the trading in securities. Its most important duties are:
(a)   the issue of licences for the securities trade,
(b)   the maintenance of suitable premises for the securities trade,
(c)   the approval of stock exchange rules and regulations,
(d)   the monitoring of the securities trade, and
(e)   the publication of daily quotations sheets.
   The *Stock Exchange Association* is composed of members licensed to engage in trading on the exchange (*Ring Banks*). Membership is mandatory for all those having a seat on the exchange. The Association's bodies are the General Assembly, the Executive Committee (Board of Governors), the Secretariat and the Court of Arbitration.

The tasks of the Association comprise:

(a) contacts with cantonal authorities,
(b) drafting and amendments of laws and regulations,
(c) examination and approval of applications for listing,
(d) supervision of stock exchange operations, and
(e) contacts with other securities markets.

The importance of the Zurich Stock Exchange

Zurich and its Stock Exchange, the latter existing for more than 100 years, have helped to develop an important international capital market in Switzerland. Zurich has thus become *the* financial centre of Switzerland. The reasons for this success are manifold.

Switzerland's political and economic stability has led to a flow of capital into the country, looking for investment possibilities. The central location of the city and an efficient airport bring Zurich within easy reach of the rest of the world.

The industrialisation of the Zurich region, resulting in highly respected and internationally known companies (Brown Boveri, Oerlikon Bührle, Sulzer), has cemented the name of Zurich not only with the international business community, but also with the international investor. The expertise acquired in the management of funds has found widespread appreciation and has aided the growth of the banks and the securities business. The international importance of the banking industry in Zurich, its worldwide contacts and its efficiency have contributed to a major extent to the expansion of the Zurich Stock Exchange. It is thus no wonder that Zurich is by far the largest and the leading stock exchange in Switzerland. With hundreds of foreign shares and bonds listed, it is in fact one of Europe's largest securities markets and ranks among the top markets in the world.

The Stock Exchange of Berne

History of the Stock Exchange of Berne

The banking industry of Berne can be traced back to the early eighteenth century, when a number of private banks were already active in international money exchange and transfer. Nevertheless, the establishment of a stock exchange came about rather late. Its roots can be found in the Association of Bernese Banks, established in January 1880. Following this loose association, the Berner Börsenverein (Bernese Stock Exchange Society) was founded in November 1884; its first trading session took place on 2 February 1885. The transactions at the exchange were executed by the *Sensale* (broker/agent). During the first decades of existence, activity on the Stock Exchange of Berne was at a very low volume. It was only after the Second World War that business improved and turnover grew larger. But it was only in 1961 that the stock exchange could enter into a long-term lease and occupy the premises still used today. Before that it had to move from one place to another. Finally, in 1972, the stock exchange was modernised through reconstruction and extension.

The organisation of the Stock Exchange of Berne

The Stock Exchange of Berne is a private institution in the form of an association (*Verein*) governed by the Swiss Civil Code. Its goal is to organise and develop securities trading in Berne by arranging regular stock exchange sessions.

Membership
Only banks that are listed in the Register of Commerce of Berne can apply for membership.

Regulatory and supervisory bodies of the stock exchange
The most important of these are:
(a)   the General Assembly,
(b)   the Board, and
(c)   the Secretariat.
   The *General Assembly*, consisting of the representatives of the member firms of the exchange, has, among other things, the rights and duties:
(a)   to elect the Board and from within it the President of the Stock Exchange Association,
(b)   to enact statutes and regulations, and
(c)   to decide on the admission or expulsion of members.
   The *Board*'s duties include the organisation and supervision of trading activities. It fixes the trading hours and elects the Secretary and his substitute. It issues guidelines regarding the publication of the official quotations list and decides on the admission of new securities for listing.
   The *Secretariat*'s most important duty is the publication of the daily price list and the supervision of trading sessions. It ensures that members live up to the rules and regulations.

The importance of the Stock Exchange of Berne

Berne, the capital of the Confederation of Switzerland, is not among the stock exchanges that are followed worldwide. Nevertheless, a considerable number of foreign shares, and even more foreign bonds, are listed on the exchange, an indication of the international appeal of this city. But the importance of this securities market lies much more on the regional level. In fact, there are quite a few Swiss securities (bonds and shares) that are quoted only in Berne. The Stock Exchange of Berne acts mainly as intermediary between the large stock exchanges and investors, and it is in the interest of the whole securities business that Berne continues to perform this important function.

The Lausanne Stock Exchange

History of the Lausanne Stock Exchange

Lausanne, with quite some pride, ranks among those stock exchanges in Switzerland that have been in existence for more than 100 years. At the beginning of the nineteenth century some securities transactions had already taken place, in which the local banks acted as intermediaries. But it was only with the 1870–71 war, and the resulting flight of capital from France into Switzerland, that the call for a stock exchange could be justified. It was on 7 July 1873 that the Lausanne Stock Exchange was founded. Its growth very much reflects the industrial development in this region. On the one hand, towards the end of the century tourism made its début in the area. On the other, companies like Henry Nestlé in Vevey, which merged with Anglo-Swiss Milk in Cham, posted one success after the other. The continuously prospering securities market forced the stock exchange to look for new premises, and in 1974 it moved to its new location at Place Bel-Air 4.

The organisation of the Lausanne Stock Exchange

Similar to Berne, the Lausanne Stock Exchange Association is a purely private institution subject only to the Swiss Civil Code.

Membership
Membership is open only to banks that are established in Lausanne and that are listed in the Register of Commerce.

Regulatory and supervisory bodies of the stock exchange
The Lausanne Stock Exchange is governed by:
(a)   the General Assembly,
(b)   the Stock Exchange Committee, and
(c)   the Stock Exchange Commissioner.
   The *General Assembly*, which consists of the representatives of the member firms, is the supreme body of the stock exchange; it fulfils, among others, the following functions:
(a)   nomination of the Stock Exchange Committee,
(b)   decisions on the admission, exclusion and suspension of members, and
(c)   elaboration and modification of statutes and regulations.
   The *Stock Exchange Committee*, elected from among the stock exchange members, is responsible for the administration of the exchange's affairs. Its most important duties are:
(a)   constantly to revise the securities that are listed,
(b)   to ensure that all rules and regulations are strictly observed, and
(c)   to represent the Stock Exchange Association outside the exchange.
   The *Stock Exchange Commissioner* directs and supervises the trading sessions. He is responsible for the editing, printing and distribution of the official quotations list.

The importance of the Lausanne Stock Exchange

The Stock Exchange of Lausanne plays, above all, an important role as a regional exchange. The most important companies headquartered or located in the Canton of Vaud appear on its quotations list and are regularly traded. In addition to this, most of the shares of the large Swiss and foreign corporations that are listed on the exchanges of Basle, Geneva and Zurich make their appearance in the price list of Lausanne. The Stock Exchange of Lausanne, therefore, is a highly respected member of the Swiss securities business.

Other stock exchanges

Neuchâtel

History of the Neuchâtel Stock Exchange

The foundation of this local stock exchange took place in 1905. Its aim was to facilitate trading in securities, especially in local shares.

At the beginning, trading sessions were held twice a week in the town hall. In 1926 the stock exchange members began to meet daily in a new location at the former hospital. Soon the exchange moved back to the town hall and it was only in 1966 that it was transferred to suitable premises, still in use.

The organisation of the Neuchâtel Stock Exchange

The Stock Exchange of Neuchâtel is a private institution subject only to the Swiss Civil Code.

Membership

According to the statutes of 1905, revised several times (the latest revision took place in 1980), membership may be granted to all banks and bankers located in Neuchâtel.

Regulatory and supervisory bodies of the stock exchange

The most important agencies of the stock exchange are the General Assembly and the Stock Exchange Committee.

The General Assembly nominates the Committee, decides on the admission or expulsion of members, establishes and amends statutes and regulations, etc. The Stock Exchange Committee's most important tasks, besides responsibility for the organisation and functioning of the exchange, are to publish the official quotations sheet and to list or delist securities. It ensures that all members observe the statutes and regulations. It also represents the stock exchange in relations with the other Swiss stock exchanges and the Association of Swiss Stock Exchanges.

The importance of the Neuchâtel Stock Exchange

Looking at the first price lists, the Neuchâtel Stock Exchange at the beginning of its existence had, for unknown reasons, a clear international character. This role diminished steadily and today its importance is purely local. Nevertheless, there are a few local shares that have become well known worldwide.

St Gall

History of the St Gall Stock Exchange

The history of the St Gall Stock Exchange began in the seventeenth century, when the merchants enacted a kind of 'market order' which served Zurich to establish its *Sensale* Law. An important date in the development of the exchange was 4 May 1887, when the Bankers' Association came into being. It was required to ensure that its members could meet regularly and exchange views and ideas regarding banking and other problems. In 1888 it also began to publish stock exchange prices, reporting from places like Paris, Frankfurt, Vienna, Basle, Geneva and Zurich. However, the official establishment of the St Gall Stock Exchange took place only in November 1933, when dealing started in the building of the Swiss Bank Corporation. After another move the stock exchange finally found a modern, well-equipped trading room in a new office building of the Swiss National Bank.

The organisation of the St Gall Stock Exchange

Membership
The St Gall Stock Exchange is a private institution whose members are all banks domiciled in St Gall and which belong to the St Gall Bankers' Association.

Regulatory and supervisory bodies of the stock exchange
The organisation of the stock exchange and of the daily trading sessions is entrusted to a Stock Exchange Commission, which is elected by the Bankers' Association. This Commission decides on the admission of securities for listing, conducts and supervises the trading sessions and is responsible for recording all quotations. The regulations governing securities trading are still those of 1933. Where no specific rules exist, the regulations of the Zurich Stock Exchange apply.

The importance of the St Gall Stock Exchange

The role of the St Gall Stock Exchange is of a purely local nature. It gives the smaller or medium-sized local companies the possibility of having their securities listed on an exchange, permitting local investors to participate in the region's economic development under adequate information policies.

Lucerne

History of the Lucerne Stock Exchange

It is since the middle of the nineteenth century that the banking circles and at a later stage the Bankers' Association of Lucerne arranged weekly meetings to discuss common problems and to deal in local securities. A formal stock exchange was founded only later.

The organisation of the Lucerne Stock Exchange

Membership
The Lucerne Stock Exchange is a private institution; only banks domiciled in Lucerne may become members.

Regulatory and supervisory bodies of the stock exchange

The regulations (the version actually in force dating back to January 1976) stipulate:

(a)   that the goal of the exchange is to stimulate and facilitate trading in securities of a local character through regular meetings,

(b)   that the Members' Assembly must organise and supervise trading and appoint the Secretary from among its members,

(c)   that trading sessions be held every Wednesday,

(d)   the minimum trading lots, and

(e)   that in all other respects the rules and regulations of the Zurich Stock Exchange be adopted.

The importance of the Lucerne Stock Exchange

The Lucerne Stock Exchange is of only local importance in the strictest sense of the word.

Chur

To complete the picture of the Swiss stock exchanges it must be mentioned that the city of Chur also used to be a market-place for securities. However, its stock exchange was closed and the Stock Exchange Association dissolved in 1970.

4 Types of securities traded

Theo Bütler

The joint-stock company

Since the most popular form of company in Switzerland is the joint-stock company (*Aktiengesellschaft*), with the typical characteristics of a fixed amount of originally issued stock and the limited liability of the stockholders (OR* 620), the most common equity paper is the share. New financing needs that have been shaped by the growth of the economy, the stability of the political system and the highly developed banking system have led to a variety of stocks that are traded on the stock exchanges. Therefore, the equity of a typical Swiss company consists of bearer shares (*Inhaberaktien*), registered shares (*Namenaktien*), non-voting stock (*Genussscheine/Partizipationsscheine*) and some other not very common specialities. Convertible and option bonds also became popular instruments for attracting risk capital.

The stock- or shareholder is a true co-owner of the corporation. He has two principal rights depending upon the number of shares he holds (OR 646):
(a) membership rights, and
(b) property rights.
The main membership right is the right to participate in the shareholders' meeting. In general, one share gives its owner one vote. The voting power of shareholders is important, mainly with regard to the election of the board of directors and the decisions concerning dividend payments (OR 689 ff).

Two important property rights accruing to owners of a stock are their claims on dividend payments (OR 660) and their right to subscribe new shares when the corporation increases its capital (OR 652). Swiss companies have been able to place new stocks at prices and conditions that are attractive both to the company and the original shareholders. The original shareholder has the option to sell his subscription rights or buy new stock at an attractive price. When a company is liquidated, the shareholder has a claim on parts of the surplus (OR 660).

---

* OR = Obligationenrecht, Switzerland's business law.

Types of shares

Shares can be either in registered or in bearer form (OR 622). The registered share is the older type because originally a share document was nothing but a certificate to be registered in the 'shareholders' book'. But bearer shares are much more popular.

Physically, securities in Switzerland consist of the actual instrument and a coupon sheet needed to collect the regular, in most cases annual, dividend payments.

Bearer shares (*Inhaberaktien*) (OR 978 ff)

Most Swiss shares are in bearer form (see Table 4.1). Holders of bearer shares are recognised as the owners of the shares on the basis of their possession alone. These certificates show no name and are 'as good as cash' when they are listed on an exchange. They carry dividend coupons which must be detached when due. If the shares are deposited with a bank in Switzerland, the dividends are cashed automatically. Bearer (and registered) shares must show a minimum nominal value of SFr 100 (OR 622/4). The usual nominal value is SFr 500 for bearer shares and SFr 100 for registered shares.

Table 4.1 Market value of the largest Swiss companies at 31 December 1984

Company	Nominal stock capital (SFr million)	Total market value (SFr million)	Market value bearer shares (SFr million)	%	Number of bearer shares
Nestlé	333.0	13,494.4	6,008.8	44.5	1,073,000
Union Bank of Switzerland	1,811.2	12,773.6	9,845.0	77.0	2,750,000
Swiss Bank Corporation	2,857.9	8,902.5	3,751.5	42.1	10,567,535
Ciba-Geigy	536.4	7,987.5	1,850.1	23.2	749,034
Crédit Suisse	1,815.0	7,629.8	6,347.7	83.2	2,730,200

Sources: Union Bank of Switzerland, *The Swiss Stock Guide 1984–85*; Zurich Stock Exchange, Annual Report 1984.

One of the advantages of the bearer form is that they are easily transferable to other holders. There are no formalities required for selling or buying. Moreover, the corporation has neither the ability to control the transfer nor the ability to monitor or influence the owners of the bearer shares. For big corporations that have a large need for capital and are also interested in a broad distribution of their stocks, the bearer form is of great importance.

Because of their anonymity and a larger number of potential buyers, bearer shares have a more liquid market and are traded with a premium relative to registered shares (see Fig. 4.1). Thus, when the Ciba-Geigy registered share was selling at SFr 1,030 in 1983, the bearer share had a market price of SFr 2,410, although both have the same nominal value and were paying a dividend of SFr 31 per share. The premiums also depend very much on the popularity of the

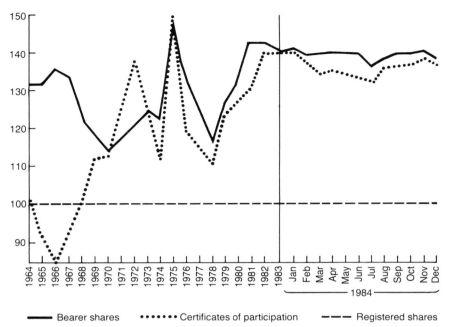

Fig. 4.1   Premium of bearer shares and certificates of participation relative to registered shares
Registered shares = 100.
Source: Zurich Stock Exchange, Annual Report, 1984.

corporations and the outstanding number of bearer shares relative to registered shares. The considerable fluctuations of the premiums of bearer shares relative to registered shares are interesting for the investor, the speculator or even the trader. Comparable to the commodity business, 'spread trading' is worth a second look.

On the average, bearer shares enjoy a premium of 25% over registered shares. Since registered shares of certain companies cannot be purchased by foreign nationals, the 25% higher price of bearer shares also reflects the larger demand of foreign investors for the specific stock of the corporation involved.

Registered shares (*Namenaktien*) (OR 974 ff)

Registered shares are recorded in the name of the owner and entered into the shareholders' book of the company concerned. To prove the legal title to the stock one owns, it is necessary to be registered in the list of shareholders. The transfer of registered shares is sometimes reserved to Swiss citizens, more often to Swiss residents and Swiss-controlled companies. New shareholders need the approval of the board of directors to obtain registration. There are various reasons why Swiss companies issue over 50% of their stock in the form of restricted registered shares, among them:
(a)   smaller corporations or traditional family companies are interested in monitoring and controlling the specific owners of their company;

(b) larger corporations do not want to lose their legal, economic or national independence; registration gives them the possibility of refusing registered stock ownership to competitors in Switzerland or abroad.

(For further details regarding restrictions on the free acquisition of registered shares, see Chapter 8.)

Foreigners have sometimes tried to acquire registered shares by using Swiss trustees as intermediaries and listing the shares under the name of a Swiss resident or friend. This solution is hardly advisable because of the legal and ownership problems that can arise. For instance, when the registered owner dies, the foreigner has difficulties proving and defending his ownership rights in court. Moreover, these stocks are merged for tax and inheritance purposes into the estate of the registered owner. Foreigners, living abroad, may participate in the forward market of registered shares, but they must close out their positions before they are due. In Switzerland, the forward market on stocks is limited to a period of nine months.

Unlike many countries (most notably the United States), there exists in Switzerland a strong link between banks and registered share transactions. The financial network of these universal banking institutions is vast, permitting an easy exchange of registered claims. A convention among banks in Switzerland regulates sales and purchases of registered shares. Under this convention, banks are permitted to execute registered share orders:

(a) when the buyer(s) fulfil(s) the requirements set by the corporation involved,
(b) if they ensure that the corporations get prompt notice of new sales or purchases.

Banks are not permitted to buy registered shares on a fiduciary basis for their clients. Since banks usually know the exact conditions under which a corporation is prepared to accept a new shareholder, the transfer of registered shares is done efficiently on the exchange.

Since most of the bearer shares have a high premium over registered shares, the latter securities enjoy the advantage of a higher yield on the invested capital. Therefore, Swiss investors generally prefer registered shares to bearer shares.

Non-voting stock (OR 657)

Non-voting stocks are certificates which generally entitle owners to all the property rights of the common shareholders, but which carry no membership rights. They can be issued in either bearer or registered form. Non-voting stock is a form of participation which is located legally somewhere between bond- and shareholders of a corporation. This security incorporates the right to participate in net profits and liquidation proceeds, as well as a preferential right to subscribe new shares in the case of a rights issue. However, the holder has no voting power and cannot attend the shareholders' meeting.

There are two different types of non-voting stock listed on the various exchanges:

(a) certificates of participation (*Partizipationsscheine*), and
(b) dividend-right certificates (*Genussscheine*).

Certificates of participation (*Partizipationsscheine*)

In the early 1960s, a few Swiss companies began to issue non-voting stock in order to raise additional risk capital. (In 1963, the corporation Gebrüder Sulzer AG placed 90,000 so-called certificates of participation. Landis & Gyr issued certificates of participation through a convertible bond in 1963.) These securities, issued in bearer form, incorporate the right to participate in net profits and liquidation proceeds and to subscribe new shares when the company raises its equity. Certificates of participation are not yet regulated by the Swiss company law. In the past, owners of certificates of participation have had to rely on the body of legislation covering dividend-right certificates (OR 657) in order to gain legal protection. It is expected, however, that the current revision of the Swiss joint-stock company law will set exact rules regarding the issuance and transfer of certificates of participation. Since these certificates are in bearer form, there are no restrictions regarding their sale or purchase. In the meantime, many major Swiss corporations have sold certificates of participation, among them the companies listed in Table 4.2.

Certificates of participation carry several remarkable advantages. And the corporations that issue them can attract capital, especially foreign capital, without giving up voting rights. They also give corporations the possibility of issuing share-like securities with a low nominal value so that the corporation has 'cheap' securities beside its 'expensive' bearer or registered shares. There is no law yet which requires a minimum nominal value.

Certificates of participation are listed on Swiss stock exchanges. Since foreigners are not restricted in the purchase of these securities, they have a rather liquid market. Certificates of participation are traded at a discount of about 10% relative to bearer shares. This fact reflects the premium for the voting power that investors are willing to pay.

Some innovative companies have issued preferred certificates of participation.

Table 4.2 Some major Swiss companies issuing certificates of participation

Company	Number of certificates of participation	Total market value (SFr million)
Union Bank of Switzerland	6,744,700	876.8
Ciba-Geigy	1,102,981	2,239.0
Sandoz	711,274	810.9
Zürich Versicherung	600,000	1,062.0
BBC	610,221	145.2

Source: Union Bank of Switzerland, *The Swiss Stock Guide 1984–85.*

Dividend-right certificates (*Genussscheine*) (OR 657)

Some companies use dividend-right certificates as compensation for services rendered when they are founded. Such certificates or 'founder's shares' (*Gründeranteilsschein/Genussschein*) are, however, rarely issued.

Other corporations use the dividend-right certificate when the company is reorganised and needs new capital. The creditors' capital is thereby transformed into share capital, e.g. dividend-right certificates.

Dividend-right certificates may also be issued when the corporation does not want to raise dividend payments above a certain percentage of the original stock (registered and bearer shares). As a result, the corporation can pay part of its earnings on the dividend-right certificates. Large issues of dividend-right certificates have the added effect of causing the average value of the original stock to diminish. Therefore, the former shareholders are always given a right to subscribe newly issued dividend-right certificates.

Important issues of dividend-right certificates over the past 20 years have been made by Maschinenfabrik Rieter AG, Winterthur; Hoffmann-La Roche, Basle: and Société Générale de Surveillance, Geneva. The Swiss-based international chemicals/pharmaceuticals giant, Hoffmann-La Roche, has by far the broadest market in this paper.

These securities are traded either over the counter or on the stock exchanges.

Specialities: preference shares, twin shares, Jumbo certificates, fractional certificates

Usually, preference shares (OR 656) carry rights that take precedence over common stock of the same corporation. This is true with regard to dividend payments, voting power or any distribution of assets on liquidation. The usual practice is for holders of preference shares to be considered first when companies are making dividend payments. Often, they are entitled to bonus (*Superdividende*) or supplementary dividends.

These shares may also be issued in the form of cumulative preference shares. This type of security entitles the owner to accumulate claims on unpaid dividends. Before a common stock dividend can be paid, these cumulative obligations to preferred shareholders must be fulfilled.

A further advantage preference shares may enjoy consists of the preferential right to subscribe to any future issues.

Preference shares are often issued when a corporation has been suffering large losses and needs new capital. In order to attract new shareholders, it is necessary to give these newly issued shares special rights. Preference shares are not as common in Switzerland as they are in the Anglo-American systems.

Landis & Gyr, an international electronics firm, has a part of its certificates of participation issued in the preferred form (*Prioritätspartizipationsscheine*).

Twin shares (*Zwillingsaktien*) are used as an instrument for co-operation between two companies. Two corporations that plan to work together issue new shares which incorporate rights of both corporations. The 'old' shareholders can exchange 'old' shares for new ones. They can also sell their shares if they do not like the new corporation in the group.

For example, the insurance company, Helvetia, placed twin shares after a co-operation agreement between Helvetia Leben and Helvetia Feuer. This new twin was 100% acquired by the shareholders of the two companies.

Twin shares are also used for the acquisition of large corporations. The Nestlé bearer and registered shares were indivisibly connected with Unilac Ltd, a

Panamanian twin company, until May 1985. Each corporation had its own dividend policy, but the two securities could not be purchased or sold separately. Another large Swiss corporation, Hoffmann-La Roche, has attached to its original dividend-right certificates the shares of Sapac Corporation of New Brunswick, Canada.

Instead of the total number of securities or shares, some corporations give their shareholders a certificate which represents a specific quantity of stocks. The company can thereby save a remarkable amount of printing expenses; the administration of the securities becomes simpler and cheaper, too. The experts refer to these as 'Jumbo certificates' when they represent 1,000 shares or a nominal value of SFr 100,000 or more. A Jumbo certificate can be converted back into smaller units and, like other Swiss securities, they are normally in safe keeping with the clearing corporation SEGA.

A special situation exists with fractional certificates for dividend-right certificates issued by Hoffmann-La Roche. The original capital consisted of 16,000 shares and 48,000 dividend-right certificates without nominal value. Due to the success of this corporation the price of both forms of securities has risen to over SFr 100,000. In order to have securities with lower market prices, the corporation proposed to its shareholders the transformation of one dividend-right certificate into ten fractional certificates. On the stock exchanges, the dealers called the partial certificates 'Baby Roche'.

Mutual fund or investment fund certificates (unit trust investment certificates)

The idea behind joint capital investments is not new in Switzerland. In fact, mutual investments have a history dating back to the last century. Numerous investors pool their funds through this financial vehicle and collectively invest under the responsibility of a professional management team. Before the Second World War, large Swiss banks and finance companies launched the first big mutual investment trustee, Société Internationale de Placement (SIP).

Today, mutual funds in Switzerland are governed by the Federal Law on Investment Funds, which entered into force on 1 February 1967. This law stipulates that the board of directors of any mutual fund is obliged to define and publish its investment policy (by-laws), but that it is the responsibility of the specific fund's administration to decide independently thereafter both on the sales or purchases of specific securities and on the issuance of new certificates. As a result, the holder of a mutual investment certificate has no right to influence the management of the fund. Furthermore, the law in question forces the managers of these funds to consider and to show discretion in choosing a reasonably diversified portfolio.

In Switzerland, open-ended investment funds have the highest popularity. Such funds are permitted to issue new shares continuously and are under the obligation to redeem them upon request. Usually, the assets of investment funds are with a custodian bank and managed by a separate entity. As Table 4.3 shows, the availability of professionally managed investment funds has attracted the

Table 4.3 Development of mutual funds in Switzerland

Year	Number of funds	Assets (SFr million)
1955	32	1,699
1965	91	6,215
1970	105	8,131
1975	118	14,130
1980	120	15,057
1984	141	19,755

Source: *Monatsberichte der Schweizerischen Nationalbank,*
Dec. 1984.

attention of many investors and has caused the funds to grow at a healthy rate
(9% p.a.).

Mutual investment funds tend to specialise in investments in real estate, in
fixed-income securities or in shares. There are funds that specialise by industry,
by currencies or by regions of the world.

Normally, the dividend payments of mutual investment certificates are subject
to a withholding tax of 35%, which can be reclaimed partly or wholly in countries
having a double-taxation agreement with Switzerland. However, dividends to
unit owners residing outside Switzerland, and funds earning 80% or more of
their proceeds abroad, are not subject to this withholding tax.

Investment fund certificates are accepted generally for listing on the Swiss
stock exchanges if there is a certain minimum amount of assets in the specific
fund (SFr 50 million). Most certificates are, however, traded over the counter.
Certificates listed on the Zurich Stock Exchange are given in Table 4.4.

Table 4.4 Mutual investment certificates listed on the Zurich Stock Exchange at 31 December 1984

AMCA, America–Canada Trust Fund
BOND-INVEST (bond fund for international investments)
CONVERT-INVEST (fund for investments in convertible bonds and notes)
EURIT (share fund for European securities)
FONSA (share fund for Swiss securities)
GLOBINVEST (investment fund for international bonds and shares)
HELVETINVEST (fund for Swiss bonds)
IMMOFONDS (investment fund for real estate)
Intercontinental Trust (investment fund for international securities)
INTERSWISS (investment fund for real estate)
PACIFIC-INVEST (investment fund for securities in the Pacific area)
SAFIT, South Africa Trust Fund
SAMURAÏ PORTFOLIO (investment fund for Japanese securities)
'Schweizeraktien' (investment fund for Swiss stocks and bonds)
SIAT (investment fund for real estate)
SIMA (investment fund for real estate)
Swissimmobil, Serie D (investment fund for real estate)
Swissimmobil, Neue Serie (investment fund for real estate)
Swissimmobil 1961 (investment fund for real estate)
Swissreal, Serie A (investment fund for real estate)
   do. Serie B (investment fund for real estate)

Source: *Kursblatt der Zürcher Effektenbörse*, Dec. 1984.

The advantages of mutual investment certificates are obvious for the small private investor, as well as for the large pension fund or insurance company. Mutual investment funds give foreign investors the chance to profit from the extensive knowledge of portfolio managers who understand the domestic market. They allow each member of the pool to invest on a more diversified basis than would be the case of investors acting alone. Furthermore, the investor has no problems of administration. The certificate holders not only earn dividend payments, but can also profit from the rising market prices of the mutual investment certificates (see Table 4.5).

Mutual investment certificates generally have high liquidity because they can be sold easily either on the exchanges or over the counter, or can be redeemed by the issuer. Since the assets of Swiss mutual investment funds have reached considerable levels, even big corporations or pension funds can participate in these markets.

Table 4.5 Total return of universal share funds (unit trusts), 1974–84

Mutual fund	Custodian*	Original issue price (SFr)	Issue price 3.1.1974 (SFr)	Total return† 74–29.6.84 (%)
Stockbar	J.B.	1,000	973	+73
Uniwert	HBNW	100	100	+72
CSF Int.	SKA	100	84.75	+37
Valca	KB	100	87	+37
Intermobilfonds	SVB	100	95	+29
Globinvest	SBG	100	82.50	+28
Universal Fund	SBV	100	107	+26

* German abbreviations.
† Change in value including distributions.
Source: HandelsBank NW Zurich, June 1984.

Stocks of foreign companies traded in Switzerland

Foreign securities are of great importance on the various stock exchanges of Switzerland. The trading volume of foreign shares amounted to 132,882 'number of quotation' in 1984 relative to 129,472 in 1983 on the Zurich Stock Exchange.* (Note that there is a minimum unit volume of foreign shares necessary for one quotation.) Swiss and many foreign investors as well are interested in trading US or other foreign stocks listed in Switzerland because the commission costs are relatively low for small amounts. The investor also has no foreign exchange transaction cost (although he bears the foreign exchange risk) because the stocks are quoted in Swiss francs. The popularity of foreign shares is further enhanced by the active arbitrage that is carried on between foreign stock exchanges.

American and Canadian shares are traded in the form of certificates that are registered in the name of one of the three major Swiss banks (UBS, SBC, CS).

* Zurich Stock Exchange, Annual Report 1984.

Table 4.6 Origin of foreign shares listed on the Zurich Stock Exchange at 31 December 1984

	Number of corporations		Number of corporations
USA	111	UK	10
West Germany	23	Japan	7
Netherlands	11	Canada	5
South Africa	8	France	4
Belgium	2	Spain	1
Norway	1	Luxembourg	1
Sweden	1	Curaçao	1

Source: *Kursblatt der Zürcher Effektenbörse*, Dec. 1984.

These certificates are endorsed in blank and are therefore transferable without restriction. Because of their registration with a Swiss bank they can circulate like bearer shares. They must be stamped when dividends are cashed.

In 1970, only 44 North American (United States, Canada) stocks were listed in Zurich. Since then, the list has risen to 116 companies that have been traded either in the spot, the forward or the premium market (see Table 4.6).

The West German and Dutch certificates traded in Switzerland are original common stock. They are in bearer form and can be transferred easily to their home countries. These securities are also quoted in Swiss francs; therefore, the investor has no additional transaction cost with foreign exchange.

Table 4.7 The five largest Swiss, West German and US companies in terms of market capitalisation, and their share of total market values at 31 December 1984

	SFr billion	%
Switzerland		
Nestlé	13.5	13.0
Union Bank of Switzerland	12.8	12.4
Swiss Bank Corporation	8.9	8.6
Ciba-Geigy	8.0	7.7
Crédit Suisse	7.6	7.4
West Germany		
Siemens	17.2	8.5
Daimler–Benz	16.6	8.2
Deutsche Bank	9.3	4.6
Bayer	8.0	4.0
Hoechst	7.9	4.0
USA		
IBM	194.8	4.7
Exxon	93.2	2.3
General Electric	66.2	1.6
General Motors	64.0	1.5
ATT	48.6	1.2

Source: Zurich Stock Exchange, Annual Report 1984.

UK stocks are original share certificates also registered in the name of one of the three big Swiss banks. In order to guarantee an easy transfer, they have a coupon of transfer attached.

The large South African gold mining corporations are traded in the same way as US stocks in Switzerland. Moreover, like UK stocks they have an attached coupon of transfer.

Table 4.7 gives figures for the five largest Swiss, West German and US companies listed on the Zurich Stock Exchange – in terms of market capitalisation and share of total market values.

An increasing number of Japanese corporations list their stocks on the main Swiss stock exchanges. Today, large companies such as Nippon Electric, Fujitsu, Honda Motor, Sanyo, Sharp and Sony are traded together with other foreign stock. These certificates are original bearer shares, deposited with SEGA (Schweizerische Effekten-Giro AG).

Equity-linked bonds and notes

Features of convertible bonds and notes

Convertible bonds and notes traded in Switzerland are mostly SFr-, US$- or DM-denominated securities which may be converted by the holder into shares or participation certificates of the same or of another company within a specified period and at a specified price. In most cases, conversion is made into shares of the same corporation, but occasionally they are exchangeable for shares of an affiliate.

Convertible bonds have advantages for both the investor and the issuing corporation. They usually carry a somewhat lower interest rate, but rising share prices offer capital gains on the bond, which are not taxed by most Swiss cantons. If the company does not perform well on the stock exchange, there is still the interest income.

The corporation enjoys the advantage of lower interest costs and the profit on the sale of shares. Conversion prices are usually substantially above the market price at the time of pricing. If stock prices rise above this level, bond owners can convert their bonds into shares; as a result, the company increases its equity on more favourable conditions than through a straight share issue.

Inasmuch as new share issues subsequent to a convertible issue dilute the stock capital, it is important for the convertible bond holder to have protection built into his ownership rights. This is accomplished by a corresponding decline in the conversion price (protection against dilution) when corporations issue new shares. The importance of this protection can be shown by the 5% Swissair 69/81 convertible bond issue, whose conversion price was set in 1961 at SFr 960. Over the past 15 years Swissair has increased its share capital many times, so that by 1981, 20 years later, the conversion price was SFr 740.

The price of convertible bonds is determined by two elements, the coupon and the conversion price. The difference between the conversion price and the share's market price at the time of the issue is called the conversion premium. It is expressed as a percentage of the share price. Therefore a premium, say, of 10% tells the investor immediately that conversion is possible at 10% above the actual market price of the shares. As a rule of thumb in Switzerland, the conversion feature loses its attractiveness if the premium is above 30% for a first-class company. If the corresponding share is in the weak currency or branch, the premium is below that. Above this level, the straight bond and the convertible bond of the same corporation tend to trade at par (i.e. the value of the conversion right is zero).

Because convertible bonds have the characteristics of both fixed-income securities and risk capital assets, they have enjoyed great success and a high popularity among Swiss investors. The more important bonds issued by large

Table 4.8 Swiss convertible bonds listed on the Zurich Stock Exchange at 30 October 1984

Coupon	Title	Term
5	Adia SA, Chéserex (conversion price SFr 2,700 nominal + SFr 539.50 = 1 bearer share)	1980–91
$4\frac{3}{4}$	Bank Leu AG, Zurich (conversion price SFr 5,000 nominal = 1 bearer share)	1980–84
4	Bar Holding AG, Zurich (conversion price SFr 5,800 nominal = 1 bearer share)	
$4\frac{1}{2}$	BBC AG Brown Boveri & Cie (conversion price SFr 2,100 nominal + 1 registered share)	1980–92
5	CKW, Luzern (conversion price SFr 1,300 nominal = 1 bearer share)	1981–93
$3\frac{1}{4}$	Crédit Suisse (conversion price SFr 2,000 nominal = 1 bearer share inclusive of 1 certificate of participation under repayment of SFr 207.55)	1978–93
$3\frac{1}{4}$	Crédit Suisse (conversion price SFr 400 nominal = 1 registered share inclusive of 1 certificate of participation under repayment of SFr 35.10)	1978–93
3	Electrowatt AG, Zurich (conversion price SFr 1,600 nominal + SFr 315 = 1.21 bearer shares)	1978–93
$4\frac{3}{4}$	Georg Fischer AG, Schaffhausen (conversion price SFr 1,000 nominal = 5 certificates of participation)	1977–89
6	LGZ Landis & Gyr Zug AG (conversion price SFr 1,000 nominal + SFr 859.70 = 2 registered shares or 20 certificates of participation)	1971–86
$5\frac{3}{4}$	Oerlikon-Bührle (conversion price SFr 2,400 nominal = 1 bearer share)	1981–91
4	Schweizerische Volksbank (conversion price SFr 2,000 = 1 bearer share + SFr 250 in cash)	1980–84
4	Gebrüder Sulzer AG (conversion price SFr 400 nominal = 1 certificate of participation)	1979–89
5	Swiss Bank Corporation (conversion price SFr 400 nominal = 1 registered share + SFr 40 in cash)	1980–84
5	Swiss Bank Corporation (conversion price SFr 300 nominal = 1 registered share + SFr 40 in cash)	1980–84
$4\frac{1}{2}$	Union Bank of Switzerland (subordinated band, conversion price SFr 3,000 nominal = 1 registered share under a repayment of SFr 247)	
5	'Winterthur' (conversion price C$1,000 nominal = 1 bearer share)	1978–86
7	'Winterthur' (conversion price US$800 nominal = 1 certificate of participation)	1981–89
4	'Winterthur' (conversion price SFr 2,400 nominal = 1 bearer share)	1983–93
5	'Zurich' (conversion price SFr 9,000 nominal = 1 bearer share)	1982–90

Source: *Kursblatt der Zürcher Effektenbörse*

Swiss and foreign corporations are listed on the stock exchanges. Foreign convertible notes are traded over the counter by both banks and brokers.

Swiss convertible bonds and notes

The first convertible bond of a Swiss corporation was issued by Landis & Gyr, Zug, in 1957. This new security had widespread appeal, both as a novel equity funding vehicle and as an attractive investment possibility for those who did not want to bear the entire risk of a share price fluctuation.

Swiss corporations issue convertible bonds in Swiss francs or in one of the other major currencies. All SFr- and some Eurocurrency-denominated convertibles are listed on the stock exchanges (see Table 4.8).

The conditions of Swiss convertibles tend to vary. They (as other Euro-convertible bonds) always show certain specifications regarding the conversion price, the issuer's option to call the bonds and the protection against dilution.

Many companies reserve the right to raise the conversion price each year by a certain amount. They intend by this policy to make the bond holder convert his bonds into equity as early as possible. Usually only growth companies are successful with this clause in convertible bonds (e.g. 5% Adia, 1980–91).

Most corporations reserve the right to call in outstanding bonds at a fixed price, starting from a certain date, in order to force conversion. Corporations give adequate notice of the recall to the bond holders.

Most (but not all) Swiss convertible bonds provide protection against dilution. This protection is essential in the case of regular share capital increases.

Foreign convertible bonds and notes

For the past few years there has been a very high demand for SFr-denominated convertible notes (bonds) issued by foreign (mostly Japanese) corporations in Switzerland (see Tables 4.9 and 4.10). These Japanese convertibles are mainly in the form of privately placed notes. Notes have a minimum nominal value of SFr 50,000 (bonds SFr 5,000). As a rule of thumb, they bear a coupon of about 1–3% below market rates for straight notes (bonds) and have a duration of five years (ten years).

Although Japanese convertible notes (or bonds) have low-interest coupons, they usually earn a higher yield than the corresponding stock. The very low premiums of Japanese convertibles is offset by their low coupons. Therefore, an investment in Japanese convertibles has all the advantages of a direct stock investment, and if the corresponding stock does not perform well, the note holders can still recoup the original investment when the notes are due.

SFr-denominated Japanese convertible notes, which are traded over the counter by banks and brokers, have the additional benefit to the investor of lower charges and commissions than a comparable direct investment in Japanese stock through a broker in Japan. The commission for the purchase of a Swiss franc note (bond) amounts to only $\frac{5}{8}$%.

Table 4.9 Some selected note placements by Japanese corporations on the Swiss capital market at 30 November 1984

Interest rate	Title	Term
$1\frac{3}{4}$	Daiwa House	1984–89
$1\frac{3}{4}$	Kao Corp.	1984–89
$1\frac{3}{4}$	Nippon Beet Sugar	1984–89
$1\frac{3}{4}$	Sonoike MfG	1984–89
$1\frac{3}{4}$	Sumitomo Electric	1984–89
$1\frac{3}{4}$	Sumitomo Real	1984–89
$1\frac{3}{4}$	Nichiboshin	1984–89
$1\frac{3}{4}$	Royal Co.	1984–89
$1\frac{3}{4}$	Chujitsuya	1984–89
$1\frac{3}{4}$	Hanwa	1984–89
$1\frac{7}{8}$	Daiki Aluminium	1984–89
$1\frac{7}{8}$	Nippon Shinpan	1984–92
$1\frac{7}{8}$	Nitto Boseki	1984–89
$1\frac{7}{8}$	Zenchiku Co.	1984–89
$1\frac{7}{8}$	Chugoku Marine Paints	1984–89
$1\frac{7}{8}$	Morita Fire Pump	1984–89
$1\frac{7}{8}$	Citizen Watch	1984–89
2	Makino Milling	1984–89
2	Mitsubishi Electric	1984–89
2	Nippon Shinpan	1984–89
2	Sumitomo Corp.	1984–89
2	Tsurumi MfG	1984–89
2	Tokuyama Soda	1984–89
$2\frac{1}{8}$	Tokai Gas	1984–89
$2\frac{1}{8}$	Mitsui Construction	1984–89
$2\frac{1}{8}$	Aoki Corp.	1984–90
$2\frac{1}{4}$	Mitsubishi Plastics Industries	1984–89
$2\frac{1}{2}$	Sogo	1984–89
$2\frac{1}{2}$	Kanemori	1984–89
$2\frac{1}{2}$	Sailor Pen	1984–89
$2\frac{5}{8}$	Meiji Seika	1984–89
$2\frac{5}{8}$	Nippon Carbon	1984–89

Source: HandelsBank NW, Dec. 1984.

Option bonds (bonds with stock warrants)

Option bonds or bonds with stock warrants are fixed-income securities which give the owner the right to purchase shares or certificates of participation of the issuing company. These warrants can be exercised only during a specified time period and at a specified price.

From the issuing corporation's point of view, an option bond is a way of getting long-term capital. The attached warrant implies the advantage of a lower interest cost and of a possible conversion of debt into equity at relatively favourable conditions. The investor gets lower interest income relative to a straight bond, but enjoys the advantage of a possible rise in the value of the stock of the corporation.

A warrant is a separate certificate which is issued with the bond. It incorporates

Table 4.10 Foreign convertible bonds listed on the Zurich
Stock Exchange at 30 October 1984

Interest rate	Title	Term
$2\frac{3}{4}$	Nippon Airways Co. Ltd, Tokyo	1984–94
$4\frac{3}{4}$	Bridge Oil Overseas NV, Curaçao	1983–93
$4\frac{1}{2}$	Générale Occidentale, Paris	1984–94
2	Nippon Shinpan Co., Tokyo	1984–92
$3\frac{1}{2}$	Fujitsu Ltd, Kawasaki	1983–93
$3\frac{1}{2}$	Honda Motor Co. Ltd, Tokyo	1983–93
$6\frac{1}{2}$	Minebea Co. Ltd, Nagano	1982–92
$4\frac{3}{4}$	Mitsubishi Chemical Ind. Ltd, Tokyo	1980–91
$3\frac{1}{2}$	NEC Corp., Tokyo	1983–93
$2\frac{1}{8}$	Nippon Oil Co. Ltd, Tokyo	1984–92
$3\frac{1}{2}$	Nissan Motor Co. Ltd, Tokyo	1983–93
$4\frac{1}{2}$	Olympus Optical Co. Ltd, Tokyo	1982–92
$5\frac{1}{2}$	Sanyo Electric, Osaka	1980–90
$3\frac{1}{2}$	Sanyo Electric, Osaka	1983–93
$3\frac{5}{8}$	Settsu Paperb. Mfg Co., Amagasaki	1983–93
$2\frac{1}{4}$	Settsu Paperb. Mfg Co., Amagasaki	1984–92
$3\frac{1}{2}$	Sharp Corp., Osaka	1983–93
$2\frac{3}{4}$	Toshiba Corp., Tokyo	1983–94
2	Toshiba Corp., Tokyo	1984–92
$4\frac{3}{4}$	Wang Laboratories	1984–94

Source: *Kursblatt der Zürcher Effektenbörse.*

the right to purchase a certain number of shares or certificates of participation of a certain corporation at a fixed price during a fixed period. The 'fixed' price is not always constant over the whole period; it is often adjusted, particularly for capital increases. The warrant can be bought either separately or together with the option bond. As a result, three quotations are made in connection with an option bond:

(a)   the price of the option bond with the attached warrant,
(b)   the price of the option bond without the warrant,
(c)   the price of the warrant alone.

The attractiveness of warrants is due to the high leverage factor. Through warrants an investor can purchase 'a large number of stocks' with a relatively low capital investment. Therefore, rising stock prices imply relatively higher gains in percentage in the warrants than in the underlying stock. Conversely, the investor is also faced with higher risk in his investment. Falling stock prices can mean a total loss of the capital invested in warrants.

Comparable to traded options on foreign option exchanges, warrants carry both an intrinsic and time value known as the premium. The intrinsic value is the difference between the actual share price and the price at which the shares can be bought through the warrant. Rarely, the warrant is traded at or below its intrinsic value. In most cases, the investors are prepared to pay a premium, because

Table 4.11 Swiss option bonds listed on the Zurich Stock Exchange at 30 October 1984

Coupon	Title	Term
4	BBC AG Brown Boveri & Cie (cum warrant) (1 option for SFr 1,000* = 3 certificates of participation at SFr 235 until 30 Sept. 88)	1983–94
$5\frac{3}{4}$	Crédit Suisse, Zurich (subordinated/cum warrant) (1 option for SFr 2,000* = 3 registered shares inclusive of certificate of participation at SFr 1,150 until 30 June 87)	1981–91
$5\frac{3}{4}$	Crédit Suisse, Zurich (cum warrant) (1 option for SFr 200* = 1 registered share inclusive of certificate of participation at SFr 230 until 30 June 87)	1982–94
$3\frac{1}{2}$	Elektrowatt A.G. Zurich (cum warrant) (2 options for SFr 3,000* = 1 bearer share at SFr 2,850 until 30 Sept. 89)	1983–95
$4\frac{1}{2}$	Huber & Suhner AG Kabelwerke, Herisau (cum warrant)	1984–96
4	Interdiscount Holding AG, Freiburg (cum warrant) (1 option for SFr 1,200* = 1 bearer share at SFr 1,200 until 15 June 88)	1983–95
$3\frac{1}{2}$	Intershop Holding AG, Zurich (cum warrant) (1 option for SFr 1,000* = 2 bearer shares at SFr 525 until 31 March 89)	1984–94
4	Konsum Verein Zurich, Zurich (cum warrant)	1983–95
4	Maag-Zahnrader & Maschinen AG, Zurich (cum warrant)	1983–95
$3\frac{3}{4}$	Maschinenfabrik Mikron AG, Biel (cum warrant) (1 option for SFr 2,000* = 1 bearer share at SFr 1,318 until 30 June 87)	1979–90
4	Mövenpick Holding, Zurich (cum warrant) (1 option for SFr 4,000* = 1 bearer share at SFr 3,300 until 30 Nov. 87)	1983–95
4	Sika Finanz AG, Baar (cum warrant) (1 option for SFr 2,000* = 1 bearer share at SFr 2,200 until 31 Dec. 85)	1983–95
$4\frac{3}{4}$	Société Internationale Pirelli SA, Basle (cum warrant) (1 option for SFr 1,000* = 3 certificates of participation at SFr 238.50 until 31 Dec. 85)	1980–90
6	Swiss Bank Corporation, Basle (subordinated/cum warrant) (1 option for SFr 3,000* = 8 registered shares at SFr 201 until 30 June 85)	1982–91
$5\frac{3}{4}$	Swissair 'Schweiz Luftverkehr-AG', Zurich (cum warrant) (1 option for SFr 1,000* = 1 bearer share at SFr 646 until 31 Dec. 86)	1981–96
$6\frac{1}{4}$	Union Bank of Switzerland, Zurich (subordinated/cum warrant) (1 option for SFr 1,000* = 1 registered share at SFr 468 until 30 Sept. 86)	1981–90
$5\frac{1}{4}$	Union Bank of Switzerland (subordinated/cum warrant) (1 option for SFr 1,000* = 1 registered share at SFr 643 until 30 Sept. 88)	1984–93
4	Zellweger Uster AG, Uster (cum warrant)	1983–95

Source: *Kursblatt der Zürcher Effektenbörse*
* Face value

warrants imply a high leverage and the right not to exercise the option. The higher the volatility of a stock, the higher the premium the investor has to pay. As a rule of thumb, premiums amount to about 5% per annum for Swiss option bonds.

Swiss option bonds

The first issue of a Swiss option bond was made in 1971 by the Union Bank of Switzerland. Since then a large number of corporations have used this new financing tool (see Table 4.11).

In Switzerland, option bonds and warrants enjoy a high popularity. Because the warrants have a maturity of one to ten years, they are an attractive investment in periods when stock prices are depressed.

The liquidity of option bonds and warrants either listed on the stock exchanges or over the counter is relatively high in Switzerland. However, in quiet markets the investor is advised to give his orders for warrants with price limits.

Foreign option bonds and notes

Japanese borrowers have also used the Swiss capital market for issuing option bonds and especially option notes. Bonds typically have a nominal value of SFr 5,000; notes cannot have a face value of less than SFr 50,000. Compared with convertible bonds, option bonds give the investor the additional advantage of purchasing the warrants only. The warrants of the bonds (notes) are traded over the counter by banks and brokers. The strength of the Japanese stock market has contributed to their great success.

As in the market for convertibles, the option bond (note) market has the advantage for the borrower of raising capital on favourable terms, not only because of the attached warrant but also because of the generally very low level of Swiss interest rates. The investor who seeks high leverage can invest in warrants of Japanese corporations instead of purchasing the stock itself. A less risky investment is the purchase of the option bond with the warrant attached.

Two Japanese corporations that have issued option bonds on the Swiss capital market are listed on the Zurich Stock Exchange. Around 30 option note issues are traded over the counter.

To conclude, Table 4.12 gives a summary of the types of securities – with their main features – which have been discussed in this chapter.

Table 4.12 Summary: types of securities and their principal features

Type	German title	Characteristics
Bearer share OR 978ff	*Inhaberaktie*	– instrument of ownership – easily transferable – name of owner not registered
Registered share OR 974ff	*Namenaktie*	– instrument of ownership – share made out in the name of the owner – shareholder registered in shareholders' book – registered transfer

Table 4.12 – cont.

Type	German title	Characteristics
Dividend-right certificate OR 657	*Genussschein*	– instrument of dividend participation without voting power – easily transferable
Certificate of participation	*Partizipations-schein*	– a dividend-right certificate
Preference share OR 656	*Vorzugsaktien*	– shares carry rights that take precedence over common stock – bearer or registered form
Twin share	*Zwillingsaktien*	– instrument for co-operation or acquisition – shares incorporate rights on two companies – bearer or registered form
Jumbo certificate	*Jumbozertifikat*	– represents 1,000 shares or a nominal value of SFr100,000
Fractional certificate	*Teilzertifikat*	– represents a part of an original share or certificate
Mutual investment certificate	*Anteilszertifikat an Anlagefonds*	– joint capital investment by numerous investors – claim against fund management
Convertible bond	*Wandelobligation*	– bond which may be converted into securities of the same or of another company at specified conditions
Option bond	*Optionsanleihe*	– bond with warrants attached – bond and warrants are traded together or separately
Warrant	*Optionsschein*	– entitles the bearer to subscribe to securities at specific conditions

5 New issue procedures

Heini P. Dubler

Types and volume of new share issues

During the last decade the Swiss capital market has seen a considerable number of new share issues by Swiss companies, both by way of initial public offerings and through share capital increases. The amounts involved are still significant, but the value of total share issues represents only 20% of all funds raised in the form of domestic bonds and shares – a sharp decline from the 50%-and-more level of the early 1960s. The methods of raising equity capital can vary; the following three methods are the most commonly used:

(a) issuance of new shares or equity instruments in the form of 'rights issues',
(b) issuance of bonds with warrants attached or convertible into the underlying equity, and
(c) initial public offerings of shares or participation certificates (PS).

Table 5.1 shows the volume of capital raised through public equity offerings both for 'primary' and 'secondary' issues since 1970.

The table accurately reflects issue activity on the Swiss equity market. Initial public offerings of any considerable size are very rare indeed. The bulk of new share issues originates from the regular users of equity markets, such as banks, insurance companies and some very large, well-established companies. The last category is now more important than in the early 1970s because of a lower cash flow due to falling profits. On the other hand, there are still companies like Hoffmann-La Roche, the fifth largest Swiss company, with an authorised share capital of only SFr 50,000 – and a market capitalisation of approximately SFr 7.5 billion at the end of December 1984, which has never used the capital market for issuance of stocks or bonds (its shares are quoted on the 'Vorbörse' – the 'pre-official stock exchange dealing').

Obstacles to new issues activity

In Switzerland, domestic companies (majority of shares owned by Swiss investors) are usually very reluctant to even consider the step of going public.

Table 5.1 Swiss share issues, 1970–84

Year	Initial public offerings		Capital increase‡ (Rights issues)		
	Number*	Amount† (SFr million)	Number	Amount (SFr million)	Total (SFr million)
1970	2	18.7	47	525.5	544.2
1971	—	—	60	998.5	998.5
1972	3	12.2	64	1,006.6	1,018.8
1973	5	100.0	65	811.6	911.6
1974	—	—	48	615.8	615.8
1975	1	—	47	1,089.9	1,089.9
1976	—	—	81	1,535.0	1,535.0
1977	—	—	77	741.7	741.7
1978	—	—	85	1,090.5	1,090.5
1979	1	27.0	81	1,322.2	1,349.2
1980	2	90.3	80	2,176.7	2,267.0
1981	3	29.3	77	2,012.0	2,041.3
1982	2	9.1	57	550.6	559.7
1983	2	27.2	48	1,001.1	1,027.3
1984	1	24.5	53	1,656.3	1,680.8

* With and without capital increases.
† Capital increases only.
‡ Quoted and unquoted public capital increases.
Sources: Swiss National Bank, Monthly Bulletin; HandelsBank NW, Zurich.

Many reasons are put forward by the owners/chief executives of privately owned companies which, considering size and acceptance, would qualify for a public opening. Not all of the following arguments apply equally to all such companies.

Growth takes more time than abroad

Because of Switzerland's small domestic economy, with a market of approximately 6.2 million people, companies reach the required size and popularity among potential investors only many years after their incorporation. In fact, during the last two decades there have been very few Swiss companies that have made a public share offering (initial public offering) within ten years of their start-up.

Non-existence of broadly developed stock market for unquoted stocks

There is no broad market for stocks to be traded outside the stock exchanges (*ausserbörslich*); companies whose stocks are traded outside the stock exchanges remain to a large extent controlled by small investors' groups, often orientated to a certain region. In most cases these are shares of regional and local banks as well as mountain railways, cable cars, ski-lifts, etc.

Anonymity, problems regarding disclosure of company data

It is in the very nature of the typical Swiss entrepreneur to start his business very cautiously and in a small way; if the company owners become successful, they usually have no interest in sharing their achievements with other investors. Unlike in the United States, a young entrepreneur's objective is not the initial public offering, thereby making a large personal fortune, but rather the 'grooming' of his company. By going public a company is subject, as in other countries, to certain obligations *vis-à-vis* the investors, e.g. publication of the annual report and organisation of annual stockholders' meetings with their sometimes awkward questions. Management is afraid that competitors might be able to get hold of important information concerning figures, profit margins, etc. The additional cost of all these obligations is often considered non-productive.

Tax law, dividend policy, capitalisation
The Swiss tax laws are not very company-friendly as far as capital market transactions are concerned (3% stamp duty on new share issues). Swiss companies, even those already officially listed, tend to have a quite restrictive dividend policy. Because of the relatively low interest level in Switzerland and a very competitive banking industry, Swiss companies tend to rely to a large extent on debt financing more than on equity. Many companies have no real need to use the capital market for raising equity because of high profitability.

Investment restrictions imposed on large domestic sources of funds
As in other industrialised countries, more and more savings are being accumulated by social security schemes, pension funds, insurance companies, etc., which have to place their funds in so-called 'conservative and safe' non-equity-related investments such as government papers (confederation, cantons, cities, etc.) and mortgages. Only a small portion is available for share investments. Even if allowed, such investments are limited to shares of well-established banks, insurance companies and possibly some large chemical or food companies (the blue chips of Switzerland). It is therefore particularly difficult to find funds among institutional investors for young enterprises with high growth potential and opportunities to create new jobs. This attitude, coupled with the mentioned shift of available capital, has up to now also limited the 'going public' of smaller companies, even if they had wished to do so.

Restrictive investment policies within the Swiss portfolio management/advisory community
Largely due to a lack of qualified and trained personnel, banks and other leading portfolio management companies have failed to encourage investors to participate in venture capital or even late-stage financings. As a first step, financial institutions or departments within existing banks might have to create, along the lines of mergers and acquisitions departments in the United States, the United Kingdom, etc., in-house organisations with the ability to judge new technologies, markets and company management. Since 1981 or so some encouraging developments have taken place in this field. In the summer of 1984 the Swiss Venture Capital Association was founded in order to promote the idea of venture capital among a wider public, in particular among the political circles of Switzerland.

Legal and other requirements for public stock issues

The Swiss capital market has usually operated with few restrictions. There are few rules and regulations to be observed; some of them were introduced on a temporary basis only.

Control of issues

According to the law governing the Swiss National Bank (Art. 16 g, h, i), the Federal Council can, in order to avoid excessive demands on the money and capital markets, declare as subject to permission any domestic public issue, in particular bonds, and certificates of deposit, shares, profit-sharing certificates (PS) and other similar instruments. The National Bank can limit the total amount of such issues to be permitted during a specific period of time.

If in a particular case there is a dispute about whether an issue requires permission, the National Bank decides. A nine-member commission appointed by the Federal Council but chaired by a member of the directorate of the Swiss National Bank rules upon individual applications. This so-called 'new issue committee' was active from January 1972 until December 1983. Since 1984 no restrictions on new issues have been in force. However, new public issues must be registered with the Swiss National Bank.

Monies from abroad

If the balanced economic development of the country is disturbed or threatened by an excessive inflow of monies from abroad, the Federal Council may limit or prohibit the acquisition of domestic securities by persons having their domicile or head office abroad. Regulations prohibiting the 'new purchase of stocks from the stock exchanges or from new issues' by foreign persons or companies were in force from 26 June 1972 until 24 January 1979. These restrictions were enacted following the extreme inflow of money from abroad that led to a very strong appreciation of the Swiss franc, with repercussions on the competitiveness of the Swiss export industry. But normally there are no restrictions.

Minimum size

Limitations in this respect are set by the listing requirements of the stock exchange commissions as well as by the number of securities to be placed among the investing public. Experience has shown that in order for a normal market to develop, the number of publicly placed shares should generally be at least 5,000–8,000. However, there are no legal requirements as to the number of shares that must be issued and offered to the public. The size of the company, the nominal value of capital, etc., are not in themselves criteria for being able to go public. To be successful in such an important step of the company's history – and in a small market like Switzerland it is even more significant – going public should result in at least a listing of the stock on the 'Vorbörse'. The real over-the-counter market (Ausserbörse) is of lesser importance because most of the shares traded over the counter are of regional character only. This market is dominated by two quite different institutions, the Swiss Bank Corporation, one of the largest banks, and Volksbank Willisau, Lucerne branch, a regional bank.

Issue price

According to Art. 624 of the Swiss Code of Obligations, shares may be issued at par or at a premium. New shares may be issued to replace any which have been cancelled. The issue of shares at a premium is permitted if the statutes provide this option or if the shareholders' meeting has so decided. The proceeds of the issue exceeding the nominal value are appropriated, after payment of the issue expenses, to the statutory reserve funds.

Public subscription

Where shares are offered for public subscription, Art. 631 and Art. 651 of the Swiss Code of Obligations stipulate that invitations to subscribers must be in the form of a prospectus signed by all the founders (or in the case of a long-existing company, by a person authorised to represent the company on behalf of the administration). *The information to be included in the prospectus must be identical with that necessary for the listing on a stock exchange* (see Chapter 7 – conditions for listing).

Legal form of issuer

There are no legal prescriptions regarding the type of corporate form. Any legal form of corporate entity can raise equity capital by way of private or public offerings.

Going public (initial public offering)

Since the mid-1970s only a handful of companies have – as already mentioned – followed the path from privately owned company to publicly owned corporation. Many companies that in principle had this avenue open (e.g. because of family problems, when no successor was available or willing to step in, etc.) finally chose to be taken over by another company, in most cases by a larger entity. This solution has further reduced the actual number of ideal candidates for going public. At present probably no more than 30–40 Swiss companies would fulfil the requirements set by the market for a public opening by way of a public issue.

Once a company has decided to go public, then even in a small market like Switzerland it is very important that the company starts early with an investor relations exercise.

The preparation of such an undertaking should be started early, including the appointment of the bank that is to manage the transaction. As in other capital market deals, the choice of a solid bank of good reputation and with investment banking activities is essential. The bank will have to perform some very important and delicate functions. Probably more than in other markets, investors rely heavily on the standing of the bank managing a share issue, as far as the quality and growth protential of the issuer is concerned.

The role of the banking community in a new issue

Of the approximately 25 major companies that have made an initial public offering since 1970, all but one have used the services of a bank or a banking syndicate for the actual issue of shares.

In such transactions banks usually underwrite the total amount of shares to be placed so that the issuer is sure of the exact net proceeds he will receive (after deduction of issue expenses, underwriting commissions, stamp taxes, etc.). The size of the transactions has varied, as has the percentage of ownership. In most cases the first round of issuing takes the form of minority stakes. There are no fixed syndicates for such new share issues (IPOs) in the Swiss market. In most cases there is only one bank handling the issue. If several banks join as co-managers, the group is usually very small. Companies that undertake the step of going public are often old established organisations of respectable size. Such companies will naturally have existing bank relationships, which will be taken into account when choosing the manager and co-manager(s) of such an important transaction. These will be the banks that have followed the particular company closely throughout its development stage and are thus well positioned to analyse and evaluate the company.

Very often a bank representative holds a directorship on the board of the company, giving him firsthand access to information on the company's performance. Under Swiss banking law, banks can perform any kind of banking business, such as portfolio management, investment banking and commercial banking, as well as foreign exchange and stock exchange business. Therefore, any Swiss bank could in principle manage new issue transactions. As it has turned out in the past, most of these deals have been managed by one of the three largest banks or a larger foreign-owned bank with some private Geneva and Zurich banks as co-managers. Because of the expected success of such transactions, the syndicate is kept very small. Some banks might receive an undisclosed invitation to participate as selling group members.

Such IPOs are set up in the traditional form, i.e. the banks underwrite the entire amount of the issue against an underwriting commission of between 2% and 3%. Two contracts are signed by the banks: (a) the purchase and placement agreement (issuer with the banks), and (b) the syndication agreement among the banks. The latter would stipulate items like allotment of shares, i.e. distribution to as many different subscribers as possible in order to ensure a widespread placement. Insurance companies, mutual funds and some other categories of large investors might be treated somewhat more favourably. Preceding the actual issue, a very detailed and well-prepared prospectus with subscription forms is produced by the leading bank, and after printing will be sent to banks and other investors. Similar to a public debt issue, the subscription period must be fixed and notified to investors. There is no fixed rule regulating the start of trading of new shares on the 'Vorbörse'. However, trading usually starts two days after the offering to the public.

The costs incurred are mainly the underwriting commission mentioned above. The 3% new issue tax is also due by the corporation if the shares offered to the public have not been issued and paid in beforehand. Costs for printing the prospectus and publication in a newspaper will amount to approximately SFr 35–50,000. A part of these expenses will not be duplicated if the stock is listed on the exchange within six months following the publication of the prospectus. Initial public offerings in the Swiss capital market have often been priced extremely conservatively. Most of the recent issues have been very successful, with stock price openings at particularly high premiums. One of the reasons for such good results was the underestimation of market forces, i.e. the investors' inclination to assume risks. Investors are looking for new firms, often to have additional diversification for their portfolios. Once a company has made its decision to go public, an immediate and substantial interest is built up by both institutional and private investors. The rarity of a new share is sometimes very quickly translated into unrealistic prices.

A listing of principal IPOs between 1970 and 1984 will be found in Table 5.2.

Table 5.2 Principal initial public offerings, 1970–84

Company	Issue amount (SFr million)	Issue price per share	Share price end-1984
Zellweger	NA	150[1]*	1,310
Cellulose Attisholz	15.0	1,350	1,050
Heuer-Leonidas[2]	3.7	925	—
Büro Fürrer	5.7	1,100	1,725
Interdiscount	6.5	608	1,510
Kuoni	11.7	1,300	8,875
Gardisette	10.0[3]	425	100
Mövenpick	2.5	2,400	3,700
Mövenpick	0.5 [4]	450†	675
Netstal	9.6	800	890
Oerlikon Bührle	100.0	500	1,260
Schweiter	7.6	950	190
Vetropack	30.0	2,500	3,200
Adia	27.0	1,630	2,255
Bär Holding	21.3	3,000	7,000
Dow Banking	69.0	1,150	1,150
Sunstar	12.0	1,200	1,150
Orsat	9.0	750	650
Surveillance	21.0	1,142*	3,800
Crossair	9.1	278†	316
Fuchs Petrolub	6.8	977	2,085
Autophon	27.2	1,550	4,200
Walter Rentsch	24.0	1,200	2,975
Carlo Gavazzi	24.5	2,400	3,930

* Profit-sharing certificates.
† Registered shares.
[1] Restricted profit-sharing certificates – for employees and existing shareholders only.
[2] Watch company, bankrupt.
[3] Private placement, approx. figure.
[4] Placed without banking syndicate, value approximate.
Source: HandelsBank NW, Zurich.

Issuance of stocks – capital increase

Under Swiss law, any increase in share capital must be approved by the shareholders' meeting in two steps. In the first meeting, shareholders must agree upon the increase in share capital. In the second meeting, *after* the issue of the shares, the shareholders must confirm their subscriptions and payment for the new shares; such procedures are inflexible, time-consuming and rather expensive.

In practice, the basic decision to increase the share capital and the confirmation of the share issue is resolved during the same shareholders' meeting. Since such proceedings are allowed only on the basis that the share capital increase is already paid in, banks play an important role because they usually have potential investors at hand and the capability to finance the payment for the share issue. In cases of public share capital increase, subscription rights must be extended to the existing shareholders. A stockholder is thereby granted the subscription right for a certain amount of new stock to be issued. This right contains the ratio in proportion to which the present shareholder can subscribe new shares – based on his present holding.

In Switzerland it is customary to sell new shares to existing stockholders at an issue price far below the market price. While, for example, an old share may sell at SFr 500 in the market, new shares of SFr 100 par value are likely to be issued at prices of perhaps SFr 150 or SFr 200 per share. Since after the issue the new shares will enjoy exactly the same rights as the old ones (except, perhaps, for a brief interim period), the subscriber may count firmly on an almost immediate and substantial profit. The right to acquire one new share of stock for, say, ten shares already held therefore has a concrete, measurable value.

In announcing the forthcoming capital increase, the company will state that the right to subscribe to new stocks may be exercised by surrendering coupon No. X (the last unused coupon attached to the share). Such coupons may then be traded as subscription rights on the exchange. Investors who are not planning to make use of their subscription rights or who wish to purchase additional rights will be able to do so at the stock exchange. The banks normally sell the subscription rights of an investor who is not reacting to the new share offering. In such a case all the remaining rights are sold at an average price on the last subscription date. All investors will therefore be credited with the same price (sales proceeds). In almost all share capital increases, the share price after the issue rises back to its old value despite the dilution effect (making up the theoretical value of the right), because companies endeavour to maintain their dividends at the previous level. The value of the right often represents a real gain, a fact that may explain the wide popularity of share capital increases.

Syndication/methods of underwriting

Firm underwriting is the most frequently used procedure for the issue of shares in Switzerland. Companies also have the possibility of direct placing, thus bearing the risk of the issue. This, however, is rather unusual in the case of a public issue. But in the case of capital increases by a banking institution, the form of direct placement without syndication and firm underwriting is used. In this manner the particular bank can save the underwriting commission of 2–3%.

Companies that raise share capital frequently have a traditional fixed bank syndicate to handle their issue by purchasing it from the issuer. The three largest banks, the cantonal bank in whose canton the company is domiciled, and perhaps another bank close to the issuer will form most of the syndicates in this domain.

As far as the many small and mostly local companies are concerned, another method is often used. A banking group acts as subscription and paying agent without taking any risk. The interested investor can send the subscription form to one of the banks mentioned in that capacity on the prospectus (sometimes on the subscription form only).

The form of private placement is used fairly frequently for small companies that have no ambition to be listed. In this case a private placement memorandum without a real prospectus will be prepared, and banks will sell the shares to only a very select number of their clientèle.

In some instances companies have made the first step towards going public by offering shares or profit-sharing certificates to their employees only. Such securities have been coupled with restrictions as to their tradeability. A listing on the stock exchange takes place several years later.

6 Share Trading Procedures and Cost

Jean-Pierre Frefel

General information on the stock exchanges

The quotations list

One of the most important tools of a trader at the stock exchange is the daily quotations list. This list will be published after each dealing day. All published information and of course the prices notified are official. Yearly subscription rates for mailing outside Switzerland vary between SFr 550 and SFr 1,000. However, most of the relevant Swiss newspapers and a variety of international publications report every day from the different Swiss market-places and indicate at least the closing prices of the more widely held stocks.

All official quotations lists are split into two major parts – bonds and stocks. In addition, there are one or two pages reserved for general information, e.g. new listings, dividends, indexes, best and worst performing share prices, closing dates of forward transactions and statistics on listed securities.

The order of equity dealing and the subsequent quotations list notification is essentially the same at all Swiss stock exchanges, starting with Swiss companies (except Basle Stock Exchange, where foreign listed securities are dealt with before Swiss shares). At the Zurich Stock Exchange the order is as follows:

	(at 31 May 1985)
Transportation companies	6
Banks	32
Finance companies	47
Insurance companies	21
Industry	69
Investment funds	22
US and Canadian shares	114
Other foreign shares (exc. W. German)	48
West German shares	25

Since a company may issue different categories of securities, there is also a strict dealing order within companies' shares. First are bearer shares, followed by registered shares and finally certificates of participation. When there is only one category listed and no specification printed in the quotations list, these securities are bearer shares. Shares that are subject to special conditions, e.g. new shares through capital increases with half dividend or non-fully paid shares (e.g. Swiss National Bank) are marked accordingly.

Registered foreign shares are traded as bearer certificates due to the registration in the name of one of the Swiss nominee banks (Crédit Suisse, Swiss Bank Corporation, Union Bank of Switzerland or Société Nominée de Genève).

A speciality of the Swiss stock exchanges is the possibility of trading securities on forward accounts. Prices paid for that type of transaction are marked as follows:

. . . †	transaction due end of current month
. . . ††	end of next month
. . . †††	end of three months
. . . d . . . †	
. . . d . . .††	forward transaction with a premium.
. . . d . . . †††	

Other symbols frequently used are:

R	transaction concluded in the second reading
L	price determined by lot

Tables 6.1, 6.2 and 6.3 give quotations lists from the Zurich, Basle and Geneva Stock Exchanges, respectively.

Trading hours

The official opening hours of the major Swiss stock exchanges are:

Zurich:	10.00 a.m. Monday to Friday
Basle:	9.55 a.m. Monday to Friday
Geneva:	10.10 a.m. Monday to Friday

Before the official listing starts all exchanges are open for pre-market dealing, usually at 9.15. Unlisted securities are dealt throughout the day on the telephone between specialised dealers. Closing hours at the stock exchanges depend upon turnover, but in general are between 1.00 and 1.30 p.m. In Zurich dealing may go on until 2.00 p.m.

Pre-market dealing

Pre-market dealing plays a very important role in the Swiss capital market. Before the official trading hour, dealers meet at the stock exchange to deal in

Table 6.1 The quotations list – Zurich Stock Exchange, 13 November 1984

Nominal value per share or certificate	Ex dividend date	Ex coupon no.	Dividend paid (SFr) 1981	1982	1983	Securities no.	Shares	Record of lowest and highest prices paid (adjusted after rights issues), 1984	Previous paid cash price	Bid	Asked	Paid
1	2	3	4	4	4	5		6	7	8	9	10
							Swiss manufacturing companies					
500	29.6.84	29	35	40	40	136,320s	Aare-Tessin AG für Elektrizität (Atel), Olten	1,300 1,405	1,310 9.11	1,300	1,320	1,300L.
200	10.5.82	5	24	0	0	136,634s	Accumulatoren-Fabrik Oerlikon, Zürich	550 760	550 1.11	550	550	
100	10.5.82	—	12	0	0	136,633	do. (nominal shares)	185 300	185 28.9	170	—	
100	3.6.77	—	0	0	0	238,497s	Aktiengesellschaft Adolph Saurer, Arbon	158 235	210 12.11	211	213	212 12† 14†††L. 13 12 R 12
20	3.6.77	45	0			238,498	do. (nominal shares, Nos. 250,001–310,000)	65 95	87 7.11	85	95	
1,000	25.5.84	8	67,50	67,50	67,50	140,840s	Aletsch AG, Mörel	1,700 1,820	1,800 10.8	1,800	1,750	
500	3.9.81	27	0	0	0	145,230s	Ateliers des Charmilles SA, Genf, A	310 490	470 12.11	461	470	R 461
100	3.9.81	13	0	0	0	145,231	do. B (nominal shares)	70 101	96 2.11	90	100	
500	22.6.82	5	25			145,201	Ateliers de Constr. mecan de Vevey SA, Vevey (nominal shares)	760 920	880 8.11	860	865	865 R 65
100	29.3.84	34	20	22	24	145,460s	Au Grand Passage SA, Genf	600 710	650 12.11	660	670	666 65 60
500	29.5.84	2	—	—	27,50	146,271s	Autophon AG, Solothurn	3,560 4,250	4,180 12.11	4,160	4,170	4,160
100	29.5.84	—	10	10	11	146,270	do. (nominal shares)	620 700	630 9.11	625	630	
500	5.6.84	28	50	30	30	238,661s	BBC AG Brown, Boveri & Cie, Baden, A	1,240 1,580	1,375 12.11	1,385	1,390	1,380 85 R 85
100	5.6.84	—	10	6	6	238,669	do. B (nominal shares)	215 255	225 12.11	224	227	
100	5.6.84	28	10	6	6	238,670s	do. (certificates of participation)	215 265	227 12.11	227	229	227 R 27
500	19.3.84	26	40	40+10	—	154,140s	Brauerei Eichhof, Luzern	1,350 1,590	1,375 12.11	1,380	1,420	
500	19.3.84	26	40	40+10	—	154,142	do. (nominal shares)	1,100 1,275	1,250 7.11	1,225	1,250	
500	15.5.84	23	30	30	30	156,318s	Buss AG, Basel (bearer shares)	800 950	870 26.10	840	880	
500	2.4.84	8	0	20	—	157,708s	Cellulose Attisholz AG, Attisholz (bearer shares)	820 1,175	1,160 9.11	1,150	1,170	
500	1.6.84	44	35	35	35	157,928s	Centralschweizerische Kraftwerke, Luzern	1,000 1,230	1,060 12.11	1,065	—	1,065
100	11.5.84	19	25	28	31	159,107s	Ciba-Geigy AG, Basel	2,080 2,560	2,470 12.11	2,480	2,490	2,485 80 R 80 500†††
100	11.5.84	—	25	28	31	159,108	do. (nominal shares)	942 1,084	1,053 12.11	1,055	1,057	1,052 R 55 90d20†††
100	11.5.84	19	25	28	31	159,109s	do. (certificates of participation)	1,640 1,980	1,970 12.11	1,975	1,980	1,970 65L. 70 80†† R 75
500	27.3.84	34	40+10	40	40	168,705s	Elektrizitäts-Gesellschaft Laufenburg AG, Laufenburg	1,800 2,450	2,145 12.11	2,150	2,160	
500	2.7.84	33	32,50	32,50	32,50	169,845s	Energie Electrique du Simplon SA, Simplon-Dorf (bearer shares)	1,240 1,300	1,270 5.11	1,270	—	

Table 6.2 The quotations list – Basle Stock Exchange, 13 November 1984

Listed capital (SFr millions)	Nominal value per share or certificate (SFr)	Dividend paid (SFr) 1983	Dividend paid (SFr) 1984	Ex dividend date	Ex coupon no.	Financial service bank	Securities no.	Shares	Record of lowest and highest prices paid (adjusted) cash and forward, 1984		Previous paid cash price		Bid	Asked	Paid
1	2	3	3	4	5	6	7		8		9		10	11	12
								Swiss manufacturing companies							
225	500	40	40	29.6.84	29	BV	136,320s	Aare-Tessin AG für Elektrizität (Atel), Olten	1,300	1,400	9.11	1,300	1,300	1,310	
2.5	200	0	0	10.5.82	5	SA	136,634s	Accumulatoren-Fabrik Oerlikon, Zürich	525	730	10.10	525	550	—	
2.5	100	0	0	10.5.82	5	BV	136,633	do. (bearer shares)	180	280	5.11	185	150	—	
20	1,000	67.50	67.50	25.5.84	8	BV	140,840s	Aletsch AG, Mörel	1,700	1,800	22.10	1,700	1,700	—	
467	500	0	0	23.4.82	22	SK	141,857s	Aluminium AG (Schweizerische), Chippis	660	935	12.11	753	755	756	753
373	250	0	0	23.4.82	27	SK	141,856	do. (bearer shares)	238	312	12.11	255	255	258	257
102.2	50	0	0	23.4.82	3	BG	141,854s	do. (certificate of participation)	62½	81	2.11	69	69½	70	
18	500	—	27.50(1/2)	29.5.84	2	BV	146,271s	Autophon AG, Solothurn	3,700+	4,430	12.11	4,175	4,175	4,180	4,175
18	100	10	11	29.5.84		BG	146,270	do. (nominal shares)	640	675	9.10	640	625	650	
366.275	500	30	30	5.6.84	28	SK	238,661s	BBC AG Brown, Boveri & Cie, Baden, A	1,240	1,585	12.11	1,370	1,380	1,385	1,380 85
73.255	100	6	6	5.6.84		SK	238,669	do. B (nominal shares)	220	253	12.11	228	225	227	
58.8720	100	6	6	5.6.84	28	SK	238,670s	do. (certificates of participation)	220	262	9.11	229	227	228	23 Jan
13	400	32+30	32+30	24.5.84	19	SA	240,180s	Brusio AG (Kraftwerke), Poschiavo	3,600	3,900	6.11	3,600	3,600	3,625	
13.2	500	30	30	15.5.84	23	SA	156,318s	Buss AG, Basel	810	945	31.10	860	850	880	
4.8	500	6	6	15.5.84	23	SA	156,316	Cellulose Attisholz AG, Attisholz	165	175	24.10	170	170	—	
8	500	20	20	2.4.84	8	BG	157,708s	Charmilles SA (Ateliers des) Genf, A	830	1,170	8.11	1,170	1,125	—	
25	500	0	0	3.9.81	27	BV	145,230s	do. B (nominal shares)	320	490	2.11	475	460	470	
5	100	0	0	3.9.81	13	BV	145,231	do. B (nominal shares)	77	98	3.10	98	90	110	
74.9034	100	28	31	11.5.84	17	BV	159,107s	Ciba-Geigy AG, Basel	2,065	2,600	12.11	2,480	2,480	2,485	2,480 85
351.203	100	28	31	11.5.84	17	BV	159,108	do. (nominal shares)	943	1,090	12.11	1,055	1,050	1,055	1,050 6oJan 55 9odtzoJan
110.2981	100	28	31	11.5.84	17	BV	159,109s	do. (certificates of participation)	1,645	2,030	12.11	1,965	1,970	1,975	1,980 75 70 75
100	500	40	40	27.3.84	34	SK	168,795s	Elektrizitär-Gesellschaft Laufenburg AG, Laufenburg	1,800	2,400	2.11	2,200	2,150	2,200	
120	500	0	0	15.5.81	9	SK	175,232s	Fischer (Georg) Aktiengesellschaft, Schaffhausen	590	750	9.11	620	610	620	
30	100	0	0	15.5.81	9	SK	175,230	do. (nominal shares)	96	122	24.10	101	98	—	
40	100	0	0	15.5.81	9	BG	175,233s	do. (certificates of participation)	95	112	12.11	100	98	—	—

Table 6.3   The quotations list – Geneva Stock Exchange, 13 November 1984

Listed capital (SFr millions)	Nominal value per share or certificate (SFr)	Last ex dividend date	Ex coupon no.	Dividend paid (SFr) 1983	Dividend paid (SFr) 1984	Securities no.	Financial service bank	Swiss shares	Record of lowest and highest prices paid	Previous paid cash price	Bid	Asked	Paid
1	2	3	4	5	5	6	7		8	9	10	11	12
								Financial, manufacturing and other companies					
30	500	30. 4.84	8	60	60	240.000s	BS	Câbleries et Tréfileries de Cossonay SA, Cossonay	1,170 1,340	29.10.84 1,220	1,270		
25	500	3. 9.81	27			145.230s	BS	Charmilles (Ateliers dos) SA, Genève 'A' = bearer shares	310 485	9.11.84 465	460	470	
5	100	3. 9.81	13			145.231	BS	'B' = nominal shares	68 100	1.11.84 90	85	100	
74.9034	100	11. 5.84		28	31	159.107s	BS	Ciba-Geigy SA, Bâle (Cp. Nº 20 att.) (bearer shares)	2,020 2,560	12.11.84 2,480	2,480	2,490	2470 2475 2480c
351.2030	100	11. 5.84		28	31	159.108	BS	do. (nominal shares)	940 1,085	12.11.84 1,055	1,055	1,057	1055c
98.2981	100	11. 5.84		28	31	159.109s	BS	do. (Cp. Nº 20 att.) (certificates of participation)	1,640 1,995	12.11.84 1,965	1,970	1,975	1970 1975c
103.367	200	2. 7.80	27			162.611s	CS	Crédit Immobilier SA, Genève	100 201	4. 9.84 201	230		
3.5	1,000	25.10.84	5			247.623s	LO	Eaux de l'Arve SA, Genève	3,800 4,500	9.11.84 3,900	3,850	4,000	
15	250	20. 6.74	11	130	130	167.211	BS	Ed. Dubied & Cie (SA) (jce Traversina SA)					
	250					167.210	BS	Ed. Dubied & Cie (SA) Ed Dubied + bon de jce Traversina (SA)	150 230	8.11.84 225	222	230	225c
5	250	20. 6.74	11			167.212s	BS	Ed Dubied & Cie (SA) (cps bon jce Traversina SA)	160 238	8.11.84 230	325	240	230 235c

shares of companies that are not officially listed but have applied for pre-market dealing. The majority of these shares are very well known and of good quality (most prominent is Hoffmann-La Roche). Apart from stocks that do not meet the official listing requirements, a significant number of companies do not want to be listed for one reason or another.

Dealing procedures are the same as for listed securities, except for a few differences. For instance, stock exchange officials do not supervise the transactions; members thus have to organise themselves to deal properly. Paid prices do not appear in the official quotations list; however, the news media and the Telekurs quotation system report the prices regularly.

Types of transactions

The most commonly used transaction is in the *cash* or *spot* market. It accounts for roughly three-quarters of total volume. The value date is the third business day following the transaction. For many years the next-day valuation was the officially established practice. However, in order to open the market more towards international settlement practices, the three-day settlement was introduced on 1 January 1985. This enables the buyers to make sure that the funds necessary for matching purchase transactions are available on time. The proposed seven-day settlement was rejected by most stock exchange members. Spot transactions are either marked by a 'c' or reproduced without special identification.

Forward transactions play a very important role in daily turnover. There are basically three different terms. Dealings on the current month's account are marked by one plus symbol (+), next month's account by two (++) and the month after by three (+++). On the floor the dealing procedure is the same as for spot transactions, but both parties must specify explicitly the account period involved. Dealing on the current month's account ends after the first reading of the quotations list on the fourth business day preceding the end of the month. A large portion of the transactions in an account period will be offset, so that the actual settlement involves only the security and the cash balance. The normal way of clearing at the month-end is delivery against payment through the clearing system.

Buying and selling shares is also possible through *premium* transactions, which are in many ways similar to call options. Account periods are the same as for forward transactions, but it is very important to know that the 'striking' prices vary according to daily market fluctuations. They are based on the cash price plus 1–5% surplus, e.g. cash price=SFr 1,090 c; striking price for a three-month premium deal=SFr 1,130. Because of this floating striking price it is nearly impossible to close open premium deals. Another difference from the international options market is the commission calculation method. Commissions are always calculated on the striking price per share, even if the deal is abandoned and only the premium is applicable. With this system the buyer has the option to purchase the shares at the striking price *or* to withdraw from the transaction by paying the seller the previously agreed premium. Premium transactions are marked by a 'd' and plus symbols +, ++ or +++. The 'd' stands for the French word *dont*; e.g. 800 d 20 ++=SFr 800 with SFr 20 premium, maturity end of next month. Categories excluded from forward and premium deals are the listed domestic banks' and insurance companies' shares as well as non-fully-paid registered shares.

Trading lots

To justify an official quotation there must be a minimum number of shares involved in a transaction, a so-called trading lot (see Table 6.4).

Table 6.4 A trading lot scale

Market value of one share (SFr)		Trading lot in shares
From	To	
	5	1,000
5	10	500
10	50	100
50	200	50
200	500	25
500	2,000	10
2,000	5,000	5
5,000	10,000	2
10,000		1

When the minimum lot of required shares in a specific range of market value is exceeded by a fraction, the trading lot price will usually be paid for this total amount of shares, e.g.

15 shares at SFr 1,500

and not 10 shares at SFr 1,500

5 shares at SFr 1,500 plus odd lot differential.

Odd lot turnover is common; however, the quotations list does not show prices for such transactions, which are usually effected with a slight difference from the officially paid price.

Price gradation

Stock prices cannot be set arbitrarily. To have a uniform gradation within the different share price categories, the stock exchange has regulated price gradations as follows:

Share price

from		to		gradation
SFr	0	SFr	10	SFr 0.05
	10		100	0.25
	100		300	0.50
	300		2,000	1.00
	2,000			5.00

The commission rates agreement

The Association of Swiss Stock Exchanges, comprising the seven Swiss stock exchanges, is responsible for maintaining an orderly market with a uniform commission rates agreement.

Companies or individuals wishing to become parties to this agreement must address their application to the Committee of the Association, which will decide on the acceptance. Admission is restricted to banks, bankers, stock exchange brokers, savings banks and certain finance companies. Insurance companies may be associate members. The applicant must prove that he is of good reputation and has the necessary technical knowledge indispensable for professional trading in the securities market. Furthermore, the local stock exchange authorities must be consulted and a balance sheet as well as profit and loss accounts presented. Foreign banks and brokers are not accepted as members. Should a member no longer fulfil the conditions upon which admission to the agreement is dependent, he will be excluded from the agreement by the Committee of the Association.

If a party is accused of any breach of the agreement, the Committee of the Association is notified and will examine the matter. If the charge turns out to be correct, a fine of up to SFr 50,000 (new proposal: up to SFr 1 million) will be imposed on the guilty party. This amount plus the costs of examination must be paid into a fund of the Association. There is of course a court of arbitration to handle the appeal of the sentenced party.

The members of the stock exchanges of Basle, Berne, Geneva, Lausanne, Neuchâtel, St Gall and Zurich have agreed to charge their counterparts the following minimum commissions.

Equity dealing in Switzerland

For shares, participation in co-operatives, investment trust units, dividend rights certificates and subscription rights the tariff is:
- $\frac{5}{8}$% of the market value, where this exceeds SFr 150 per security,
- 1% of the market value, where this is SFr 150 or less per security.

Commissions on the very few remaining partly paid-up securities in the market are charged on the full market value. This tariff is also applicable when dealing in pre-listed and unlisted securities.

Proposal for new Swiss stock exchange commissions

In 1982 the Board of the Association of Swiss Stock Exchanges appointed a committee of experts to prepare a new commission rate agreement. The first draft presented in 1983 was rejected by a majority of the members and a new proposal was presented in June 1985.

The major features of this new proposal are as follows:
1.   The admission of professional (domestic) portfolio managers to the commission rate agreement in addition to the member banks and insurance companies.
2.   A new revised tariff system with:
    (a) decreasing rates with rising volume,

(b) somewhat higher rates for small orders,
(c) a higher minimum commission rate for very small transactions, and
(d) in order to comply with the worldwide ongoing deregulation of the securities business, the possibility of negotiating commission rates for large transactions.

A comparison of the most important rates of the Swiss stock exchange commissions is given in Table 6.5.

Table 6.5 Comparison of old and new Swiss stock exchange commissions

Old	New (starting 1 December 1985)		
Shares	(a) *Domestic shares*		
1%: share price up to SFr 150	until	SFr 50,000	0.8%
⅜%: share price over SFr 150	for the next SFr 50,000		0.7%
	for the next SFr 50,000		0.6%
	for the next SFr 150,000		0.5%
	for the next SFr 300,000		0.4%
	for the next SFr 400,000		0.3%
	for the next SFr 1 million		0.2%
	over	SFr 2 million	free
	(b) *Foreign shares*		
	until	SFr 50,000	1.0%
	for the next SFr 50,000		0.9%
	for the next SFr 50,000		0.7%
	for the next SFr 150,000		0.5%
	for the next SFr 300,000		0.4%
	for the next SFr 400,000		0.3%
	for the next SFr 1 million		0.2%
	over	SFr 2 million	free
Domestic mutual funds			
1%: price up to SFr 150	until	SFr 500,000	0.3%
⅜%: price over SFr 150	for the next SFr 500,000		0.2%
	for the next SFr 1 million		0.1%
	over	SFr 2 million	free

The ideas and counterproposals of the Association's members will be examined by the Committee and a new final agreement will be presented for approval before the end of 1985. A new tariff system to be agreed upon is expected to become effective at the end of 1985.

Equity dealing on foreign stock exchanges

In addition to the commissions with which the parties to the agreement are debited themselves, they may charge the following minimum rates:

For transactions on *West German* and *Austrian* exchanges
– ⅜% of the amount involved plus the official German or Austrian commission applicable to customers
– ½% of the amount involved if the transaction is executed net of foreign commissions.

For the *London* exchange
- one-half of the full official London commission; the discount London commission scale, when dealing in a specific security within an account period, has to be taken into consideration.

For the *Canadian* exchanges
- if the market value is

under C$40	½% of the Canadian commission
C$40 but under C$70	⅝% of the Canadian commission
C$70 and over	¾% of the Canadian commission

For transactions on *all other foreign market-places* (excluding the United States)
- ½% of the amount involved.

Special commission scale for transactions in the *United States*.

The commission schedule consists of the commission paid to US correspondents plus the Swiss commission. Under the heading 'US/Swiss commission', the *combined* amount appears on contract notes addressed to the customers. After the introduction of the negotiated commission rates in the United States, the commission rates agreement was subject to a revision with the aim of passing on to the customer a certain portion of the US rebate. The schedule is structured in the following way:

1.   Lots of 1 to 100 shares of stock

Amount involved	Minimum commission
From $100 to $799.99	3% plus $10
From $800 to $2,499.99	2% plus $20
From $2,500 and over	1½% plus $35

However, the commission cannot exceed $130 per transaction.

2.   Lots of 101 shares of stock and over

Amount involved	Minimum commission
From $100 to $2,499.99	2½% plus $20
From $2,500 to $19,999.99	1¾% plus $40
From $20,000 to $29,999.99	1¼% plus $150
From $30,000 and over	¾% plus $310

In addition, $0.07 per share will be charged.

The commission for multiple round-lot transactions must not exceed that for each lot of 100 shares of stock. This rule is very important when dealing in stocks with a low share price because the additional charge of 7 cents can, in percentage terms, be significant in relation to the share price. For example:

(tariff 1) 100 shares at \$5=\$25
(tariff 2) 200 shares at \$5=\$59   =2×\$25=\$50 max.
          300 shares at \$5=\$78.50 =3×\$25=\$75 max.
          400 shares at \$5=\$98   (4×\$25=\$100)

---

3. For orders exceeding \$100,000 per day, per stock and per client, scheduled commission rates may be waived; nevertheless, the Swiss commission must not be lower than $\frac{1}{2}$% of the gross amount involved in the transaction.
4. For transactions net of US commission (e.g. over the counter), a commission of not less than 50% of the rates given under item 1 or 2 of the schedule must be charged to clients. Again, the minimum charge cannot be less than $\frac{1}{2}$% of the gross amount involved in the transaction.
5. Deviating from the principle of combined commission calculation, the commission on call and put option transactions must be calculated with the US commission paid, plus separately a minimum of 50% of this US commission as Swiss commission.
6. Commissions on transactions of less than \$100 are left to the discretion of members to the agreement.

Proposal for new equity commissions when dealing on foreign stock exchanges:

	Until SFr 50,000	For the next SFr 50,000	For the next SFr 150,000
USA	2.5%	1.5%	1.0%
Japan	2.0%	1.5%	1.3%
West Germany	1.4%	1.3%	1.2%
Great Britain	2.7%	1.7%	1.3%
Netherlands	1.8%	1.7%	1.6%
Canada	2.7%	1.7%	1.3%
Australia	2.0%	1.5%	1.3%
Others – Europe	1.6%	1.5%	1.4%
Others – overseas	2.5%	1.5%	1.0%

The foreign charges are included in the above rates (*Globaltariff*).

For transactions over SFr 250,000 the tariff in Table 6.5 will be charged in addition to the commission calculated by the foreign broker.

Minimum rates

For each transaction in Switzerland or abroad, a minimum commission of SFr 10 per contract note is charged. This is in addition to the commission paid to the foreign stock exchange counterpart. For amounts below SFr 100 the commission may be reduced to SFr 5. (New proposals for minimum rates: SFr 30 for shares; SFr 10 for mutual funds; no commission for amounts below SFr 250.)

Dealing with reduced commission

The parties to the agreement are permitted to reduce their commission by one-half while dealing with:

(a)   parties that are signatories to the commission rates agreement,
(b)   recognised professionals engaged in securities trading for the account of third parties, domiciled in Switzerland, entered in the Register of Commerce and keeping the securities turnover register.

Transfer fee for registered Swiss shares

The minimum rates for the transfer of registered Swiss shares (listed or unlisted) must be charged to the purchaser as well as to the seller.

Price per share	Fee per share
Over SFr 500	SFr 1
Over SFr 100 but under SFr 500	SFr 0.50
Over SFr 50 but under SFr 100	SFr 0.10
Under SFr 50	SFr 0.05
Minimum fee SFr 2.50 } per statement Maximum fee SFr 50	

(Under the new tariff, transfer fees will not be charged any more.)

Exempt from the fee are shares of the Swiss National Bank and registered certificates issued in the name of a nominee and endorsed in blank.

All the commission rates given above represent the strict minimum and are applied in most instances of securities transaction contract notes.

Nevertheless, every party is free to charge more than these minimum rates. Special expenses for telecommunication fees, securities delivery, etc., will usually be charged on the contract note in a separate column.

Stamp duties, cantonal tax and stock exchange fees

For all securities transactions performed by a professional securities dealer in Switzerland there are charges for stamp duties, cantonal tax and stock exchange fees. Such charges are levied with each change of beneficial ownership.

Federal and cantonal tax inspectors regularly audit the stamp register, where all transactions are recorded on a daily basis. An infringement of the regulations will be prosecuted by the tax authorities.

The charges are calculated on the purchase price (in the case of bonds, plus accrued interest and are split into a tariff for domestic and foreign securities. Purchasers and sellers are charged equally:

Domestic securities	
Federal stamp duty	0.075%
Cantonal tax (rounded up to the next SFr0.10)	0.01%
Stock exchange fee (rounded up to the next SFr0.05)	0.005%
Foreign securities	
Federal stamp duty	0.15%
Cantonal tax (rounded up to the next SFr0.10)	0.01%
Stock exchange fee (rounded up to the next SFr0.05)	0.005%

The duties, taxes and fees are charged on all orders executed through one of the Swiss stock exchanges. As the only exception, transactions on the Lausanne stock exchange are free of cantonal taxes but stock exchange fees of 0.01% will be charged.

Examples of contract notes

Sample contract notes for the following types of transaction appear on pages 84–90.

1. Purchase of shares in Zurich
2. Sale of shares in Zurich
3. Purchase of shares in New York
4. Purchase of shares in London
5. Sale of shares in Toronto
6. Sale of shares in Frankfurt
7. Purchase of shares in Zurich (forward transaction)

Dealing at the stock exchange (or how to buy an officially listed share at a Swiss stock exchange)

After doing some research or consulting an investment adviser, the customer decides to place an order through his Swiss bank. If the bank is not a member of one of the Swiss stock exchanges, the order will be passed on to one of the 'ring banks' (stock exchange floor members). The transaction costs are in any case the same due to the uniform commission rates agreement. The order ends up with one of the ring banks and will be passed on from the telephone room straight to the dealer on the floor. The floor consists of a room with one or more so-called 'rings' (trading areas); there the traders stand at specific places allotted to the bank they represent. They are aided by an assistant who carries order sheets and other information from the ring to the telephone room and vice versa. Order sheets differ from one bank to another but have the main characteristics in common. For example, sale or purchase intentions should not be visible to other traders (neutral paper colour). Inside the ring the stock exchange commissioner, the stock exchange clerk and the price reporter of the Telekurs TV network take up their places. The stock exchange clerk opens the trading session by calling out the first security listed in the official quotations list, releasing one security name after the other in the order they are recorded. He notes all prices called out by the

Telefon 01/214 51 11 Telex Allgemein 812186/813701 Telefax 01/214 53 96
Telex Börse 815486 Telex Emissionen 814020 Effektenhändler Nr. 805215

HandelsBank N.W.

YOU HAVE	PURCHASED	8022 Zürich, 08.01.1985 Ref. No.
IN ZURICH	ON 08.01.1985	Konto / Compte / Account

			VAL. NO.	0000000
NOMINAL	SHS X Y Z – BEARER –			
25	AT THE PRICE OF	2,450.00	Fr.	61,250.00
COMMISSION		382.80		
STAMP DUTY		45.95		
CHARGES		9.30	Fr.	438.05

Saldo Konto/Solde compte/Balance Acc.   Val.

THE SECURITIES WILL BE PUT	11.01.1985	Fr.	61,688.05
INTO YOUR SECURITIES ACCOUNT			TO YOUR DEBIT

Mit freundlichen Grüssen Avec les meilleurs compliments With the best compliments

HandelsBank N.W.

WE THANK YOU FOR THIS ORDER

BEARS ONE SIGNATURE ONLY

Contract note: purchase of shares in Zurich

Telefon 01/214 51 11 Telex Allgemein 812186/813701 Telefax 01/214 53 96
Telex Börse 815486 Telex Emissionen 814020 Effektenhändler Nr. 805215

HandelsBank N.W.

YOU HAVE IN ZURICH	SOLD ON 08.01.1985	8022 Zürich, 08.01.1985	Ref.	No.

Konto
Compte
Account

		VAL. NO.	0000000

| NOMINAL 100 | SHS X Y Z | | |
| | AT THE PRICE OF | 575.00 | Fr. | 57,500.00 |

COMMISSION	359.40
STAMP DUTY	43.15
CHARGES	8.70

| | | Fr. | 411.25 |

Saldo Konto/Solde compte/Balance Acc.   Val. 11.01.1985   Fr. 57,088.75

TO YOUR CREDIT

Mit freundlichen Grüssen   Avec les meilleurs compliments   With the best compliments

HandelsBank N.W.

BEARS ONE SIGNATURE ONLY

WE THANK YOU FOR THIS ORDER

Contract note: sale of shares in Zurich

Telefon 01/214 51 11   Telex Allgemein 812186/813701 Telefax 01/214 53 96
Telex Börse 815486 Telex Emissionen 814020 Effektenhändler Nr. 805215

HandelsBank N.W.

YOU HAVE	PURCHASED			
IN NEW YORK NYSE	07.01.1985	02/0002	8022 Zürich, 08.01.85	Ref. 022 No. 0002

Konto
Compte   ACCOUNT
Account

			SEC.NR.	000000.0
NOMINAL				=========
1500 SHS	XYZ	AT 20.00	$	30,000.00
		FOREIGN CHARGES	$	15.00
		SUB TOTAL	$	30,015.00
COMMISSION USA/CH		$ 640.00		
STAMP DUTY		$ 49.52		
CHARGES		$ 1.03	$	690.55

Saldo Konto/Solde compte/Balance Acc.   Val.

THE SECURITIES WILL BE PUT		14.1.85	$	30,705.55
INTO YOUR SECURITIES ACCOUNT				TO YOUR DEBIT

Mit freundlichen Grüssen   Avec les meilleurs compliments With the best compliments

HandelsBank N.W.

WE THANK YOU FOR THIS ORDER

BEARS ONE SIGNATURE ONLY

Contract note: purchase of shares in New York

Telefon 01/214 51 11. Telex Allgemein 81 2186/813701 Telefax 01/214 53 96
Telex Börse 815486 Telex Emissionen 814020 Effektenhändler Nr. 805215

HandelsBank N.W.

YOU HAVE	PURCHASED			
IN LONDON	ON 07.01.1985	02/0001	8022 Zürich, 08.01.85	Ref. 022	No. 0001

Konto   ACCOUNT
Compte
Account

SEC. NR.   000000.0

NOMINAL				
2000 SHS	XYZ	AT	10.00	£	20,000.00
		FOREIGN CHARGES		£	301.70
		SUB-TOTAL		£	20,301.70
COMMISSION			130.00		
STAMP DUTY			33.50		
CHARGES			0.81	£	164.56

Saldo Konto/Solde compte/Balance Acc.   Val.

	21.01.85	£	20,466.26

TO YOUR DEBIT   Avec les meilleurs compliments With the best compliments

THE SECURITIES WILL BE PUT   Mit freundlichen Grüssen
INTO YOUR SECURITIES ACCOUNT   HandelsBank N.W.

WE THANK YOU FOR THIS ORDER   BEARS ONE SIGNATURE ONLY

Contract note: purchase of shares in London

Telefon 01/214 51 11 Telex Allgemein 812186/813701 Telefax 01/214 53 96
Telex Börse 815486 Telex Emissionen 814020 Effektenhändler Nr. 805215

HandelsBank N.W.

YOU HAVE	SOLD	02/0004	8022 Zürich, 08.01.85	Ref. 022	No. 0004
IN TORONTO	07.01.1985		Konto ACCOUNT		
			Compte		
			Account		

			SEC. NR.	000000.0
				====
NOMINAL				
3000 SHS	XYZ	AT 5.00	CAN$	15,000.00
		FOREIGN CHARGES	CAN$	462.50
		SUB TOTAL	CAN$	14,537.50
COMMISSION		CAN$ 225.00		
STAMP DUTY		CAN$ 23.99		
CHARGES		CAN$ 1.32	CAN$	250.31

Saldo Konto/Solde compte/Balance Acc. Val.

THE SECURITIES WILL BE TAKEN	14.01.85	CAN$	14,287.19
FROM YOUR SECURITIES ACCOUNT		TO YOUR CREDIT	

Mit freundlichen Grüssen Avec les meilleurs compliments With the best compliments

HandelsBank N.W.

WE THANK YOU FOR THIS ORDER   BEARS ONE SIGNATURE ONLY

Contract note: sale of shares in Toronto

Telefon 01/214 51 11 Telex Allgemein 81218 6/813701 Telefax 01/214 53 96
Telex Börse 815486 Telex Emissionen 814020 Effektenhändler Nr. 805215

HandelsBank N.W.

YOU HAVE IN FRANKFURT	SOLD 07.01.1985	02/0011	8022 Zürich, 08.01.85	Ref. 022	No. 0007

Konto
Compte
Account

			SEC. NR.	000000.0
NOMINAL 500 SHS	XYZ	AT 50.00	DM	25,000.00
		FOREIGN CHARGES	DM	275.00
		SUB TOTAL	DM	24,725.00
COMMISSION		DM 92.71		
STAMP DUTY		DM 40.80		
CHARGES		DM 3.05	DM	136.56

Saldo Konto/Solde compte/Balance Acc.   Val. 09.01.85

THE SECURITIES WILL BE TAKEN
FROM YOUR SECURITIES ACCOUNT

DM	24,588.44

TO YOUR CREDIT

Mit freundlichen Grüssen Avec les meilleurs compliments With the best compliments

HandelsBank N.W.

WE THANK YOU FOR THIS ORDER

BEARS ONE SIGNATURE ONLY

Contract note: sale of shares in Frankfurt

Telefon 01/214 51 11 Telex Allgemein 812186/813701 Telefax 01/214 53 96
Telex Börse 815486 Telex Emissionen 814020 Effektenhändler Nr. 805215

HandelsBank N.W.

YOU HAVE	PURCHASED	8022 Zürich, 08.01.1985 Ref.		No.
IN ZURICH	ON 08.01.1985			
LIQUIDATION	ULTIMO MARCH	Konto		
		Compte		
		Account		

		VAL. NO. 000000

NOMINAL   SHS X Y Z – BEARER –
20

                 AT THE PRICE OF   5,300.00   Fr.   106,000.00

COMMISSION   662.50
STAMP DUTY   79.50
CHARGES   15.90   Fr.   757.90

Saldo Konto/Solde compte/Balance Acc.   Val.
                                        ULTIMO   Fr.   106,757.90
                                        MARCH   TO YOUR DEBIT

Mit freundlichen Grüssen Avec les meilleurs compliments With the best compliments

HandelsBank N.W.

WE THANK YOU FOR THIS ORDER   BEARS ONE SIGNATURE ONLY

Contract note: purchase of shares in Zurich (forward transaction)

traders; at the end of the trading session his notes are the basis for the official quotations list. In the meantime, the price reporter feeds all the prices into the Telekurs computer so that subscribers to the system can follow the price listings on their screens.

When a stock is released for trading, the traders call out their dealing intentions by stating a *Geld* or *je prends* (bid) or *Brief* or *je donne* (asked) price. It is usual to mention only the last one or two digits of the price, e.g. 30 *Geld/je prends/* bid or 40 *Brief/je donne/* asked, assuming that all parties involved are well aware of the preceding figures (1,130 *Geld*–1,140 *Brief*). Transactions are completed when parties agree on a price; this might be the bid, asked or sometimes the middle price. A paid price will be called out as *bezahlt/payé* and the stock exchange clerk will repeat it to make sure that everyone has a chance to intervene in case of disagreement. When bid and asked quotations are stated without any specification of the amount of shares involved, the price is good for a round lot; otherwise the dealer must mention the number of shares involved. With stocks of large trading size it sometimes takes up to half a minute before a paid price on which all trading participants can agree will emerge.

When conditions are such as to make it impossible for all buyers and sellers involved to participate in a deal with at least one trading lot, the shares are allocated by electronic lot drawing. The allotting system will operate in the event of a lack of sufficient trading lots from the seller or lack of demand from the buyer side. Parties involved in such a deal will press a key and their bank symbol will light up on a screen located in the centre of the ring. The electronic allotting system will designate the 'winner', and the name of the bank making the deal will flash on the screen, visible to everyone around the ring. Prices of securities traded in this way are marked in the quotations sheet by an 'L'.

Once a security is released for trading, it is possible to revert on the quoted bid and asked price within the lecture (round) of that specific category of securities. In this way one security after the other is released for trading and dealers trade back and forth. For the dealers, this method requires a high degree of concentration, especially when they are concerned with a large number of price limits.

The stock exchange clerk passes through the whole list of securities, category by category. When all securities have been traded in a first round, they will be taken up again in a second round. The usual turnover in the first reading accounts for over two-thirds of the total transaction volume; it is much more animated than the second reading, called the *reprise* or *zweite Lesung*.

At the end of the second reading, the stock exchange clerk rings a bell to inform everyone that the official dealing session is closed. Right after the closing, dealers will check with each other the transactions noted on their order sheets. At that stage any differences between parties can be settled easily. The most frequent problems are wrong counterparts, differences in the number of shares and unclear forward period.

The over-the-counter market

Besides official dealing at the stock exchange and pre-market dealing, there is an over-the-counter market in Switzerland organised by a number of banks and finance companies. Transactions are conducted almost exclusively by telephone. With the exception of some well-known stocks of widely held companies that are not listed, most of the market-makers concentrate on local and regional companies. Turnover in the latter category is thin, with the bid-only situation prevailing. Inexperienced investors discuss their investment move with the specialist at their bank and operate with limited orders. Applicable commissions in the over-the-counter market are regulated by the uniform commission rates agreement.

Shares traded in the over-the-counter market are from various sectors: banks, breweries, finance companies, industries, hotels and thermal spas, and a wide range of transportation companies.

Transportation companies are a particularly popular investment among the customers of such companies. Shareholders are very often granted a reduction in fares instead of a cash dividend. Half of the stocks traded in the over-the-counter market are registered securities and are not usually available to foreign investors.

The specialised market-makers publish bulletins with the prices of the stocks they have available for the market. Once a week, financial newspapers list the prices of a representative selection of over-the-counter stocks.

The clearing system

To facilitate the safe keeping and clearing of securities transactions, Swiss banks founded a clearing organisation called SEGA Schweizerische Effekten-Giro AG in 1970. In addition to dealing with the safe keeping of all securities traded in Switzerland, with the exception of domestic registered shares and some convertible notes, SEGA is the clearing agency for Swiss banks. On the settlement day, usually the third working day after the transaction day, the clearing agency will effect the book transfer from one securities account to the other according to the joint instructions of the parties involved. The money balance of cleared securities transactions will be debited or credited to each member's account with the Swiss National Bank.

7 Listing of shares on Swiss stock exchanges

Heini P. Dubler

This chapter deals with the listing of domestic as well as foreign stocks. It explains the various listing steps and the three types of markets.

As already mentioned, there are eight different stock market-places in Switzerland, of which only three (Zurich, Geneva and Basle) have a strong international character. The organisation and functioning of these three stock exchanges are only marginally different from each other (see Chapter 3). The procedure to be adopted for listing stocks again differs only slightly from one place to another. Reference therefore is made in the following outline (unless otherwise mentioned) to the listing procedure of the Zurich Stock Exchange, since it handles the highest trading volume.

As explained in Chapter 6, there are three trading methods in Switzerland:

1. Over-the-counter trading includes the trading of both listed and unlisted stocks outside the floors of the various stock exchanges. This market covers the shares of many hundreds of local companies such as banks, railways, etc. In connection with a public offering this market would normally trade new stocks out of an initial public offering on an 'if and when issued' basis. It consists primarily of telephone calls among participating banks, and will not be dealt with in any detail here.
2. Unofficial trading commences with a new issue on the stock exchange two days following the close of the subscription period.
3. Official trading in listed securities starts on the stock exchange after all the formalities have been complied with, normally two to three months following the issue.

Listing for 'pre-stock exchange trading' *(also referred to as 'unofficial trade' or 'Vorbörse')*

Stocks not officially listed, and those to be listed in the near future, are traded unofficially on the 'Vorbörse'. Stocks that have been placed among the investors through a public offering must first be traded at the unofficial or pre-stock exchange. This rather complicated system is a result of the somewhat particular way settlement and delivery of securities in new issues are handled in Switzerland. The physical stock or bond certificates are printed and distributed to the subscribers only two to three months following an issue, although payment has been made long before. As long as the underlying certificates are not distributed, the official listing cannot be applied for.

The Zurich Stock Exchange Association has issued rules concerning the trading and *listing* of stocks/bonds at the 'Vorbörse'. In summary these rules are as follows:

1. Trading starts about one half hour before the normal opening of the official stock exchange, depending on the amount of transactions expected.
2. Trading is executed on separate rings (one for stocks and one for bonds).
3. The price gradations are the same as on the official stock exchange. There are no limitations for prices below SFr 5 per share. Trading lots are also identical. Registered shares which are not fully paid-in cannot be traded forward (this includes stocks of banks and insurance companies) – as with an official listing.
4. Securities can be put forward for acceptance on the pre-stock exchange only if they have already been trading regularly outside the stock exchange, i.e. over the counter.
5. The Executive Committee of the stock exchange must be informed 20 days prior to the proposed listing. If the Committee has any objections to the listing, the applicant must be informed not later than three days before the first trading date.
6. The stock exchange member firm, in Zurich normally a bank introducing the listing, must provide all members of the stock exchange with some basic information about the new security, not later than three days before the first trading date. Such information should include:
    (a) corporate name, domicile and purpose,
    (b) date of incorporation,
    (c) latest available balance sheet and profit and loss statements, including auditors' report; summary statement of guarantees and contingent liabilities if any (off-balance-sheet items),
    (d) amount and nature of capital and reserves,
    (e) information on dividend distribution.
7. Conditions mentioned under 4, 5 and 6 are not applicable for new issues of publicly placed bonds/stocks or for capital increases of companies that are already quoted on the official or unofficial stock exchange.
8. In cases where shares from a new issue have not been allotted on the basis of 'rights', the trading in such stocks can start only after the allotment date.
9. The Committee will establish a list of all securities traded on the 'Vorbörse', with details such as the first trading date and the name of the member firm that introduced the security.
10. The Committee delegates a member to supervise the trading activity.
11. The Committee has the right to suspend trading in a security if this appears to be appropriate because of unusual circumstances.

The actual 'Vorbörse' trading session takes place from about 9.30 to 10.00 a.m.

In Geneva and Basle there are no special rulings for pre-stock exchange trading since in those centres stocks and bonds are dealt with either officially on the exchange or 'off the floor' (Ausserbörse).

If the applicant company can fulfil the relevant requirements of these rules and wishes to put its shares up for pre-stock exchange trading, it will have to mandate one of the 24 members of the stock exchange. The member will prepare a memorandum on the company, including all the information required by the admission rules. If the listing is unrelated to a public issue, there will be a wait of about four weeks. The costs involved are modest and banks in charge of such operations will normally not charge any commission. No fees are payable to the stock exchange commission.

The advantages of having stocks listed for pre-stock exchange trading are obvious:

(a) regular quotation in the newspapers of companies' stock prices (under separate heading),
(b) wider distribution of stocks, and
(c) better transparency of the stock price thanks to the regulated trading environment.

Full listing for trading on the stock exchanges

Legal provisions

Art. 12 of the Law on Professional Trading of Securities of the Canton of Zurich stipulates that:

Whoever wishes a security admitted for trading on the stock exchange (of Zurich) must obtain permission from the Stock Exchange Association.
The application shall be made known by posting it for at least four days on the premises of the stock exchange. The Stock Exchange Association may revoke the admission. Appeal to the Department of Economics (of the Canton of Zurich) is possible against such decisions of the Stock Exchange Association.
The Department of Economics is also entitled, after consulting with the Board of the Stock Exchange Association, the Stock Exchange Commissioners' Office, and the Stock Exchange Commission, to forbid on its own initiative the admission of a security, or to cancel an existing listing.

The regulations governing the admission of securities for trading and listing on the Zurich Stock Exchange (Listing Regulations) cover in detail the listing of both domestic bonds, stocks and other securities, and their foreign counterparts.

Excerpts from the regulations (for domestic shares)

1. *Application for Listing*

Para. 1 – Designation of admission office and applicants
Application for admission of securities for official trading and listing on the Zurich stock

exchange shall be addressed to the Board of the Zurich Stock Exchange Association, as admission office. An application shall be filed through the intermediary of at least one bank or stock exchange firm admitted to the stock exchange and licensed to trade on the floor of the stock exchange.

Para. 2 – *Contents of application for listing*

Application for listing must include the following information:

1. Information as to whether final certificates have been issued, or provisional certificates have been issued in the interim;
2. Designation of the office where admission and listing fees shall be collected;
3. Indication of the newspaper and the issue number in which the prospectus was published;
4. Assurance by the firm submitting the application that annual reports will be provided regularly, and that any changes in the articles of incorporation will be reported.

Para. 3 – *Supporting documentation for the listing for application*

The application shall include:

1. 12 copies of the introductory memorandum or prospectus on issuance;
2. 12 copies of the latest annual report or the financial statements of the company;
3. 12 copies of the current articles of incorporation;
4. A specimen or a photostat copy of the provisional certificates, if any, and of the final certificates.

2. *Conditions for Listing*

Para. 4 – *Introductory prospectus*

Prior to the listing of a security, an introductory prospectus shall appear in a daily newspaper published in Zurich in one of the three national languages. This publication requirement applies by analogy to the recording of subscription rights to stocks or bonds of companies not yet listed on the Zurich stock exchange. If the listing application has been preceded by an offering for public subscription, the prospectus on issuance published on that occasion may serve as an introductory prospectus, provided its publication is not more than six months old.

The introductory prospectus as well as the prospectus on issuance must include the necessary information for an assessment of the security to be introduced and moreover must conform with the listing regulations set out hereinafter.

The company for whose securities a stock exchange listing is sought shall certify by its signature the accuracy of the information contained in its prospectus. The prospectus of admission shall in its concluding part contain the application for listing filed by the sponsoring banking institute or security trading firm. If a subscription prospectus of a new issue is accepted as the basis of consideration for listing, the application shall be filed by one or more members of the stock exchange (normally banking institutes) which are licensed to trade at the stock exchange trading rings and have officially participated (*en nom*) in the issue concerned. The prospectus shall contain:

1. Details of the articles of association of the company and the planned use of the proceeds of the issue;
2. Nominal amount of the issue: in case parts of the issue are temporarily suspended from trading by any embargo, this fact shall be stated;
3. Characteristics (type, par value, series, numbers, fractioning, etc.) of the securities, as well as indication whether such securities are registered securities or issued to bearer; in the case of registered securities the modalities of transfer and number of coupons attached to each certificate shall be specified;
4. Indication of whether shares are partially or fully paid up, whether certificates for the

payment of call on shares exist and in which amounts and the manner of payment of such calls;
5. Name of the official paying agent in Zurich with regard to dividends;
6. Undertaking to publish in good time all official communications to holders of securities in one or more Zurich daily newspapers.

Para. 5 – *Other disclosure for commercial companies*

For joint stock companies the prospectus shall provide the following additional information:
1. Date of registration;
2. Corporate name, domicile and purpose;
3. Duration of company, as well as description of concession, if any;
4. Amount and nature of capital and reserves, indication of preferential rights, if any, as well as existence of non-voting stock outstanding, if any;
5. Voting rules;
6. Membership of Board of Directors, name of auditors;
7. Ordinary dividends distributed in the preceding five years or since the company's formation;
8. Bond issues made by the company, date of final maturity;
9. Company fiscal year and by-laws governing the preparation of financial statements, depreciation practices, as well as details of appropriation of net earnings;
10. Copy of the most recent financial and earnings statements, summary statement of guarantees and contingent liabilities, if any, as well as auditors' report;
11. List of major group companies and subsidiaries, together with indication of their issued capital and bond issues outstanding;
12. Summary report on current business developments if more than six months have elapsed since the most recent annual general stockholders' meeting.

Para. 6. – *Further terms of admission*

The admission and listing of securities and their maintenance shall be subject to the following additional regulations:
1. The total nominal amount of one specific issue of securities shall not be less than SFr 10 mill.
2. As a rule, listing of stocks shall not be applied for until the company concerned has completed at least one full business year and has issued its first annual report.
3. Dividends as well as securities called, shall be payable in Zurich free of charge.
4. Exchange of temporary certificates for definite certificates and procurement of new coupon sheets shall be possible in Zurich free of charge.
5. Payments of calls on shares and the exercise of subscription rights to new shares shall be possible in Zurich free of charge.
6. The company whose securities are to be listed shall publish its accounts and issue a printed annual report which shall be held at the disposal of stockholders by the sponsoring banking institute filing the listing.
7. Any alterations to the securities listed which may result in modifications of the type of listing shall be notified to the Zurich Stock Exchange Association either directly or through the intermediary filing the application for a listing.

Para. 7 – *Exceptions*

On the assumption that the issuer of the securities is well known and that its securities are already traded on the Zurich stock exchange, the Executive Committee may exceptionally waive the requirements for publication of a detailed prospectus and accept the listing on the strength of a founded application, a summary prospectus and the supporting documents to be submitted in conformity with Para. 3 of the regulations.

The content of the summary prospectus shall be decided upon individually by the

Executive Committee (of the stock exchange) in each case. Similarly, the Executive Committee shall be authorized in special cases to waive the requirements for compliance with individual provisions of the regulations if it considers such action as being in the interest of the security holders or of trading procedures in general as opportune and useful.

The Committee can authorize waivers of the provisions of Para. 6, sections 4, 5 and 6 and can permit nominee banks to debit security holders with reasonable charges for foreign registered shares of stocks registered in their names and assigned by them in blank, provided that in conformity with the usages in its country the issuer of the securities is unable to pay such commissions and provided that there exists a substantial interest among the Swiss investing public for the stock concerned.

3.   *Admission and Listing Authority*

Evaluation of applications for admission and listing shall be performed by the Executive Committee of the Stock Exchange Association, in its capacity as admission authority, on the basis of the supporting documents submitted together with the application. The admission authority shall further have the power to demand additional information complementary to that contained in the prospectus. Following the approval of the application by the Committee the application together with the Committee's recommendation will be posted for a period of four days on the notice board on the stock exchange floor. If no objections are filed, the security in question may be listed without delay.

4.   *Fees* (Para. 9)

The Executive Committee of the Stock Exchange Association shall have the right to collect, in respect of its consideration and evaluation of listing applications, a non-recurring admission fee for each security, payable to the Stock Exchange Association. The following fees are approved by the Government of the Canton of Zurich.

Stocks
Domestic corporations
(a) with an issued capital of up to SFr 10 mill.	SFr 400
(b) with an issued capital exceeding SFr 10 mill.	SFr 600
Foreign corporations	SFr 1,000

Para. 10 – Annual Listing Fee
If a stock is accepted for trading and listing on the stock exchange, an annual listing fee established by the Cantonal Advisory Committee on Securities Trading shall be charged, payable to the Cantonal Treasury at the beginning of each year. Only half the annual fee is due when listing takes place in the second half of the year.
The current fees, adopted since January 1967, are as follows:

Stocks incl. non-voting stocks
1. Domestic corporations	
(a) issued capital of the corporation of up to SFr 10 mill.	SFr 400
(b) issued capital of the corporation exceeding SFr 10 mill.	SFr 600
2. Foreign corporations	SFr 1,000

The above charges can be reduced to half if the corporation in question has already listed another category of its stocks.

5. *Suspension of trading and cancellation of listings*
Paras. 11 and 12 deal with the subject of suspension of trading and cancellation of listings. If the sponsoring bank or the issuer fails to meet any obligation, or if the turnover (the holding of stocks of a particular company on the Swiss stock exchanges) becomes negligible, then the Executive Committee may order the deletion of a security.

How to proceed in practical terms

If all the above requirements can be met by a Swiss stock company, the normal procedure is to entrust a member of the stock exchange where the listing is to be made with the preparation of the necessary documentation. Since in almost all cases a capital market transaction will have preceded such an application, there is no need to publish a new prospectus. In summary, the bank in charge of the listing procedure will assume all the responsibilities for a successful listing and will also be keenly interested in seeing that the securities do well on the market.

Costs involved

Apart from the one-time application fee and the annual recurring fees on the various stock exchanges, the cost of printing and publishing the prospectus amounts to approximately SFr 50,000 (the amount depending on whether the listing is sought for one or several stock exchanges). Table 7.1 gives a summary of the total listing costs encountered at the larger exchanges.

Table 7.1 Summary of stock exchange listing costs

	Stock Exchanges of		
	Zurich	Geneva	Basle
		(SFr)	
Admission fee (one-time)	400–600	—	350–500
Listing fee (annual)	400–600	500*	350–500
Prospectus†			
Newspaper publication†	25,000	25,000	25,000

* A one-time lump sum payment of SFr 5,000 can be paid instead.
† In most cases no extra costs, since already incurred in connection with the preceding new issue/capital stock increase. One full page of a prospectus in the *Neue Zürcher Zeitung* costs about SFr 8,500. In the corresponding newspapers in Geneva and Basle the price amounts to about SFr 6,000.

Advantages for a Swiss company in having its shares listed

1. The publicity effect which follows the opening to the capital market and subsequent listing of the stock is of great value to a company. Not only will the prospectus (for the new stock issue or the listing itself) be published in one or several newspapers, but also the financial press will write about the

company and its products. In addition, a small communiqué will normally appear in most newspapers throughout the country.

2. For institutional investors, it is important that new stocks be listed officially on the stock exchanges:

(a) Quite a large number of institutional investors are allowed to purchase listed stocks only. Very few institutional investors can buy unlisted stocks, and the amounts so invested are very limited. Foreign investors also prefer to invest in fully listed stocks rather than in those traded on the pre-stock exchange.

(b) It is much easier for listed companies to arrange a capital increase at a later stage. There is also the opportunity to float a public bond issue at more advantageous terms than would otherwise have been possible (again, institutions will follow such companies more closely and probably invest in their bond issues).

(c) The general marketability of the stock will increase with better price transparency.

(d) Credit standing almost certainly benefits, leading to better credit terms from banks.

(e) The company-owned shares may be given as collateral against a loan at more favourable terms than would otherwise have been possible (usually done through a holding company, since under the Code of Obligations, Art. 659, a joint-stock company cannot own its own stocks).

Table 7.2 shows the number of new listings of domestic stocks on the Zurich Stock Exchange, as well as the total nominal value of stocks so listed (the actual market value is, however, substantially higher).

Table 7.2 New listings of domestic stocks on the Zurich Stock Exchange

	No. of first-time listings	No. of companies	No. of categories of stocks	Nominal value (SFr million)
1980	1	23	25	1,071.4
1981	6	22	24	1,298.4
1982	4	23	24	1,389.8
1983	1	23	25	749.8
1984	6	26	28	727.5

Source: Zurich Stock Exchange, Annual Reports 1980–84.

Listing of shares of foreign companies on the Swiss stock exchanges

Importance of the Swiss capital market for major foreign companies

Over the past 25 years, the Swiss capital market has also become very important for foreign companies that wish to raise share capital either through stock exchange listings or through outright over-the-counter sales. For the average investor, listing has the advantage of much lower purchase costs, given Switzerland's low stock exchange commissions; for the corporation, there is the advantage of the low listing fee and the greater publicity effect. Zurich in fact appears to be the most important stock exchange in Europe for US corporations' shares. Corporations that have their stocks listed on the Swiss stock exchanges – in most cases it is done simultaneously on the exchanges in Zurich, Geneva and Basle – are followed more closely not only by the international investors' community in Switzerland but also in some neighbouring countries. If such companies are raising capital through issues in other capital markets such as the Eurobond market, and particularly if they raise capital through a public or private Swiss franc issue, many of the regular Swiss investors and their investment advisers are likely to be more familiar with them. Since a large proportion of Eurobonds eventually find their way into Swiss-managed portfolios, it can be quite useful to have the stock listed in Switzerland.

Procedure and conditions for listing

As a general rule, only shares of quality companies well known to Swiss investors, with a high marketability and already widely distributed on the Swiss market, are acceptable for trading in Switzerland. Furthermore, unrestricted arbitrage transactions with the stock exchanges of their country of origin must be possible.

The criteria which serve as a basis for discussion with regard to applications for admission are as follows:

1. The number of shares deposited with a selection of the larger banks must be big enough to ensure a sufficiently large trading volume on the Swiss stock exchanges after their introduction; this condition is regarded as being fulfilled if the total of the shares of a company deposited with a number of Swiss banks attains a stock market value of at least 10 to 15 million Swiss francs spread among a considerable number of clients.

2. The application is submitted by the proposing bank and will be processed after examination and consideration by a syndicate arranged by the lead bank.

3. If the syndicate agrees to sponsor the listing, a letter will be sent to the Swiss National Bank to obtain authority for the admission of the shares to the Swiss stock exchanges. The Swiss National Bank makes its decision in the light of the prevailing monetary and economic situation, similar to the procedure for bond/notes issues. But it would take an extraordinary situation for the SNB to decline.

4. Following Swiss National Bank approval, the lead bank will submit a similar application to the Swiss Admission Board.* Approval of the request represents the final step prior to actually approaching the Swiss stock exchanges to which admission is being sought. These are usually the three principal exchanges in the country, namely Zurich, Geneva and Basle, and sometimes Lausanne.

Application for admission of the shares is then made simultaneously to each

* The Swiss Admission Board is a special body, the members of which are partly delegated by the Association of Swiss Stock Exchanges and by the Federal Department of Finance.

stock exchange concerned. It is based on a prospectus to be prepared by the proposing bank and contains information provided by the company that must conform to the quite strict requirements of the various Swiss stock exchanges and those of the Swiss Admission Board.

In addition to the information needed for a domestic stock listing (see beginning of chapter), the names of the non-Swiss stock exchanges on which the shares are already listed or to which admission is being sought must be provided.

The bank in charge of the listing operation will undertake the preparation of the prospectus in English and/or German and French (depending on the situation), in co-operation with the company to be listed.

All later publications of the company intended for the shareholders, such as those relating to ordinary dividends, stock dividends, capital increases, rights issues, splits, mergers, etc., must also appear in one of the daily newspapers in the city where the shares are listed; such advertisements are made at the company's expense.

The bank introducing the share listing is responsible for furnishing the stock exchange authorities regularly with the company's reports and must communicate any change affecting the shares.

To admit the shares of a foreign company to the Swiss stock exchanges, the bank handling the application requires, in addition to the information specified for domestic stock listings:

(a)   30 copies of the latest annual report,
(b)   30 copies of both the By-Laws and Certificate of Incorporation (or Memorandum of Association and Articles of Association), and
(c)   15 specimens of the security to be admitted.

Trading can take place only in the form of *original share certificates* (except Japanese and French shares, which are traded in the form of depositary receipts). Registered shares are normally registered in the name of one or several banks of the syndicate and are issued in a number of specific denominations as required by the market.

Charges for admission are as follows:

(a)   Non-recurring charges
       SFr 85,000 lump sum for handling charges and expenses of the lead bank.
       SFr 30,000 to SFr 50,000, the approximate cost of placing a condensed version of the prospectus in the various local newspapers (as per invoice).
       SFr 500 introductory fee levied by the Swiss Admission Board.
       Introductory fee for the stock exchanges of:*

       Zurich   SFr 1,000
       Basle   SFr 750
       Geneva   SFr 750
       Lausanne   None

(b)   Recurring annual charges
       The annual listing charges are as follows:

       Zurich   SFr 1,000
       Basle   SFr 875

* Subject to change.

Geneva   SFr 750*
Lausanne   SFr 700
(c) Expenses related to quarterly/annual information for shareholders.
The costs of small advertisements (if and when necessary) in one local newspaper in the city of listing must be paid by the company.

Investor relations campaign

In most cases the listing of a foreign stock is preceded by advertisements in various Swiss newspapers, giving information about the corporation (including some brief financial data).

On the day of the first listing, a presentation takes place in Zurich and Geneva. Some 100–130 investment advisers, portfolio managers from the insurance and pension fund industry, bankers and security analysts, etc., are invited for a luncheon presentation. These meetings, to which the press is also invited, are often followed by a special press conference. Normally the chairman and a few senior executives give the presentation. These meetings are often professionally prepared by specialist organisations. The arranging of the presentation, including the invitations, is almost always done by the bank sponsoring the listing.

Volume of listed foreign shares

At the end of 1984, some 181 foreign stocks of 175 different corporations were listed on the Zurich Stock Exchange. Stocks from the United States and Canada totalled over 108. The Federal Republic of Germany had the second largest number, with 22 stocks listed (the first three figures compare with 170, 164 and 100 respectively in 1983).

During 1984, 14 new stocks were listed. In addition, nine companies listed new shares from a capital increase. Three corporations withdrew some or all of their listed securities (the respective figures for 1983 were 12, 4 and 5 – see Table 7.3).

Table 7.3 Newly listed foreign stocks on the Zurich Stock Exchange (inc. capital increases)

	Categories of stocks withdrawn	US stocks	Other stocks	Total
1980	2	4	5	9
1981	5	4	11	15
1982	5*	—	9	9
1983	5	5	11	16
1984	3	11	12	23

* Of which four nationalised French companies.
Source: Zurich Stock Exchange, Annual Reports 1980–84.

Table 7.4 shows the various foreign shares listed on the Zurich Stock Exchange at the end of 1984, with a breakdown of US, West German and other shares.

* Or the option of a lump-sum payment of SFr 7,500 for the entire duration of the listing, including introductory fee (subject to amendment).

Table 7.4   Foreign shares listed on the Zurich Stock Exchange (1st January 1985)

United States and Canada
Abbott Laboratories, North Chicago
Aetna Life and Casualty Company, Hartford
Alcan Aluminium Limited, Montreal
Allied Corporation, Morris Township
Aluminum Company of America, Pittsburgh
Amax Inc., New York
American Brands, Inc., New York
American Cyanamid Company, Wayne (NJ)
American Express Company, New York
American Hospital Supply Corporation, Evanston
American Information Technologies Corporation, Chicago
American Medical International, Inc., Beverly Hills
American Telephone & Telegraph Co., New York
Archer-Daniels-Midland Company, Decatur
Atlantic Richfield Company, Los Angeles
Baker International Corp., Orange (California)
Baxter Travenol Laboratories, Inc., Deerfield (Illinois)
Beatrice Companies, Inc., Chicago
Bell Atlantic Corporation, Philadelphia
Bell Canada Enterprises, Inc., Montreal
The Black and Decker Manufacturing Co., Towson (Maryland)
The Boeing Company, Seattle
Borden, Inc., New York
Bowater Incorporated, Darien (Connecticut)
Burlington Industries, Inc., Greensboro
Burroughs Corporation, Wilmington
Canadian Pacific Ltd, Montreal
Caterpillar Tractor Co., San Francisco
Chrysler Corporation, Wilmington
Citicorp, New York
City Investing Company, Dover (Delaware)
The Coca Cola Company, Wilmington
Colgate-Palmolive Company, New York
Consolidated Natural Gas Co., New York
Control Data Corporation, Wilmington
Corning Glass Works, Corning
CPC International Inc., City of Dover (Delaware)
Crown Zellerbach Corporation, San Francisco
CSX Corporation, Richmond
Dart & Kraft, Inc., Wilmington
Diamond Shamrock Corporation, Dallas
Walt Disney Productions, Burbank
Dow Chemical Company, Midland (Michigan)
E. I. du Pont de Nemours & Co., Wilmington
Eastman Kodak Company, Rochester (NY)
Engelhard Corporation, Edison
Exxon Corporation, New York
Fluor Corporation, Dover (Delaware)
Ford Motor Company, Dearborn (Michigan)

General Electric Co., Schenectady
General Foods Corporation, Wilmington
General Motors Corporation, Detroit
Genstar Corporation, Vancouver, with Cps. No. 23 & ff.
Genstar Corporation, Vancouver, registered shares
The Gillette Company, Boston
Goodyear Tire & Rubber Co., Akron (Ohio)
W. R. Grace & Co., New York
GTE Corporation, New York
Gulf & Western Industries, Inc., New York
Halliburton Company, Dallas (Texas)
Homestake Mining Company, Wilmington
Honeywell Inc., Minneapolis (Minnesota)
Inco Limited
International Business Machines Corp., New York
International Paper Company, New York
ITT Corporation, New York
Lilly (Eli) and Company, Indianapolis
Litton Industries Inc., Beverly Hills
Lockheed Corporation, Burbank
Minnesota Mining & Manufacturing Co., St Paul
Mobil Corporation, Wilmington
Monsanto Company, St Louis (Missouri)
National Distillers and Chemical Corp., New York
NCR Corporation, Dayton
NYNEX Corporation, New York
Occidental Petroleum Corporation, Los Angeles
Owens-Illinois, Inc., Toledo (Ohio)
Pacific Gas & Electric Co., San Francisco
Pacific Telesis Group, San Francisco
Pennzoil Company, Houston
PepsiCo, Inc., New York
Pfizer Inc., New York
Philip Morris Inc., New York
Phillips Petroleum Company, Bartlesville
The Procter & Gamble Company, Cincinnati (Ohio)
Rockwell International Corporation, Wilmington
Schlumberger Limited, Curaçao
Sears, Roebuck and Co., Chicago
SmithKline Beckman Corporation, Philadelphia
Southwestern Bell Corporation, St Louis
Sperry Corporation, New York
Squibb Corporation, New York
Standard Oil Company (Indiana), Chicago
Sun Company, Inc., Radnor (Pennsylvania)
Tenneco Inc., Houston
Texaco Inc., New York

Transamerica Corporation, San Francisco
Union Carbide Corp., New York
Uniroyal Inc., New York
United Energy Resources, Inc., Houston
United States Gypsum Company, Chicago
United States Steel Corporation, Wilmington
United Technologies Corporation, Hartford
US WEST, Inc., Englewood
Wang Laboratories, Inc., Lowell B
Warner-Lambert Company, Wilmington
F. W. Woolworth Co., New York
Xerox Corporation, Rochester NY
Zenith Electronics Corporation, Chicago

Federal Republic of Germany
AEG-Telefunken AG, Berlin and Frankfurt
a.M.
Allianz-Versicherungs-AG, Berlin and Munich
(registered shares)
BASF Aktiengesellschaft, Ludwigshafen
a.Rhein
Bayer Aktiengesellschaft, Leverkusen
Bayerische Motoren Werke AG, Munich
Commerzbank Aktiengesellschaft, Düsseldorf
Daimler-Benz Aktiengesellschaft, Stuttgart
(ordinary shares)
Degussa Aktiengesellschaft, Frankfurt a.M.
Degussa Aktiengesellschaft, Frankfurt a.M.
($\frac{1}{2}$ dividend)
Deutsche Babcock Aktiengesellschaft,
Oberhausen (ordinary shares)
Deutsche Bank Aktiengesellschaft, Frankfurt
a.M.
Dresden Bank Aktiengesellschaft, Frankfurt
a.M.
Gutehoffnungshütte Aktienverein AG,
Oberhausen
Hoechst Aktiengesellschaft, Frankfurt a.M.
Kraftübertragungswerke Rheinfelden AG,
Rheinfelden
Mannesmann Aktiengesellschaft, Düsseldorf
Mercedes-Automobil-Holding AG, Frankfurt
a.M.
Rheinisch-Westf. Elektrizitätswerk AG, Essen
(ordinary shares)
Rheinisch-Westf. Elektrizitätswerk AG, Vorzug
Schering Aktiengesellschaft, Berlin and
Bergkamen
Siemens, AG, Berlin and Munich (ordinary
shares)
Thyssen-Aktiengesellschaft, formerly A.
Thyssen-Hutte, Duisburg
VEBA Aktiengesellschaft, Bonn and Berlin
Vereinigte Elektrizitätswerke Westfalen AG, B
Volkswagenwerk Aktiengesellschaft, Wolfsburg

Other countries
AEGON NV, The Hague (bearer ordinary
shares)

AKZO NV, Arnhem (bearer ordinary shares)
Algemene Bank Nederland NV, Amsterdam
(bearer ordinary shares)
Amsterdam-Rotterdam Bank NV, Amsterdam
(bearer ordinary shares)
Anglo American Corp. of South Africa Ltd,
Joh'burg (ordinary shares)
Anglo American Gold Investment Co. Ltd
(ordinary shares)
Barlow Rand Limited, Sandton (South Africa)
(ordinary shares)
BAT Industries PLC, London (ordinary
shares)
Beghin-Say, Thumeries
Bowater Industries PLC, London (ordinary
shares)
The British Petroleum Company PLC,
London (ordinary shares)
BSN-Gervais Danone, Paris
Compagnie des Machines Bull, Paris
Cia Sevillana de Electr., Seville
Consolidated Gold Fields PLC, London
(ordinary shares)
Consolidated Gold Fields PLC, London
(registered ordinary shares)
Courtaulds PLC, London (ordinary shares)
De Beers Consolidated Mines Ltd, Kimberley
(ordinary shares)
De Beers Consolidated Mines Ltd (registered
ordinary shares)
Driefontein Consolidated Limited,
Johannesburg
Fujitsu Ltd, Kawasaki (ordinary shares: bearer
depository receipt – Basle)
General Mining Union Corp. Ltd, Joh'burg
(ordinary shares)
General Mining Union Corp. Ltd, Joh'burg
(registered ordinary shares)
General Shopping SA, Luxembourg (in
liquidation)
Gold Fields of South Africa Limited,
Johannesburg
The Great Universal Stores PLC, London
(ordinary shares 'A')
Honda Motor Co. Ltd, Tokyo (ordinary
shares: bearer depository receipt – SEGA,
Basle)
Imperial Chemical Industries PLC, London
(ordinary shares)
Kloof Gold Mining Company Limited,
Johannesburg
Kojninkl. Nederl. Hoogovens en Staalfabr.
NV. Ijmuiden (ordinary shares: bearer
certificates – Administratiekantoor)
NEC Corp., Tokyo (ordinary shares: bearer
depository receipt – SEGA, Basle)
Norsk Hydro A/S, Notodden (registered
ordinary shares)
Olympus Optical Co. Ltd, Tokyo (ordinary

Table 7.4 – cont.

shares: bearer depository receipt – SEGA, Basle)

NV Philips' Gloeilampenfabrieken, Eindhoven (bearer ordinary shares)

The Rio Tinto-Zinc Corp. PLC, London (ordinary shares)

The Rio Tinto-Zinc Corp. PLC, London (registered ordinary shares)

ROBECO NV, Rotterdam (bearer ordinary shares)

Rolinco NV, Rotterdam (bearer ordinary shares)

Rorento NV, Sint Maarten (bearer ordinary shares)

Royal Dutch Petroleum Company, The Hague (ordinary shares)

Sanyo Electric Co., Ltd, Osaka (ordinary shares: bearer depository receipt – SEGA, Basle)

Sharp Corporation, Osaka (registered ordinary shares – bearer depository receipt – SEGA, Basle)

Sidro, Brussels (Nos. 1–1,000,000: 'issued after 6 Oct. 44')

Sté Nationale Elf Aquitaine, Courbevoie

Solvay & Cie. Societe Anonyme, Ixelles-Brussels ('issued after 6 Oct. 44')

Sony Corporation, Tokyo (ordinary shares: bearer depository receipt – SEGA, Basle)

Unilever NV, Rotterdam (ordinary shares)

Source: *Kursblatt der Zürcher Effektenbörse*, 28 December 1984.

8 The foreign investor and the Swiss equity market: legal and fiscal aspects

Dr Urs W. Benz

Opening a bank account for securities transactions

Since they are dealers on the Swiss stock exchanges, banks carry out virtually all transactions concerning Swiss shares. The banks delegate their securities dealers to the stock exchanges and execute customer orders for stock exchange transactions. Orders are accepted from their clients, which include individuals, companies and other banks. These other banks may deal on their own account or on behalf of their clients. While a large degree of confidentiality can be guaranteed by dealer banks, Swiss regulations stipulate that they accept orders only from people they know.

The easiest way to initiate and maintain an active stock portfolio is to enter into a contractual relationship with a Swiss bank. This is normally done by opening both a current and a securities safe custody account. The combination of these two accounts provides investors with the necessary tools to invest in almost any instrument worldwide. This solution also accommodates the banks, because before executing a transaction at the stock exchange the bank wants to be sure that the investor who intends to buy shares has sufficient funds at his disposal to pay the purchase price, and that the investor who intends to sell is able to furnish the securities sold.

A Swiss bank account can be opened by correspondence or by visit. Banks usually require the following forms:
(a) a signature card,
(b) a signed copy of the bank's general conditions,
(c) a signed copy of the bank's regulations governing deposits, and
(d) a signed declaration of acceptance or rejection of Convention XVI regarding insider dealings (see below).

If the client is a company, the following documents are also required:
(a) an extract from the commercial registry (or certificate of registration or certificate of good standing),
(b) Memorandum and Articles of Association, and

(c)   a resolution of the board of directors re the opening of an account.

The signature of the account holder must be authenticated. This can be done by a Notary Public, by a well-known bank, or by the client during a visit to the bank.

Swiss banks are forbidden to open a bank account without first ascertaining the identity of the account holder and of the person who is beneficially entitled to the funds in the account. Thus if the account holder acts on behalf of a third party, the bank must be informed, by means of a special form, of the third party's name and residence. If the account is opened in the name of a domiciliary company, the bank must be informed of the name and residence of the controlling individuals.

While the disclosure of an individual's identity is the norm, there are ways for investors to remain anonymous. The identity of the beneficial owner need not be revealed if the account holder acts through a person domiciled or with a registered office in Switzerland who is bound by a legally protected professional secrecy (particularly attorneys-at-law and notaries), or who is a member of an association affiliated with the Schweizerische Treuhand- und Revisionskammer. Such person must declare to the bank, on a special form, that he knows the beneficial owner of the account and that, to the best of his knowledge, the funds to be deposited are not connected with any unlawful transaction. (For further details, see the 'Agreement on the observance of care by the banks in accepting funds and on the practice of banking secrecy', an agreement concluded between the Swiss banks, the Swiss Bankers' Association and the Swiss National Bank. The full text of the agreement will be found in Appendix 2.)

In order to facilitate stock exchange transactions (and, of course, any other banking business), the account holder may grant *powers of attorney* to one or several persons. Signatories are entitled to represent the account holder in all kinds of banking transactions and such rights may be granted individually or jointly (two signatories). Unless cancelled by the account holder or later by his executor or his heirs, powers of attorney remain valid beyond the account holder's lifetime.

If he prefers, the account holder may grant so-called *powers of administration*, which are limited powers of attorney. The holder of a power of administration may give buying or selling orders on behalf of the client, but he is not allowed to withdraw funds or securities from the account. Such powers of administration are quite usual with Swiss banks.

Restrictions on transfer of shares

Swiss corporate law provides for both bearer shares and nominal shares. The free transfer of nominal (=registered) shares may be restricted by a special provision in the Articles of Association. On the other hand, bearer shares are freely transferable without any formalities; the person who holds the share at a certain time must be accepted as owner. From this it follows that the free transfer of bearer shares can be restricted only by a contractual agreement of the shareholders. This is not practical for large corporations and it is also not very effective since a shareholder agreement is not binding upon third parties.

There are instances where restrictions on the free transfer of shares are in the interest of corporations and/or their shareholders. Most often one finds transfer restrictions in the charters of so-called closed corporations or family corporations. Such transfer restrictions are designed to maintain the original balance of control, avoiding the sale of shares to outside persons, or to ensure that shares can be held only by members of one or a few families.

There are also reasons for medium-sized or large publicly owned corporations to maintain or introduce transfer restrictions. Medium-sized corporations may, for instance, find it necessary to ensure that none, or not too many, of their shares are acquired by competitors. Similarly, large corporations operating in international markets may consider it desirable to preserve their national character and to avoid becoming dependent on foreign enterprises. In some fields of business, the motive is the intention to bid for governmental contracts that may be awarded only to domestic contractors. Consequently, such companies introduce the restriction that their shareholders must be Swiss citizens. During the Second World War, the fear of being put on the blacklist of foreign countries during wartime, for example in connection with the US's Trading with the Enemy Act, caused a first wave of such charter amendments in Switzerland.

As a result, foreign investors who wish to buy shares of publicly traded Swiss corporations may be prevented from acquiring nominal shares. Publicly traded bearer shares, on the other hand, may be bought without restrictions.

The acquisition of nominal shares has indeed been restricted by many large Swiss companies. One of the following restrictions is usually present:

(a)   Only Swiss citizens may be registered as shareholders.
(b)   Foreigners and foreign companies may not be registered as shareholders. Swiss companies that are controlled by foreigners are regarded as foreign companies.
(c)   Only Swiss citizens and foreigners who are domiciled in Switzerland may be registered as shareholders.
(d)   The board of directors may refuse a new shareholder without stating a reason.
(e)   The board of directors may refuse a new shareholder if one of certain enumerated grounds applies.
(f)   The board of directors may refuse a new shareholder 'on important grounds'.
(g)   A foreigner may not acquire more than a certain number or percentage of nominal shares.

By way of illustration, the restrictions on the transfer of nominal shares by some important publicly traded Swiss companies are listed below. In some of these examples, only a summary of rather complex provisions is given.

Alusuisse, Bank Leu, Brown Boveri, Ciba-Geigy, Hasler Holding, Holderbank, Nestlé, Oerlikon-Bührle Holding, Schweiz. Bankverein, Schweiz. Rückversicherung, Sibra Holding, Sulzer, Swissair, Winterthur. Foreigners and foreign companies are excluded from buying nominal shares of these companies.

Ateliers de Constructions Mécaniques de Vevey SA. Foreigners and foreign companies may acquire up to 50 nominal shares per shareholder.

Banca della Svizzera Italiana. Foreigners with a permanent domicile (Permit C) in Switzerland are accepted; foreigners with a residence Permit B and foreign companies are excluded.

Georg Fischer. Foreigners and foreign companies may acquire nominal shares up to a maximum of 10,000 shares, but in no case more than 10% of all nominal shares.

Globus. Foreigners domiciled in Switzerland are accepted, with the exception of competitors; other foreigners and foreign companies are excluded.

Sandoz. Foreigners and foreign companies are excluded with the exception of foreigners domiciled in Switzerland for at least 15 years, who may acquire up to ten nominal shares per shareholder.

Schindler. Foreigners with a permanent domicile of at least ten years are accepted; other foreigners and foreign companies are excluded.

Schweiz. Allgemeine. Foreigners may acquire up to 60 nominal shares per shareholder; foreign companies are excluded.

Schweiz. Bankgesellschaft. Citizens of the United States and persons domiciled abroad, as well as foreign companies, are excluded; other foreigners with permanent domicile in Switzerland (Permit C) are accepted.

Schweiz. Kreditanstalt. Citizens of the United States and persons domiciled abroad, as well as foreign companies, are excluded; other foreigners with permanent domicile in Switzerland (Permit C) may acquire up to 5,000 nominal shares per shareholder.

Zürich Versicherung. Foreigners may under certain conditions acquire a limited number of nominal shares; foreign companies are excluded.

The internal regulations or the practice of some – but not all – of these companies provide that a foreigner may be registered as a shareholder if he acquires nominal shares:
(a)   by succession,
(b)   by marital property law, or
(c)   by exercising his pre-emptive right based on nominal shares already registered in his name in the course of an increase of the company's share capital.

When a purchase of nominal shares does not get the approval required under a consent restriction, the question arises as to what happens to the shares which the rejected investor bought. From the point of view of the corporation, the legal situation is clear: Art. 685 al 4 of the Swiss Corporation Law states that the person whose name appears in the share register shall be regarded as a shareholder *vis-à-vis* the company. The company will continue to consider the seller – who is still registered – as a shareholder and to allow him all the rights a shareholder has under the law.

Thus, the selling shareholder is still in a position to exercise the rights of a shareholder of the company. Having sold and transferred his shares, he is of course no longer in a position to sell the shares a second time. Financially, he does not own the shares any more. The sales contract between the selling and the buying shareholder (or the sales contracts between the selling shareholder and his bank, between his bank and the bank of the buyer, and between the buying shareholder and his bank) is valid between the parties, although the buying shareholder has been rejected by the company. The rejected shareholder owns the share certificates. As a consequence, only he is in a position to sell them. This is the only way out of the unsatisfactory situation which has arisen through the company's refusal to register the new shareholder. He will have to resell the shares, if and when possible, to a person who will be acceptable to the company.

It should be noted that situations such as those described above are not very frequent, at least not with regard to the restricted nominal shares of large companies. As we have seen from the above list, the transfer restrictions of these companies are unambiguous and do not usually leave much discretion to the company's management. Due to the normally clear wording, banks are, in most cases, able to advise their foreign clients as to whether they may buy nominal shares of a certain company.

Swiss bank secrecy

For a foreign investor in shares, the question may be vital as to what extent he is protected under Swiss bank secrecy.

Principle

In general

Bank secrecy as a principle is as old as banks themselves. The statutes and by-laws of the earliest banks in Europe contained rules compelling bank employees to keep silence concerning their clients' affairs.

In later years, private legal provisions were laid down in many countries focusing both on the bank's own right to its business secrecy and/or on its clients' right to privacy with regard to their financial affairs.

Still later, bank secrecy became part of the criminal law providing the sanction of imprisonment for bank secrecy violation.

In Switzerland

Today's Swiss bank secrecy has its basis both in private and in criminal law.

In private law, the client's right to secrecy is both part of the contractual relations between the bank and its client and an aspect of every person's right to privacy. This right of the client results in an obligation of the bank to keep secrecy. Any breach of bank secrecy gives the client the right to claim damages from the bank.

In 1934 the efforts of the German National Socialist authorities to get hold of fugitive Jewish assets in Switzerland prompted the Swiss legislature to strengthen the protection of bank secrecy by means of criminal provisions. Art. 47 of the Swiss Bank Act, which came into force on 1 March 1935, reads as follows (unofficial translation):

Art. 47

1. Whoever divulges a secret entrusted to him in his capacity as an officer, employee, mandatory, liquidator or commissioner of a bank, as a representative of the Banking Commission, officer or employee of a recognised auditing company, or who has become aware of such a secret in this capacity, and whoever tries to induce others to violate professional secrecy, shall be punished by a prison term not to exceed six months or by a fine not exceeding 50,000 francs.

2. If the act has been committed by negligence, the penalty shall be a fine not exceeding 30,000 francs.

3. The violation of professional secrecy remains punishable even after termination of the official or employment relationship or the exercise of the profession.

4. Federal and cantonal regulations concerning the obligation to testify and to furnish information to a government authority shall remain reserved.

Swiss bank secrecy is, as a rule, extremely far-reaching since it covers all facts not generally known. Moreover, it protects the client even after the termination of his contractual relation with the bank.

For the investor, these legal provisions impose upon the bank a duty to keep silence not only concerning his stock exchange transactions and the balance in his bank account, but also with regard to the fact that he is a client of the bank.

Exceptions

Contrary to what some clients may think, Swiss bank secrecy is by no means an absolute right. It has its limits as well.

Inheritance

When a person dies, most of his rights pass, by law, to his heirs and, to a lesser degree, to his executor. As a consequence, the executor and all heirs are entitled to be informed by the bank of the balance in the deceased client's account at the time of his death.

At the same time, the bank is not obliged – nor in fact allowed – to furnish any information to fiscal or other state authorities.

Debt collection, bankruptcy and legal attachment

In the event of bankruptcy in Switzerland, the bank is obliged to make a declaration of the bankrupt's assets and to distribute them to the receiver in bankruptcy.

In the event of debt collection and attachment proceedings in Switzerland, the bank must block all assets and, when a distraint has been issued, furnish the required information and release all assets. According to recent court rulings, if the banks assert rights of their own with regard to the assets, such as a lien or a right of set-off, they must give this information immediately after the opening of the proceedings.

The law on debt collection and bankruptcy is governed by the principle of national territoriality. As a rule, information and assets are not given, in principle, to official receivers and other agencies abroad.

Exceptions are possible for some countries on the basis of an applicable treaty of mutual assistance in such proceedings. And there are indications that the principle of national territoriality in debt collection and bankruptcy matters might sooner or later be softened.

Civil proceedings in Switzerland

Because Switzerland is a confederation of 26 cantons and half-cantons, there exist 26 different cantonal codes of civil procedure and an additional code for federal civil proceedings. In some cantons, the law on civil procedure stipulates an obligation of the bank to furnish information in civil lawsuits, while the law of other cantons allows the bank the right to withhold information. In Zurich and some other cantons, as well as in federal civil proceedings, the law leaves it with the courts to decide whether bank secrecy is to be maintained or whether the bank must disclose the information requested by the party to a lawsuit. It goes without saying that information concerning persons who are not involved in the particular lawsuit must be protected.

Criminal proceedings in Switzerland

The interest of the state in criminal matters is much greater than in civil proceedings. As a consequence, the law on criminal proceedings of all cantons and of the federation stipulates that bank secrecy does not extend to persons accused in Swiss criminal proceedings. Under these circumstances, banks must send representatives to testify and to disclose relevant bank documents. Nevertheless, the rights of third persons who are not accused themselves continue to be protected as far as possible.

Tax proceedings

Here, we must distinguish between normal tax assessments and tax offence procedures.

With regard to both federal and cantonal tax assessments, bank secrecy is kept. The banks are not obliged to furnish bank statements or other information directly to the tax authorities. This rule applies both during the lifetime of the taxpayer and with regard to the tax inventory to be established after his death. In Switzerland, it is the duty only of the taxpayer or his heirs to deal with the tax authorities and to provide the required evidence.

As far as tax offences are concerned, Swiss law distinguishes three different types, each of which carries a different sanction:
(a) A tax infringement is the non-observance of procedural obligations; it is punished with a fine.
(b) Tax evasion is the payment of insufficient taxes as a result of filing an incomplete tax return; it is punished with a penal tax and a fine.
(c) Tax fraud is tax evasion by means of deceiving the tax authorities with false or forged documents with the intent to evade taxes; it is punished by a penal tax and fine or imprisonment.

As far as tax infringements and tax evasion are concerned, bank secrecy is kept with regard to cantonal taxes and to the federal income tax. With regard to other federal taxes such as stamp duties, withholding taxes, turnover tax on sales and customs duties, bank secrecy is not protected. In such matters, banks must give the required information to the competent federal authorities.

Tax fraud is a criminal offence. In such procedures bank secrecy is superseded by the bank's obligation to disclose any information required with regard to the accused client.

International legal assistance in civil proceedings

Concerning legal assistance in civil lawsuits abroad, the rules of the relevant code of civil procedure apply. As outlined above, bank secrecy is either maintained, left to the discretion of the court or not maintained.

International legal assistance in criminal matters

The rules for international legal assistance in criminal matters are laid down in the federal law of 20 March 1981 on international assistance in criminal proceedings, in bilateral treaties, and in the European Convention on Mutual Assistance in Criminal Matters of 20 April 1959.

The fundamental principle in Switzerland has always been that full assistance in foreign criminal proceedings is granted on the condition that the particular offence is punishable under both foreign and Swiss criminal law. As a consequence, no legal assistance is possible in matters involving violation of currency regulations and political, military or tax offences.

Further, no legal assistance is granted:

(a)   if giving the requested information might endanger Swiss security, public order or other important national interests, or if it might result in a significant disadvantage to the Swiss economy, or

(b)   if the Swiss authorities consider the incriminating act of the accused to be a trivial matter.

On the other hand, there are exceptions to the normal refusal to grant legal assistance with regard to tax offences. According to the new federal law of 1981, assistance may be granted if the incriminating act is, under Swiss law, considered as tax fraud. Further, the Treaty on Mutual Assistance in Criminal Matters between Switzerland and the United States provides that, under certain conditions, assistance is granted with regard to US tax offences as far as organised crime is concerned.

Whenever the Swiss authorities decide that legal assistance should be granted and, as a consequence, that bank secrecy is not to be protected, the following two principles must be maintained. First, the country requesting legal assistance must guarantee that it will use the information obtained only for the particular criminal act for which it was requested. Thus, material acquired in connection with a criminal offence may not be used in proceedings involving violation of currency regulations or tax offences. Second, the bank and the Swiss authorities must ensure that the rights of third persons who are not accused are protected. This may require eliminating part of the information before the documents are given to the foreign authorities.

The right of all parties affected to be heard before a decision becomes final is a fundamental principle in Swiss law. This means that both the bank and its client, whose right to bank secrecy might be jeopardised by the granting of legal assistance, will be given the opportunity to object. If the administrative authority overrules such objections and decides that the requested information must be given, the bank and/or the client may appeal to the Federal Court in Lausanne, which is the court of last resort in Switzerland.

A final remark might be made with regard to the exchange of information provided for in many double-taxation treaties. A double-taxation treaty is never applied unless the client himself intends to make use of its provisions in order to obtain a refund of deducted withholding taxes or if he wants to prevent double taxation in other tax matters. Only if a taxpayer makes explicit use of the advantages of a double-taxation treaty may the authorities of the two countries concerned exchange the information necessary for a correct application of the treaty. And even in such situations, the obligation of the Swiss authorities to furnish information is subject to standard legal provisions. As a consequence, bank secrecy remains protected.

Insider dealings

Most important for foreign buyers of shares on Swiss stock exchanges is the present situation regarding insider dealings.

Much has been said and written recently about the problems arising with insider dealings. Such dealings involve the sale or purchase transactions of shares or options by a person who has confidential information likely to have an influence on the value of these securities in the near future.

Two major cases were responsible for raising this topic in Switzerland. In 1981, the United States Securities and Exchange Commission (SEC) discovered that in the take-over cases involving Santa Fe International Corporation/Kuwait Petroleum Company and St Joe Minerals Corporation/Seagram and Co., some insider dealings at US stock exchanges had been transacted indirectly through Swiss banks.

Requests by the SEC for legal assistance were unsuccessful because most insider dealings are not a criminal offence in Switzerland. As noted above, a prerequisite for any international legal assistance in criminal matters is that the act must be a criminal offence in both countries.

Although insider dealings are regarded as unethical or immoral, only a small portion of insider transactions are punishable in Switzerland. It must be shown that fraud, unfaithful business management or breach of business secrets were elements in the transaction.

It is well known that the SEC and other US authorities put much emphasis on having a 'fair' securities market. Understandably, they request foreign investors to follow their rules when dealing on US stock exchanges. Further, they want to prevent investors who do not obey their rules from hiding behind foreign secrecy laws.

Switzerland is not the only country where insider dealings are not treated as a criminal offence. However, Swiss banks very frequently execute stock exchange transactions in the United States, both for Swiss and foreign investors. That is why in 1982 the US authorities put pressure on Switzerland to find a solution that would enable Swiss banks – despite Swiss bank secrecy – to give information to the SEC about clients accused of insider dealings.

Following short but intensive negotiations, the two governments executed the 'Memorandum of Understanding' on 31 August 1982. This agreement gave the necessary frame for closer co-operation between the SEC and the competent Swiss authorities in order to let the SEC have information requested from Swiss banks during insider-dealing investigations.

At the same time, all Swiss banks signed an agreement (Convention XVI) setting forth details of when and how information on possible insider dealings could be forwarded to the SEC. In principle, the system involves having the Swiss banks request that their clients give a pledge not to make use of any insider knowledge when dealing on US stock exchanges.

Should they not adhere to this agreement, their names and the details of the transactions might – upon request of the SEC and after the case has been checked by a special Swiss investigation commission – be passed on to the US authorities.

For investors dealing on Swiss stock exchanges, the following aspects should be pointed out:

1. The Memorandum of Understanding and Convention XVI cover only securities transactions that are performed on a US stock exchange. With regard to transactions on any of the Swiss stock exchanges, bank secrecy remains intact – even if the transactions involve the sale or purchase of shares in an American company.

2. A new law is under preparation which will make insider dealings a criminal offence in Switzerland. This amendment will most likely be in the form of a rewording of Art. 161 of the Swiss federal penal code. As soon as this new law is in force, the rather complicated Memorandum of Understanding and Convention XVI will become obsolete. Information could then be given to the SEC on insider-dealing investigations under the normal international legal assistance procedures since the prerequisite that the offence be a criminal act in both countries would be met.

3. When the new law is in force, insider dealings on a Swiss stock exchange will be investigated and punished under Swiss criminal law.

A final remark might be in order. As mentioned above, the SEC in 1981–82 tried in vain to get legal assistance from Switzerland in the Santa Fe takeover. This case became one of the main reasons for the execution of the Memorandum of Understanding. In 1983 the SEC introduced a new request for legal assistance, giving evidence that the investigation involved a breach of business secrets which is, as we have seen, a criminal offence in Switzerland. The Swiss federal authorities decided that the new request could be accepted and obliged the banks involved to furnish the necessary information. Their decision was upheld by the Swiss Federal Court on 16 May 1984.

Withholding tax on dividends

A federal withholding tax is levied on all capital income originating in Switzerland. The withholding tax, which amounts to 35%, is deducted at source. The Swiss corporation is obliged by law to deduct the withholding tax from its dividend payments and from all other distributions to its shareholders, as well as from its interest payments to bondholders. The amounts deducted must be paid to the Federal Tax Administration.

For residents of Switzerland, the withholding tax deducted is not lost. They can claim it back upon filing their tax returns. If they declare the respective capital income, the deducted withholding tax is either set off against their ordinary income taxes due or is reimbursed in cash.

Investors who are not residents of Switzerland may file for a refund of all or part of the withholding tax according to the provisions of an applicable double-taxation treaty. Switzerland has in fact concluded double-taxation treaties with

Table 8.1 Withholding tax relief available in double-taxation treaty countries

Countries	Relief (%)	Net tax* (%)
Australia	20	15
Austria	30	5
Belgium	20	15
Canada	20	15
Denmark	35	0
Finland		
Individuals	25	10
Legal entities	30	5
France	30	5
Germany	20	15
Great Britain	20	15
Hungary	25	10
Ireland	25	10
Italy	20	15
Japan	20	15
Korea	20	15
Malaysia	20	15
Netherlands	20	15
New Zealand	20	15
Norway	30	5
Portugal	20	15
Singapore	20	15
South Africa	27.5	7.5
Spain	20	15
Sri Lanka	20	15
Sweden	30	5
Trinidad and Tobago	15	20
USA	20	15

* In most of these countries, the remaining net tax can be offset against domestic income tax.

many countries. Table 8.1 indicates the amount which investors residing in these countries may claim back.

The claim for tax relief based on an applicable double-taxation treaty must be filed with the competent tax authorities at the investor's place of residence. The tax relief is usually granted in the form of a retrospective refund. The complexity of the formalities and the time required to obtain the refund vary from country to country.

9 Corporate financial reporting in Switzerland and accounting principles

A. Pauchard

Causes for inadequacies in reporting

Financial reporting in Switzerland is not always readily understandable. The lack of transparency in annual reports as compared, for instance, with the better-defined US accounting principles, often gives rise to questions. The historical background and the philosophy of the people offer the clue to understanding the contrasting systems of reporting between Switzerland and, for example, Anglo-Saxon countries.

The Swiss accounting rules are set forth in the Swiss Code of Obligations, which in its revised form became effective on 1 July 1937. The rules appear to be loosely worded, and at first sight seem somewhat sketchy. At the time, in a politically unstable Europe threatened by the power of the Third Reich, these rules were assumed to be most useful to the Swiss entrepreneur, protecting his company and his interests against alien intrusion, but also reflecting to a considerable degree the priority Switzerland gives to privacy. The basic tendency is to report as little as possible and, at the same time, build up as many 'hidden reserves' as necessary.

The average size of Swiss companies has played an important role too. Companies with more than SFr 1 million in share capital in 1981 represented only 5% of the total. Some 48% were companies with SFr 50,000 nominal capital.* A very large percentage of firms are still controlled by family groups. Even among the large corporations, such as Hoffmann-La Roche and Oerlikon-Bührle, family-controlled interests are very much a reality that is reflected in financial reporting. Consolidated reporting is still not expressly requested in Swiss company law.

Company reporting becomes more open, with more definite details on the balance sheet and profit and loss accounts, when a company goes public. But no precise scheme of regulations exists for the composition of the balance sheet and the profit and loss account, and the reporting of companies with a broad

* *Bundesamt für Statistik*, Stat. Quellenwerk, Heft 688.

Table 9.1 Ranking list of corporate reporting policies. Evaluation of Swiss companies' financial reporting by the SSFA

	Weighting	Ems-Chemie	Ciba-Geigy	Galenica	Roche	Sandoz	Globus	Interdiscount	Jelmoli	Konsumverein ZH	Merkur	Mövenpick	Pressefinanz	Usego	Hero	Jacobs Suchard	Lindt and Sprüngli	Nestlé	Rinsoz and Ormond	Sibra	Alusuisse	Holderbank	Schindler	Von Roll	Zürcher Ziegeleien	Autophon	BBC	Bobst	Oerlikon-Bührle	Georg Fischer	Landis and Gyr	Mikron Holding	Saurer	Sulzer	Adia	Forbo	Holzstoff	Walter Rentsch	Sika	Swissair	Average
1. Management																																										
1.1 Management, sphere of responsibility, organigram	2	0	0	2	0	0	1	2	2	2	2	2	2	2	2	2	0	2	2	2	2	2	2	3	3	3	3	2	3	0	3	3	0	3	3	2	2	2	2	1	62
1.2 Comments on the changes in the board of directors and management	1	1	1	3	2	3	3	3	2	3	3	0	3	3	1	3	3	3	3	0	3	3	3	3	3	3	2	1	2	2	3	3	3	3	3	1	3	2	3	3	3	79
1.3 Structure of shareholders	2	0	1	1	0	1	0	3	3	0	3	0	3	0	0	3	0	2	1	3	1	0	0	3	0	1	3	0	1	0	3	0	0	1	0	0	0	1	1	2	34
2. General information on the operation																																										
2.1 Development of the main divisions and markets	3	2	3	2	3	3	2	2	2	3	3	2	2	3	3	3	3	2	2	3	3	3	2	3	3	3	2	1	2	3	3	3	2	2	2	3	3	3	3	3	81
2.2 Order inflow	3	0	1	1	1	1	0	1	1	1	1	2	1	1	1	1	1	1	1	1	1	1	1	3	1	3	3	0	1	1	3	1	2	3	1	1	1	1	1	1	50
2.3 Share of revenue of the different production sectors	3	0	3	3	3	2	3	3	3	3	2	3	3	3	2	2	3	2	3	3	2	3	2	3	3	3	3	0	2	3	2	2	2	0	2	2	2	0	2	3	73
2.4 Geographical division of production	3	1	2	0	2	2	0	0	0	0	0	0	0	0	0	0	2	0	0	1	3	1	1	3	2	0	2	0	0	3	3	3	1	2	1	3	3	0	3	1	58
2.5 Geographical division of revenue	2	0	3	1	2	3	0	0	0	0	0	0	0	0	1	0	2	0	0	3	2	3	3	2	1	0	3	0	1	2	2	2	1	0	2	2	3	1	2	3	61
2.6 Research and development (e.g. project results, number of employees)	2	0	3	1	2	3	0	0	0	0	0	2	0	1	2	2	2	0	0	3	2	2	2	2	0	2	3	0	0	2	3	2	1	0	2	2	3	1	3	3	58
2.7 New products with applications	3	2	2	1	3	3	1	1	1	1	1	1	1	1	1	2	2	2	1	1	3	1	2	2	1	2	3	0	2	2	1	1	2	2	1	1	2	0	0	1	58
2.8 Order backlog	4	2	1	2	3	2	1	1	1	1	1	2	1	1	0	1	1	2	0	3	2	2	2	2	0	2	2	0	2	2	3	0	3	2	1	2	2	1	2	2	64
2.9 Outlook	4	1	2	2	2	2	3	2	2	1	1	2	3	0	1	3	0	1	1	0	1	1	1	0	1	0	2	0	1	2	3	1	2	2	2	2	3	1	1	2	57
2.10 Number of employees	2	2	2	2	2	3	2	2	2	2	2	2	1	2	1	1	3	2	3	3	3	3	2	3	2	2	3	1	3	1	2	2	2	2	2	2	2	1	3	3	68
3. Balance sheet																																										
3.1 Assets																																										
3.1.1 Fixed assets	3	0	3	2	3	3	2	2	2	2	2	3	3	0	0	3	1	2	2	3	3	3	3	2	3	1	0	0	3	1	3	1	0	3	1	1	2	3	0	3	60
3.1.2 Participation and loans to non-consolidated subsidiaries	2	0	2	1	1	3	1	3	3	2	3	3	1	0	0	2	3	3	2	2	3	3	3	3	3	0	0	0	3	1	3	1	0	3	1	3	0	1	3	3	58
3.1.3 Raw materials, finished and semi-finished goods	3	0	3	1	3	3	3	3	3	2	2	3	3	2	1	3	2	2	2	3	2	2	2	2	2	2	0	0	2	3	3	3	3	1	1	2	3	3	2	3	64
3.1.4 Accounts receivable	2	0	2	1	3	3	3	3	2	2	2	2	2	2	0	3	2	2	2	3	2	2	2	3	3	2	0	0	2	3	3	2	0	3	0	2	2	2	3	3	62
3.1.5 Liquid assets	3	0	2	2	3	3	3	3	2	2	3	3	2	0	1	1	3	2	2	3	3	2	2	3	3	3	0	0	3	3	3	3	0	3	0	3	3	2	2	3	62
3.2 Liabilities																																										
3.2.1 Capital structure	3	0	2	2	2	2	3	3	3	3	2	3	3	0	2	3	3	2	2	3	3	3	3	3	3	3	0	0	3	3	3	3	3	1	3	3	3	3	2	2	82
3.2.2 Other equity	3	0	3	3	2	2	2	3	2	2	2	2	2	1	1	3	3	2	2	2	2	2	2	3	3	0	0	0	3	3	3	0	3	3	0	2	3	3	3	3	63
3.2.3 Minority interests	2	0	3	1	3	3	2	2	2	2	2	3	3	3	3	1	3	2	3	3	2	3	1	3	3	1	0	0	3	3	3	1	0	3	3	1	3	0	3	2	82
3.2.4 Provisions	2	0	0	1	0	1	3	3	3	3	3	0	3	3	3	1	0	0	3	3	2	2	2	3	3	1	0	0	3	3	3	1	0	3	3	1	0	1	0	1	42
3.2.5 Medium- and long-term liabilities	2	0	2	2	2	1	3	2	2	2	1	2	1	1	2	1	3	1	2	3	3	2	2	3	3	2	0	0	3	3	3	1	0	0	0	1	2	3	2	2	62
3.2.6 Liabilities due one year or less	3	0	2	2	1	2	3	3	2	3	3	3	2	2	2	2	2	2	2	2	3	3	3	3	3	3	0	0	3	3	3	3	0	1	0	3	3	3	2	2	60

	important data	
4.1		
4.1.1	Revenue of the year	85
4.1.2	Cash flow	57
4.1.3	Results	62
4.2	Details	
4.2.1	Production	44
4.2.2	Material costs	63
4.2.3	Personnel costs	59
4.2.4	Depreciation	61
4.2.5	Capital expenditure for research and development or advertising	25
4.2.6	Services to third parties and income from licences (royalties)	17
4.2.7	Services from third parties and licence costs	22
4.2.8	Income and interest on unconsolidated participations	28
4.2.9	Financial income	35
4.2.10	Financial costs	72
4.2.11	Taxes	46
4.2.12	Extraordinary income	32
4.2.13	Extraordinary expenditure	37
4.2.14	Account for the distribution of profit	78
5.	*Investments*	
5.1	Description of investments in the fiscal year	79
5.2	Capital expenditure	62
5.3	Investment projects	39
5.4	Financing of investment projects	32
6.	*Other information*	
6.1	Sources and applications of funds	69
6.2	Review with comparable data for the last 5 years (balance sheet, profit and loss account)	71
6.3	Overview with important data at the beginning of the annual report	83
6.4	Comments on the closing of accounts (principles and consolidation method)	83
6.5	Report of the auditors	54
6.6	Percentage participation of the most important subsidiaries	75
6.7	Stock market data	72
6.8	Important data per share	
6.8.1	Cash flow	65
6.8.2	Net income	74
6.8.3	Book value	63
6.9	Rapid publication	66

shareholder base is, at best, as good as in other continental European countries, where accounting standards have probably not affected the economy negatively.* Switzerland has no 'accounting principle board'; however, independent accountants apply a set of rules which have arisen out of practice. Moreover, the Swiss Society of Financial Analysts (SSFA) has set up a series of regulations which it recommends for application to the larger and internationally orientated corporations. Every year this society, which represents (loosely and on a self-designated basis) the interests of shareholders and financial analysts, evaluates the information policies of the leading companies. However, its recommendations are not legally binding.

For a number of years, the request for more realistic and more sophisticated accounting standards has grown steadily. The Swiss company law is now in the process of being revised, taking into account the need for in-depth information because of the rapid expansion of international activity and the interrelationships among international capital markets; the reform bill is currently under discussion.

A central theme of recent debates about the draft company law are the 'hidden reserves'. To the great majority of people it seems obvious that some sort of change must take place, i.e. that the present rule on hidden reserves must be revised. But a straight prohibition of such reserves is not feasible politically.

A brief glimpse at the statistical data† shows that because of the sheer increase in the number and size of companies, better rules for financial reporting are required. From the end of 1937 the number of incorporated companies rose from 20,173 to more than 113,000 in 1981; 63 companies have a total nominal capital of over SFr 20 billion. However, they represent only 0.1% of the total number of companies.‡ The basic aims of the reform are (a) to increase clarity and transparency of financial reports, (b) to increase shareholder protection, (c) to improve the structure and function of the organs in the company, (d) to combat abuses, and (e) to facilitate the acquisition of capital. The reform bill will above all help to augment the informative value of the reports.

The draft bill tries to achieve this not only by making consolidated reporting compulsory but also by setting up a clear-cut layout scheme for balance sheets and profit and loss statements, by legalising generally accepted accounting principles and by making the publication of the dissolution of secret reserves compulsory.

According to the Swiss Society of Financial Analysts, the disclosure practices of Swiss corporations are improving every year. The criteria set out in Tables 9.1 and 9.2 are applied every year of the SSFA when working out its report on activity. The information flow from Swiss companies to the shareholder and the interested public is evaluated on the basis of these criteria.

---

* G. Behr, *l' Expert-comptable Suisse*, 3/1984.
† *Statistisches Jahrbuch der Schweiz*, 1937.
‡ *Bundesamt für Statistik*, stat. Quellenwerk, Heft 688.

Table 9.2 Ranking list on the information flow to share-holders (Published in the SSFA 18th report on activity, 1984)

Company	1984 (%)	1983 (%)
1. Landis & Gyr	90.4	89.6
2. Interdiscount	88.9	75.6
3. Sibra	85.1	77.0
4. Swissair	84.2	86.4
5. Jelmoli	82.4	80.9
6. Mövenpick	82.4	80.8
7. Jacobs Suchard	80.2	72.1
8. Globus	78.9	77.7
9. Von Roll	78.6	78.6
10. Ciba-Geigy	78.5	77.1
11. Holzstoff	78.2	72.4
12. Walter Rentsch	73.4	—
13. Sandoz	72.7	72.4
14. Merkur	71.7	51.6
15. Forbo	71.4	71.4
16. Holderbank	69.6	67.8
17. Alusuisse	68.9	68.9
18. Nestlé	68.7	67.2
19. Hoffmann-La Roche	68.3	67.8
20. Georg Fischer	66.1	47.4
21. Zürcher Ziegeleien	65.5	62.4
22. Oerlikon-Bührle	64.3	63.5
23. Pressefinanz	62.8	47.8
24. Mikron	59.9	58.5
25. Sika	56.9	46.4
26. KVZ	54.1	38.0
27. Schindler	53.1	51.3
28. Sulzer	49.7	50.5
29. Rinsoz & Ormond	47.7	47.6
30. Autophon	46.6	—
31. Hero	44.9	50.0
32. Adia	42.6	40.1
33. Galenica	40.6	40.9
34. Lindt & Sprüngli	39.4	32.7
35. Usego	36.5	30.8
36. BBC	34.4	33.9
37. Saurer	25.4	27.1
38. Ems	15.4	16.5
39. Bobst	13.3	13.3

Note: For the detailed point system see Table 9.1, 'Ranking list of corporate reporting policies'.

Consolidation and hidden reserves in Swiss corporate reporting

At present, a number of corporations do not publish consolidated reports: for example, Maag Zahnräder AG. Since there are no formal balance sheet schemes and filing is not required (listed companies, banks, insurance companies and railways excepted), a comparison and evaluation, particularly for a longer period of time, is rather difficult. On the other hand, the information received verbally from Swiss management is assumed to be somewhat more valuable than that disclosed in other countries, particularly in the United States. The quantitative elements and the ratios of financial data are very seldom overstated, which is more or less the result of a conservative accounting approach.

In the following sections, the more important elements of the balance sheet and profit and loss account are discussed. The most important aspect in Swiss financial reporting is the item 'hidden reserves', an extensively discussed topic. Hidden reserves are not included in the annual reports, in contrast to 'open reserves'. The former are associated in most cases with real estate, machinery, equipment and stocks. By definition*, hidden reserves are the difference between the book values and the objectively calculated market values. Hidden reserves are produced (a) when assets are undervalued, either by exaggerated depreciation or by a massive increase in the values of assets, for which a re-evaluation cannot be considered due to accounting regulations; (b) by reduction of assets to zero through depreciation; (c) by an overvaluation of liabilities, by creation of provisions which exceed the real risk, or by not dissolving the provisions when the risk no longer exists; (d) by creating fictitious debts.

The reader of a Swiss annual report should, therefore, closely examine the items 'real estate, land, equipment', and compare them with the 'insured value', which is mentioned in the commentary on the accounting policies or in the footnote. A few examples may illustrate this:

Galencia Group As at 31 December 1983
Fixed assets

Machinery and equipment	SFr 7,180,000
Office equipment	SFr 1
Equipment for handling stocks	SFr 1
Computer hardware	SFr 1
Trucks	SFr 1

However, for those items, the insured value amounts to SFr 45,700,000. The assets are obviously substantially undervalued.

Sandoz Ltd Balance sheet as at 31 December 1983
Long-term assets

Land	SFr 1
Buildings	SFr 292,308,113
Plant and equipment	SFr 110,178,889

Land (acres): 446.3; insured values: buildings: SFr 1.9 billion; plant and equipment: SFr 1.7 billion. The insured values are in this case well above the

* Botschaft über die Revision des Aktienrechtes vom 23. Februar 1983.

book value. From this information one may gather that Sandoz has substantial hidden reserves.

Structure of share capital

Companies do not readily provide information on the structure of the issued share capital. However, Sibra Holding SA offers an excellent example of an open and transparent presentation:

	As at 31 December 1983		
Registered shares	No. of shareholders	No. of shares at nom. SFr 100	%
Public institutions (Confederation, cantons, cantonal banks)	3	2,359	0.4
Industry, commercial, holding companies and financial groups	87	45,558	7.6
Banks and insurance companies	18	8,651	1.4
Trust institutions and pension funds	29	28,625	4.8
Private shareholders	2,086	314,807	52.5
Bearer shares		200,000	33.3
Share capital		600,000	100.0

Operational reports

General information concerning the description of operations, product lines, divisions and marketing sectors has improved tangibly during the last few years. Management also informs the public on these topics at press conferences during the fiscal year. All major corporations publish interim reports where, in general, more qualitative elements are disclosed. With regard to research and development, the data published are somewhat more restricted for obvious reasons. Comments on the outlook are not so ample in the reports, primarily due to the rather difficult economic environment and because forecasting is an inherently difficult task.

Stating fixed assets

Fixed assets: The Swiss Code of Obligations distinguishes two kinds of assets (CO para. 665) – physical assets (machinery, real estate, land and tools) and non-material assets (goodwill, patent licences and development rights). Both categories must be evaluated by the same method. The SSFA recommends that the method of evaluation be precisely stated – original costs before depreciation, or the insured value, and repurchase value. According to the law, assets may be evaluated in the balance sheet at acquisition cost or production cost at the most.

Sandoz Ltd states values in the following way: fixed asset values are translated into Swiss francs at the average exchange rate in the year of acquisition of the asset and are then subject to straight-line depreciation. Land is valued at acquisition cost.

Hoffmann-La Roche, in the 1983 consolidated report, published a transparent outline of 'long-term assets' according to geographical regions for a period of five years. There is an interesting observation in the annual report of F. Hoffmann-La Roche & Co. AG, Basle; Assets:

– Land and buildings	SFr 1
– Machinery and equipment	SFr 1
– Patents	SFr 1

The item 'liquid assets' is defined in the notes to the consolidated statement in some well-itemised reports. A good example is shown in Sibra Holding. It differentiates between cash (states the exact amount) and securities, and comments on the evaluation method of the latter. An important factor in Swiss balance sheet reporting is the currency aspect, which can change corporate data enormously, particularly when foreign subsidiaries are consolidated. Geographical location makes quite a difference (weak or strong currency region), as does the method applied. Not only can the balance sheet items be affected substantially, but also cash flow and net profit. No rigid accounting rule is in force. However, the current-rate method is widely used in Swiss reporting.

Foreign exchange valuation

Example: Hoffmann–La Roche (Consolidated Income Statement)			
	1983	(SFr million)	*(1982)*
Foreign exchange losses	−87.1		−67.4

Currency translation: 'The income statements of foreign subsidiary companies are translated into Swiss francs at the average annual rate of exchange; net fixed assets are translated at the rate prevailing at the time of acquisition; all other assets and liabilities are translated at the year-end current rate.'

The Oerlikon-Bührle Group states the following under 'foreign currencies':

The figures in the Statement of condition of the Group's foreign companies were converted into Swiss francs at the exchange rates prevailing at the end of the year, whereas those in the Statement of Income were translated into the Swiss currency at the average rates for the year. This way short-term ups and downs, which are naturally reflected if reporting date rates are used in translating income figures, could be largely eliminated. The following exchange rates were applied in the case of the currencies of greatest importance to the Group:

Swiss francs	Average rate		Year-end rate	
	1983	1982	1983	1982
1 US$	2.10	2.03	2.18	2.00
1 £	3.18	3.55	3.16	3.24
100 DM	82.30	83.70	80.00	84.00
100 FFr	27.60	31.00	26.15	29.70
100 L	0.139	0.15	0.132	0.145
100 BFr	4.12	4.45	3.90	4.28
100 Cruz	0.37	1.143	0.222	0.796

Capital structure and provisions

In the item 'capital structure', the SSFA demands the disclosure of nominal value in the different categories of shares, as well as the approved capital for the eventual use of convertible issues, with details. In the case of provisions – about which the shareholder is not so widely informed – the SSFA requests that the amount be divided into short- and long-term provisions and that the purpose of the taxable part be stated in order to evaluate the risk. Provisions have different functions. The item can also assume the character of potential secret/latent reserves. The Sandoz Group provides a good example:

Provisions and accrued expenses: in addition to provisions for taxes, personnel and other current expenditure, this item includes provisions for customary or statutory severance payments in various countries. It also includes appropriate provisions for potential risks.

Under the item 'production', a good example is given in the 1983 annual report of Landis & Gyr, Zug, where the value of production is disclosed. The report is an excellent example of a Swiss company publication. It presents a number of ratios, defines the cash flow and gives a detailed account of the operating cost structure. The group has been outstanding in following liberal information policy for many years.

Investments, financing and cost structure

Corporations provide fair information on the description of investments, but the disclosure of the financing method for investment projects has progressed only moderately. The Sandoz Group outlines its investment activity clearly, by geographical area and by divisions.

Information on cost structure, an important field for the analysis of the operation, has improved markedly in the past years, but there is still considerable room for hiding particular aspects of costs. Nestlé for instance, does not disclose its advertising expenses, a substantial item in the profit and loss account. Moreover, the reader should look closely for bench-marks. Items in this category, such as guarantees and obligations, could have a significant influence.

Ratios

In its 1983 report, Hoffmann-La Roche published a set of very useful ratios for the shareholder – which is, unfortunately, not too common:

		1979	1980	1981	1982	1983
Liquidity:	acid ratio	98.6	80.7	83.6	83.2	106.1
	quick ratio	178.9	161.1	181.3	171.6	189.0
	current ratio	280.7	253.9	280.4	253.3	275.4
Finance:	shareholders' equity as % of:					
	– total assets	72.2	69.0	69.0	65.1	63.9
	– long-term capital	86.1	85.1	83.0	80.2	78.3
Profitability:	net income as % of:					
	– sales	4.2	4.0	3.7	4.0	4.4
	– shareholder's equity	3.4	3.5	3.7	4.0	4.5
	– assets	2.4	2.4	2.5	2.6	2.9

Depreciation

With regard to depreciation, different methods apply. But they are not always amply disclosed in the reports. Maag Zahnräder AG, Zurich, effects the depreciation in the year the capital expenditure is executed. For this reason the following items have only *pro memoria* value in the balance sheet.

	Statement at 31 December 1983 *SFr*
Machine tools and equipment	
(insured value: SFr 106,873,000)	1
Tools and equipment	1
Office equipment	1

Cash flow statements

Sources and application of funds: of the firms analysed by the SSFA for the fiscal year 1983, the following published a realistic flow-of-funds account:

Alusuisse	Mikron
Autophon	Mövenpick
Ciba-Geigy	Nestlé
G. Fischer	Oerlikon-Bührle
Globus	Sandoz
Hoffmann-La Roche	Sibra
Holzstoff	Sulzer
Jacobs-Suchard	Swissair
Jelmoli	Von Roll
Landis & Gyr	Zürcher Ziegeleien
Merkur	

Reporting losses

The following is an example of how 'red figures' have been published in the past by some companies:

From the annual report of Roco, 1978:*

	SFr million
Profit and loss statement	
Results before reorganisation	
Swisscol Roco	+2.26
Reorganisation	−9.99
Dissolution of stated reserves	+1.30
Partial dissolution of hidden reserves	+7.65
Profit	+1.22

This company (Roco) publishes even the dissolution of the stated and hidden reserves, thereby following an unusually liberal information policy.

In the 1982/83 report of Ems-Chemie AG (statement of condition), the following comments were published:

The item 'land' has been valued at Fr 35,707,000. The revaluation profit has been applied partly to cover the loss carry forward and partly to effectuate extraordinary depreciations. These extraordinary depreciations are necessary due to losses in the engineering sector for commenced projects, which presently cannot be realized for reasons of financing.

Because of the risky financial situation, the company has taken this extraordinary step, and the auditors have accepted it. One has to bear in mind that the revaluation has gone beyond the original cost value.

Bank reporting

The publication of annual reports in the banking sector is somewhat different. The law prescribes a definite structure for the presentation of the balance sheet and the profit and loss accounts. This basis is set forth in the Federal Law on Banks and Savings Banks dated 8 November 1934, which covers 'Banks, Private Banks and Savings Banks'. The term 'Banks' also includes financial corporations and companies that publicly solicit deposits. This legal edifice was created in the rather risky environment of the early 1930s, in the midst of a world recession.

The Federal Bank Law was revised in 1971. However, the basic concepts of 1934 were preserved. In early 1985, an amended set of rules was under discussion in the Swiss Parliament. Control and supervision of banking operations are executed by the Federal Banking Commission and the Swiss National Bank, which receive very detailed information. The publication of information in the annual reports of banks is, however, still relatively sparse and leaves considerable room for the improvement of information flows to the public. A comparable 10-K report (annual report of a US company to the SEC) does not

* Dr Max Boemle, *l'Expert-comptable Suisse*, 9/79.

exist. During the last few years some progress has been made in this direction, although banks are slow to respond to the challenge. The trend, however, is towards a more liberal information policy for all banks worldwide. A rapid expansion in the international activity of banks and other financial institutions is taking place. Competition from other financial centres is increasing, and bad experience with international debts has introduced yet another element. At the same time, an increasingly critical public is putting heavier pressure on the financial sector for more information.

So far, little effort has been made by the banks to present consolidated accounts. Even more than in industrial reports, hidden reserves are of prime importance in bank statements. Swiss banks have a very large equity base. Their equity ratio is considerably higher than in any other country, without even taking hidden reserves into consideration. In the loan sector, the information given is not ample in general; no indication is given of non-performing loans, and the loss ratio is not disclosed. Since the mid-1970s, the large banks have expanded rapidly in foreign countries and their foreign assets have grown substantially. As consolidated accounts are not published, evaluation and comparison are quite difficult. In the network of foreign subsidiaries, there is thus ample room for secret reserves or potential risks. In the profit and loss account only the most important elements are disclosed. Information on operating investments is published fairly seldom. The real earnings potential is therefore not easy to discern.

But in general terms, some improvement in informing the shareholder has been made above and beyond the legal requirement. For example, the Cantonal Bank of Zug has published a comprehensive review of its main activities since 1892; the Appenzell Innerrhodische Kantonalbank (AIK), in its 1983 report,

Table 9.3 Open portfolios disclosed by the AIK

	1983	1982
	(SFr million)	
Swiss securities and accounts		
Savings books	60.3	46.2
Medium-term notes	50.6	52.5
Bonds	30.1	30.7
Shares	33.0	29.4
Mortgage bonds		
(at nominal value)	17.8	15.2
Precious metals	1.0	1.2
	192.8	175.2
Foreign securities		
Bonds	30.9	27.3
Stocks	7.3	6.5
	38.2	33.8
Total	231.0	209.0
Included: clients		
in foreign countries	13.6	12.3

presents a relatively detailed account of sources and application of funds and gives information on the number of open portfolios the bank managed, with their market value – which is information of considerable value. This element, and more precisely the off-balance-sheet business, is an important part of Swiss banking activity. Among most Swiss banks, the operating data on investment counselling are still considered top secret. The market value of managed portfolios is very substantial and well beyond balance sheet totals.

By the end of 1983, the AIK had managed 3,603 (preceding year 3,536) open portfolios for its clients at market value (see Table 9.3).

The Swiss Bank Corporation has taken a good step in the right direction, showing Swiss moratorium agreements in the loan section of its 1983 annual report (see Table 9.4). It is, however, of no real help in calculating the loss ratio.

In its 1983 annual report, the Spar- und Leihkassa Kaltbrunn disclosed its liquidity account and gave some hints as to the hidden reserves:

Table 9.4 Support provided by the Swiss Bank Corporation to customers in Switzerland

	Year(s)	Industry	Construction	Trade	Tourism	Total
			(SFr million)			
Moratorium agreements	1976–83	589.4	71.9	26.8	10.6	698.7
Credit line totals	1983	152.0	3.1	3.3	—	158.4
Financial contributions	1976–83	77.0	5.8	19.6	0.6	103.0
Loan charge-offs	1983	27.8	—	—	0.2	28.0
Conversion of debt	1976–83	160.1	0.7	10.0	—	170.8
to equity	1983	133.3	—	—	—	133.3
Debt converted into	1976–83	48.2	—	—	—	48.2
subordinated loans	1983	48.2	—	—	—	48.2
Interest reduction or	1976–83	3.1	3.4	1.0	0.3	7.8
cancellation	1983	0.4	0.1	0.1	0.1	0.7
	1976–83	288.4	9.9	30.6	0.9	329.8
Total	1983	209.7	0.1	0.1	0.3	210.2

Statement of liquidity and reserve ratio at 31 December 1983
(in accordance with the regulations of the Federal Law on Banks and Savings Banks)

(a)   Statement of liquidity

Liquid assets should amount to	SFr 1,147,000
Available liquid assets total	SFr 4,657,000
Liquid assets and easily realisable assets together should amount to	SFr 7,880,000
Available liquid and easily realisable assets total	SFr 11,005,000

(b)   Reserve ratio

The requisite total for capital and reserves is	SFr 6,872,000
The total calculated is	SFr 8,099,000

Over the past few years, the Union Bank of Switzerland has followed a somewhat more liberal information policy, too. In the annual statement of 1983, UBS reports on the utilisation of customer credit lines. The number of customer accounts is also presented, which gives a good picture of the client structure of the bank.

Number of customer accounts	1982	1983	Change
Demand deposits	442,373	459,797	3.9
Time deposits	51,978	47,346	−8.9
Savings books and accounts	1,254,035	1,303,772	4.0
Deposit books and accounts	405,896	421,644	3.9

Customer credit lines were utilised as follows:

Credit drawn	End of 1982	End of 1983	End of 1982	End of 1983
	Number of customers		SFr million	
Up to SFr 20,000	86,708	90,771	400.9	405.1
SFr 20,001 – SFr 50,000	20,791	20,698	979.8	974.7
SFr 50,001 – SFr 100,000	20,535	20,447	1,943.2	1,971.6
SFr 100,001 – SFr 500,000	44,874	46,624	11,570.7	12,468.0
SFr 500,001 – SFr 1,000,000	6,048	6,221	4,847.3	5,237.1
SFr 1,000,001 – SFR 5,000,000	4,456	4,568	10,574.6	10,647.5
SFr 5,000,001 and over	891	945	16,725.6	17,343.5
Total	184,303	190,274	47,042.1	49,047.5

The Gotthard Bank, Lugano, in its statement of operations for 1983, also published more than just the information required by law:

Business and office expenses:	SFr million
– Rental and sundry costs paid to third parties	4.1
– Maintenance of machinery, real estate, and rebuilding of rented space	1.1
– Telephone and mailing	3.4
– Insurance premiums and other costs	6.7

The information policy of Swiss companies is at a crossroads. For the fiscal year 1984 the Swiss Society of Financial Analysts, for the first time, evaluated the interim reports of the leading companies. With this move it has recommended that corporate management offer a more in-depth and continuous information flow to the stockholder during the fiscal year, and adopt generally accepted standard statements. The reform of the company law and its public discussion should eventually bring about a more liberal information policy too. A similar picture presents itself in the banking sector, as demand for more meaningful information comes from different directions.

Nevertheless, it is of some comfort to the investor that, generally, leading Swiss corporations tend to present a rather less favourable picture than reality: understatements are the rule!

Appendix 1 Analysis of the shares of leading companies in Switzerland

A. Pauchard

The following are outlines, in concise form, of 14 important corporations from different sectors in Switzerland; the shares of these companies are quoted on the stock exchanges. The reports contain much valuable information for institutional and private investors. Under the subheading 'Activity', the basic elements of operations are explained, with a breakdown of group sales, whereas under 'Outlook' the prospects and investment conclusions for the foreseeable future are presented. A detailed stock analysis, however, is not included. To visualise the development of share prices in the past, short- and long-term charts (published by Verlag Hoppenstedt & Co., Havelstrasse 9, D-6100, Darmstadt) were incorporated.

The financial data are based above all on annual reports and on generally accessible information sources, while some qualitative information in the Outlook has been received through management contacts. Some per share data are on an adjusted basis, in order to get a comparable set of figures after rights issues. Further details can be obtained from the author in writing.

Union Bank of Switzerland

Activity

Union Bank of Switzerland was formed under its present name in 1912 through the merger of the Bank in Winterthur (est. 1862) and the Toggenburger Bank (est. 1863). As a universal bank, UBS effects all types of banking transactions. Within Switzerland, UBS currently operates 245 branch offices and agencies, and abroad is represented through 8 branches, 7 subsidiary institutes and 22 representative offices in all important financial centres around the world. The principal domestic subsidiaries and participatories are: AKO-Bank, Zurich; Bank Aufina, Brugg; Bank Cantrade Ltd, Zurich; Bank of Saudi-Swiss Trade & Investment Ltd, Geneva; Orca Bank Ltd, Geneva; Mortgage and Commercial Bank of Winterthur, Winterthur; Swiss Mortgage and Commercial Bank, Solothurn; and Eidgenössische Bank, Zurich. UBS is also the custodian bank for Intrag Ltd, Management of Investment Trusts, Zurich (est. 1938), which manages 22 investment trusts. Union Bank of Switzerland (Underwriters) Ltd, Hamilton (Bermuda), and especially UBS (Securities), London, as well as UBS Securities, New York, founded in 1978, give UBS a leading position in international underwriting, while Union Bank of Switzerland (Luxembourg) SA and UBS (Panama) Inc. concentrate on international banking business.

Outlook

The strong international position, the well-diversified services and the dynamic management are a good basis for further growth. Balance sheet total has advanced at a relatively fast pace during the last few years, while net profit has also increased quite favourably. Due to the bank's wide income base, a continued earnings advance may also be expected for the longer term. The enlarged international debt risk should cause no problems, as the bad loan factor is amply covered by provisions, and the loan portfolio is well diversified. Rationalisation and automation should further enhance the profit margin. The shares are good medium-term investments.

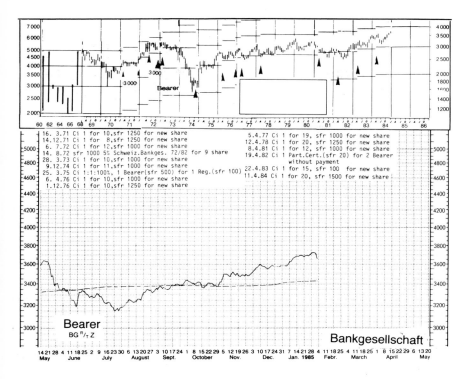

Price range (adjusted) and dividend (actual) of bearer shares and registered shares in SFr

		1984	1983	1982	1981	1980
Bearer shares	H	3,650	3,499	3,066	3,148	3,177
	L	3,145	2,927	2,490	2,513	2,627
Dividend		115	110	100	100*	100
Registered	H	676	643	547	566	578
shares	L	600	524	445	419	504
Dividend		23	22	20	20†	20

* plus ½ PC.
† plus ¹⁄₁₀ PC.

Stock exchange listings: Zurich, Basle, Geneva, Berne, Lausanne, Neuchâtel, St Gall

Stockholders' equity at 31 December 1984: SFr 6,673 million

	SFr par.	SFr mill.
2,750,000 bearer shares	500	1,375
2,750,000 registered shares	100	275
6,745,280 participation certificates	20	135
Declared reserves incl. profit carry-forward		4,888

Market value at 28 December 1984: SFr 12,603 million

Principal balance sheet items in million SFr

	1984	1983	1982	1981	1980
Assets					
Cash	4,283	3,572	3,286	2,994	2,871
Due from banks	39,268	34,216	30,917	24,710	23,177
Loans and advances	57,686	49,048	47,042	43,085	38,359
Liabilities and equity					
Due to banks	30,518	28,155	25,182	26,735	20,330
Due to customers	82,844	72,449	67,393	54,926	46,579
Stockholders' equity	6,673	5,890	5,475	5,311	4,713
Balance sheet total	131,031	115,142	106,353	93,738	77,527
Stockholders' equity as % of balance sheet total	5.1	5.1	5.1	5.7	6.1
Income statement in million SFr					
Net interest income	510	486	394	278	294
Bills and money market paper	822	675	673	574	380
Net commissions	1,075	947	807	716	607
Other income	749	709	696	599	624
Gross income	3,157	2,817	2,570	2,167	1,905
Salaries and other personnel expenses	1,136	1,050	1,002	895	790
Business and office expenses	592	533	490	436	407
Taxes	312	285	255	226	202
Total expenses	2,040	1,868	1,747	1,557	1,399
Gross earnings	1,117	949	823	610	506
Loan losses, writedowns, depreciation and provisions	534	444	386	227	173
Net earnings	583	506	438	382	334

Board of Directors: Dr A. Schaefer, Honorary Chairman; Dr R. Holzach*, Chairman; H. Rüegg*; Vice-Chairman; Dr G Tobler*, Vice-Chairman; U. Ammann; H. André; Dr C. Blocher; Dr H. Braunschweiler*; J. Carbonnier; C. R. Firmenich; Dr M. Junger; B. de Kalbermatten; M. Kündig; Dr G. Lombardi; F. Milliet*; Dr H. Munz*; Dr H.-P. Schaer*; Dr S. Schmidheiny; H. P. Schulthess*; Dr H.-P. Sigg; Dr R. Sorato; P. G. Sulzer; P. de Weck*
* Member of Board of Directors' Committee

Swiss Bank Corporation

Activity

Swiss Bank Corporation, founded in 1872, is one of Switzerland's big universal banks. The company operates a network of 197 branches and 9 banking subsidiaries in Switzerland and 13 branches, 13 banking subsidiaries and 22 representative offices abroad. The principal domestic subsidiaries specialising in consumer credit and investment business are: the Schweizerische Depositen- und Kreditbank, Basle; Ferrier Lullin & Cie SA, Geneva; Bank Finalba AG, Zurich and Bank Prokredit AG, Fribourg. Among the financing companies are: Industrie-Leasing AG, Zurich; Indelec Finanz AG, Basle; and Basler Handelsbank Beteiligungs- und Finanzgesellschaft, Basle. The most important affiliates not connected with banking business are the Indelec Schweizerische Gesellschaft für elektrische Industrie, Basle, and the Schweizerische Elektrizi- täts- und Verkehrsgesellschaft, Basle. In the services sector, Swiss Bank Corporation has a 100% holding in Métaux Précieux SA, Neuchâtel and Schweizerische Treuhandgesellschaft, Basle. A number of management companies offer a broad range of investment opportunities in unit trusts. The scale of SBC's international activities can be seen from the fact that, at the close of 1984, foreign assets accounted for 59% of its balance sheet total. The principal foreign subsidiaries, which specialise mainly in international credit operations, are the Swiss Bank Corporation (International) Ltd, London; Société de Banque Suisse (Luxembourg) SA, Luxembourg; Banque de Placements et de Crédit, Monte Carlo; Swiss Bank Corporation (Canada), Toronto; Swiss Bank Corporation (Overseas) Ltd, Nassau; Swiss Bank and Trust Corporation Ltd, Grand Cayman; Swiss Bank Corporation (Overseas) SA, Panama; SBC Finance (Asia) Ltd, Hong Kong; and SBC Australia United, Sydney.

Outlook

The SBC has a long-established position internationally, with a broad range of services which are offered to a large institutional clientèle as well as to private clients. The corporation has, therefore, a good basis to produce a consistent growth rate, in the longer term as well. Of increasing importance is the loan portfolio, which is well diversified. Moreover, provisions have been increased markedly during the last few years, taking into account the expanded bad loan factor, which is amply covered. Rationalisation and cost-cutting programmes, partly by computer systems, should also help to increase the profit margin. This quality stock can be bought primarily for the conservative investor with a longer-term view.

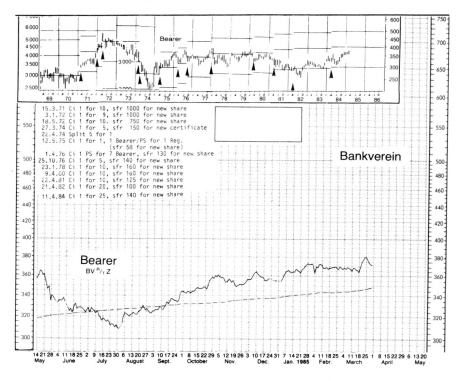

15.3.71 Ci 1 for 10, sfr 1000 for new share
3.1.72 Ci 1 for 9, sfr 1000 for new share
18.5.72 Ci 1 for 10. sfr 750 for new share
27.3.74 Ci 1 for 5, sfr 150 for new certificate
22.4.74 Split 5 for 1
12.5.75 Ci 1 for 1, 1 Bearer/PS for 1 Reg.
        (sfr 58 for new share)
1.4.76 Ci 1 PS for 7 Bearer, sfr 130 for new share
25.10.76 Ci 1 for 5, sfr 140 for new share
23.1.78 Ci 1 for 10, sfr 160 for new share
9.4.80 Ci 1 for 10, sfr 160 for new share
22.4.81 Ci 1 for 10, sfr 125 for new share
21.4.82 Ci 1 for 20, sfr 100 for new share
11.4.84 Ci 1 for 25, sfr 140 for new share

Bankverein

Bearer
BV ᴿ/₇ Z

Price range (adjusted) and dividend (actual) of bearer shares and registered shares in SFr

		1984	1983	1982	1981	1980
Bearer shares	H	365	319	309	346	358
	L	308	289	247	275	304
Dividend		12	11	10	10	10
Registered	H	271	248	218	251	277
shares	L	240	216	181	174	226
Dividend		12	11	10	10	10

Stock exchange listings: Zurich, Basle, Geneva, Berne, Lausanne, Neuchâtel, St Gall, Frankfurt (part. certificate)

Stockholders' equity at 31 December 1984: SFr 5,907.6 million

	SFr par.	SFr mill.
10,567,535 bearer shares	100	1,056.7
10,969,587 registered shares	100	1,097.0
6,083,438 participation certificates	100	608.4
		3,145.5
Open reserves incl. profit carry-forward		

Market value at 28 December 1984: SFr 8,601 million

Principal balance sheet items in million SFr

	1984	1983	1982	1981	1980
Assets					
Liquid assets	4,585	3,661	3,222	3,025	3,502
Due from banks	31,848	27,504	31,783	27,268	22,036
Loans	53,851	44,312	39,562	38,271	36,048
Liabilities and equity					
Due to banks	23,249	23,123	21,103	25,516	21,793
Due to customers	82,901	71,347	65,294	52,833	43,619
Stockholders' equity	5,908	5,259	5,047	4,804	4,345
Balance sheet total	119,027	105,156	96,816	87,555	74,109
Stockholders' equity as % of balance sheet total	5.0	5.0	5.2	5.5	5.9
Income statement in million SFr					
Net interest income	−46	288	482	275	358
Bills and money market paper	933	520	496	533	229
Net commissions	875	744	623	528	454
Other income	898	837	621	530	585
Gross income	2,661	2,389	2,195	1,865	1,626
Salaries and other personnel expenses	945	889	845	759	681
Business and office expenses	462	428	419	349	338
Taxes	230	221	200	197	140
Total expenses	1,637	1,538	1,464	1,305	1,159
Gross earnings	1,003	851	731	560	467
Loan losses, writedowns, depreciation and provisions	500	423	362	239	180
Net earnings	503	429	369	322	287

Crédit Suisse

Activity

Founded in 1856, Crédit Suisse is the oldest of Switzerland's three leading big banks. As a universal bank it not only operates in all sectors of commercial banking, consumer and mortgage loan business, but also conducts underwriting, stock market and foreign exchange operations. Specialised affiliated companies handle Euromarket underwriting operations, as well as leasing, factoring and non-recourse financing transactions. Domestic operations have played a significant role in the rapid growth in business volume in recent years. On the other hand, the sharp expansion of foreign operations, which was evident in previous years, has been curbed in line with the more balanced risk policy. There are currently 166 branch offices and agencies in Switzerland's most important economic and tourist centres, working together with the head office in Zurich to ensure that customer needs are met. Besides the Texon Group, the main companies affiliated with Crédit Suisse are Bank Hofmann Ltd, Zurich; Bank Neumünster, Zurich; Finance Ltd, Zurich; Compagnie de Gestion et de Banque Gonet SA, Nyon; Société Internationale de Placements, Basle; Electrowatt Ltd, Zurich; and Fides Trust Company, Zurich. Crédit Suisse's organisation abroad comprises at the present time 12 branch offices, 12 subsidiaries and their outlets, and 20 representative offices in the world's most important financial centres. Through Crédit Suisse First Boston, the bank has become very prominent on the Euromarket in particular. A number of investment trust companies offer a wide range of investment possibilities.

In 1982 Crédit Suisse decided to restructure its organisation. To this end the bank transferred its interest in the Financière Crédit Suisse–First Boston Group and part of its stake in Electrowatt Ltd to the newly established Crédit Suisse Holding. In return for these assets, Crédit Suisse Holding issued participation certificates which were distributed by Crédit Suisse to its shareholders as a stock dividend inseparably linked to Crédit Suisse shares. Today the bank's stock is traded as a twin security comprising one share of Crédit Suisse linked with one of Crédit Suisse Holding's participation certificates.

Outlook

The bank's total assets have expanded quite rapidly in recent years. At the same time it has strengthened its international position and at present it has a broad basis for a relatively consistent growth rate in the longer term. Rationalisation and cost-cutting measures have been passed, which should improve the operating margin somewhat. Earnings prospects for 1985 are favourable and in the majority of the large divisions, operating profit should increase markedly in the medium term. The stocks can be bought for the longer term.

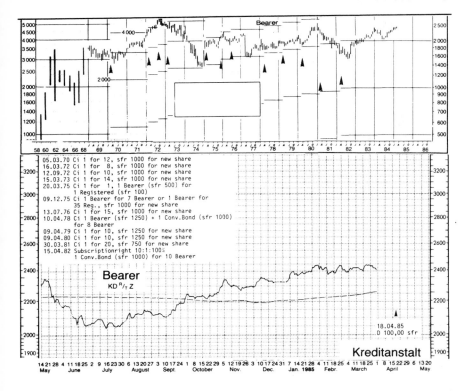

Price range (adjusted) and dividend (actual) of bearer shares and registered shares in SFr

		1984	1983	1982*	1981	1980
Bearer shares	H	2,400	2,310	1,975	2,599	2,506
	L	2,040	1,885	1,535	1,815	1,891
Dividend		100	94	82	80	80†
Registered	H	454	432	360	448	434
shares	L	395	350	300	340	359
Dividend			18.80	16.50	16.00	16.00†

* beginning of CS Holding (incl. participation certificate)
† plus a bonus of SFr 9.28 (bearer) and SFr 1.87 (registered)

Stock exchange listings: Zurich, Basle, Geneva, Berne, Lausanne, Neuchâtel, St Gall

Stockholders' equity at 31 December 1984: SFr 5,096 million

	SFr par.	SFr mill.
2,730,200 bearer shares	500	1,365
2,849,000 registered shares	100	285
Open reserves incl. profit carry-forward		3,446

Market value at 28 December 1984: SFr 7,366 million

Principal balance sheet items in million SFr

	1984	1983	1982	1981	1980
Assets					
Cash	3,301	3,355	3,010	3,373	3,274
Due from banks	22,260	18,601	16,264	16,248	15,017
Bills discounted and money market paper	4,656	4,308	2,687	4,104	2,232
Loans	37,900	35,445	36,171	36,996	33,468
Securities and holdings	5,382	4,912	4,891	5,336	5,454
Liabilities and equity					
Due to banks	18,028	18,467	17,412	22,437	19,830
Due to customers	56,711	50,559	47,811	43,180	36,394
Share capital	1,650	1,650	1,650	1,500	1,335
Reserves and profits carry-forward	3,446	3,187	3,077	2,981	2,795
Total stockholders' equity	5,096	4,942	4,812	4,541	4,210
Balance sheet total	84,028	77,268	73,497	73,579	63,475
Shareholders' equity as % of balance sheet total	6.1	6.4	6.5	6.2	6.6
Income statement in million SFr					
Net interest income	386	306	141	−84	102
Bills and money market paper	343	329	394	454	257
Net commissions	732	664	566	520	430
Other income	725	691	723	670	611
Gross income	2,186	1,991	1,825	1,561	1,399
Salaries and other personnel expenses	819	774	745	681	600
Business and office expenses	350	312	315	292	267
Taxes	154	144	103	120	91
Total expenses	1,323	1,229	1,164	1,092	958
Gross earnings	863	761	662	469	441
Loan losses, writedowns, depreciation and provisions	446	409	359	193	160
Net earnings	417	352	303	276	281

Board of Directors: R. E. Gut, Chairman; Dr R. R. Sprüngli, Vice-Chairman; Dr O. Aeppli; Dr E. L. Keller; P. Dutwyler; Dr U. Albers; Dr S. Koechlin; A. Baltensweiler; P. Hummel; E. Matthey; H. C. M. Bodmer; F. Gerber; Dr M. Moret; J. Zumstein; A. Frauenfelder; H. B. Saemann; T. Schmidheiny; Dr F. Honegger; F. Hoegger; H. Maucher

Bank Leu AG

Activity

Bank Leu AG, whose predecessor was founded in 1755 in Zurich, is considered the oldest bank in Switzerland. It had total assets of SFr 11.6 billion at the end of 1984. The bank's activities have traditionally focused on domestic mortgage and commercial lending operations. Today Bank Leu must be classified as a multi-service bank, specialising in the commercial and mortgage loan business as well as in foreign exchange operations and the gold trade. Its numismatics department is one of the most important of its kind on the international scene. In recent years the bank has expanded its foreign activities considerably; the bank's representative office in New York was upgraded to a full branch in January 1984. The office is expected to concentrate primarily on foreign exchange and money market operations and the precious metals trade. The principal area of activity is still Switzerland and the Zurich region in particular. In addition to six branches and one agency in the city of Zurich itself, it has over 14 branch offices and an agency in other communities of the Canton of Zurich.

Its most important subsidiaries and holdings are Bank Gutzwiller, Kurz Bungener SA, Geneva; Bank Heusser & Co. Ltd, Basle; Bank Leu International Ltd, Nassau; Swiss Investment Company, Zurich; and Merkur Immobilien AG, Zurich. At the end of 1984 Bank Leu AG had a staff of 1,194 (1983: 1,113).

Outlook

The bank expanded rapidly during the five years 1979–84. From 1980 to the end of 1984, assets have grown at an annual rate of 16.5%, whereas profits advanced by 9.7% p.a. During this period a large investment programme was executed, which should bear fruit in the longer term. The broad spectrum of activities provides a good foundation for continued earnings development in the coming years. The company has formed considerable provisions in order to cope with higher credit risks at home and abroad. Earnings increase should be somewhat less strong for 1985 after this phase of expansion. However, this quality stock is considered as a good longer-term investment.

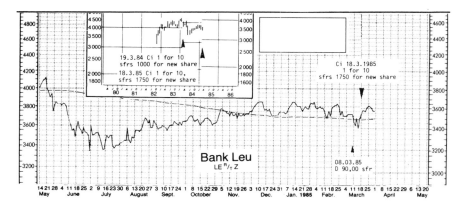

Price range (adjusted) and dividend (actual) of bearer shares and participation certificates in SFr

		1984	1983	1982	1981	1980
Bearer shares	H	4,328	4,092	3,955	4,749	4,536
	L	3,350	3,581	2,651	3,711	3,398
Dividend		90	90*	80	80	80
Participation	H	608	624	595	718	760
certificates	L	515	509	425	565	575
Dividend		18	18†	16	16	16

* bonus of SFr 10 in 1983 incl.
† bonus of SFr 2 in 1983 incl.

Stock exchange listings: Zurich, St Gall

Stockholders' equity at 31 December 1984: SFr 725.8 million

	SFr par.	SFr mill.
128,980 bearer shares	500	64.5
128,980 registered shares	500	64.5
106,480 registered shares	100	10.6
512,435 participation certificates	100	51.2
Open reserves incl. profit carry-forward		535.0

Market value at 28 December 1984: SFr 1,166 million

Principal balance sheet items in million SFr

	1984	1983	1982	1981	1980
Assets					
Cash	214	260	251	233	152
Due from banks	5,473	4,600	3,958	3,719	2,268
Bills discounted and money market paper	82	40	36	33	47
Loans	3,346	3,163	3,049	2,863	2,440
Securities and holdings	966	730	682	733	839
Liabilities and equity					
Due to banks	4,252	3,851	3,443	2,997	1,736
Due to customers†	6,174	5,556	4,955	4,698	3,907
Share and PC capital	191	168	168	149	126
Reserves and profits carry-forward	535	511	472	433	361
Total stockholders' equity	726	679	640	582	487
Balance sheet total	11,648*	10,445*	9,346*	8,590†	6,429*
Stockholders' equity as % of balance sheet total	6.6	6.5	6.8	6.8	7.6
Income statement in million SFr					
Net interest income	35.3	30.1	17.9	7.6	12.3
Bills and money market paper	3.5	2.7	4.0	5.0	3.3
Net commissions	57.6	51.9	37.8	30.6	27.8
Income from foreign exchange and precious metals	39.6	42.2	51.4	43.4	34.1
Income from securities	48.7	32.7	33.0	31.7	28.4
Other income	17.6	17.3	16.6	17.3	15.2
Gross income	202.3	176.9	160.6	135.6	121.1
Salaries and other personnel expenses	86.3	75.9	70.3	61.9	54.6
Business and office expenses	39.1	32.3	31.2	28.0	26.1
Taxes	9.1	7.9	8.3	7.2	6.6
Total expenses	134.5	116.1	109.8	97.0	87.3
Gross earnings	67.8	60.8	50.8	38.6	33.8
Loan losses, writedowns, depreciation and provisions	28.4	25.8	19.1	8.7	6.8
Net earnings	39.4	35.0	31.8	29.8	27.0

* Precious metals accounts included in balance sheet total as from 1981 (1981: SFr 960 million; 1982: SFr 1,323 million; 1983: SFr 1,493 million; 1984: SFr 1,337 million).
† Incl. bonds and loans granted by Central Mortgage Bond Instit.

Board of Directors: Dr Dr h.c. Arthur Fuerer*, Chairman; Eric von Schulthess*; Dr Thomas W. Bechtler; Bertrand Jaquiéry; Siegfried Keller; Robert E. Koch; Hans H. Mahler*; Claus Nuescheler; Heinrich Pestalozzi; Dr Heinz Portmann*; Dr Stephan Renz; Dr Eugen Roesle; Alfred E. Sarasin; Felix Schnyder; Dr Herbert Schoenenberger*; Dr Dr h.c. Edwin Stopper*; Dr Heinz R. Wuffli*
* Member of Board of Directors' Committee

Winterthur Insurance Ltd

Activity

Winterthur Insurance Company, founded in 1875, is the parent company of one of Europe's foremost multi-line insurance groups. Its operations are concentrated primarily in the major European countries and North America. The life insurance sector is managed 89% by the most important and internationally active subsidiary, Winterthur Life Insurance Company, whereas the parent company is responsible for roughly two-thirds of the premium income generated by the group's remaining insurance operations. There are numerous other subsidiaries and affiliated companies located in Switzerland, such as Federal Insurance Company Ltd, Zurich, Winterthur Rechtsschutzversicherungs-Gesellschaft, Winterthur; and abroad Citadel General Assurance Company, Toronto, Provident Life, London, Winterthur Compagnia Italo Svizzera di Assicurazioni SpA, Milan. In order to attend to the group's growing international reinsurance business and direct underwriting abroad, Winterthur-Norwich (45% minority interest) was founded in 1976 as a joint venture in co-operation with British and Japanese partners. In 1982 Winterthur-Norwich's net premium income amounted to SFr 636 million. In 1983 Winterthur strengthened its position in the US insurance market through the acquisition of Republic Group, which focuses mainly on property and third-party insurance in Texas, New York and California; it recorded consolidated gross premium income of roughly SFr 1,415 million in 1982.

Outlook

During the last several years expansion has advanced quite rapidly – the results of a more dynamic management policy. The group at present has a strong marketing base, and is well diversified geographically and by sector, which should offer a stable growth rate in the longer term. Efficient control of operating expenses will help to improve the earnings margin, while low inflation should have a favourable impact on losses and costs. Moreover, the life insurance sector should register a continued profit growth. Underwriting volume developed favourably in almost all divisions in the fiscal year 1984. For the group as a whole, good results can also be expected for 1985.

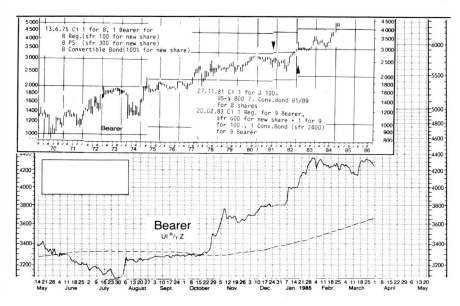

Price range (adjusted) and dividend (actual) of bearer shares and registered shares in SFr

		1984	1983	1982	1981	1980
Bearer shares	H	3,775	3,600	2,895	2,649	2,654
	L	3,080	2,871	2,135	2,258	2,096
Dividend			53	50	50	46
Registered	H	2,100	2,017	1,687	1,528	1,554
shares	L	1,820	1,669	1,155	1,155	1,311
Dividend			53	50	50	46

Stock exchange listings: Zurich, Basle, Berne, Geneva, Lausanne, Neuchâtel

Stockholders' equity at 31 December 1983: SFr 1,390.3 million

	SFr par.	SFr mill.
270,000 bearer shares	100	27
630,000 registered shares	100	63
200,000 participation certificates	100	20
Open reserves incl. profit carry-forward		1,280

Market value at 30 November 1984: SFr 2,974 million

Selected consolidated balance sheet data in million SFr	1983	1982	1981	1980	1979
Investments	16,031	13,164	12,351	11,316	10,341
Underwriting reserves: non-life	5,573	4,242	3,988	3,978	3,592
life	9,470	8,581	7,650	6,750	6,060
Authorised capital	110	90	90	80	80

Selected consolidated profit and loss statement data in million SFr					
Net premiums: non-life	3,449	2,494	2,319	2,307	2,007
life	1,677	1,537	1,332	1,230	1,153
Earnings before tax: non-life	155	101	89	85	99
life	66	30	38	27	21
Net earnings	138	74	72	69	68

Board of Directors: Dr H. Branschweiler, Chairman*; Dr H. Kundert, Vice-Chairman*; Dr P. Spälti*; P. Borgeaud; Dr M.-H. Chaudet; Prof. Dipl.-Ing. Dr h.c. M. Hilti; G. Kaiser; Dr L. von Planta; J. Revaclier; Dr H. R. Schwarzenbach; Dr N. Senn*; R. Staubli
* Member of Executive Committee

Swiss Reinsurance Company

Activity

Swiss Reinsurance Company, Zurich, founded in 1863, is the parent company of one of the largest insurance groups worldwide. It is the world's second largest reinsurer after the Munich Reinsurance Company. Swiss Reinsurance Company controls, through Swiss Re Holding Ltd, Zurich, 11 reinsurance companies of which the following are the most important: the Bavarian Reinsurance Company, the North American Reassurance Company (life), the North American Reinsurance Corporation (non-life) and the European General Reinsurance Company. Additionally, it holds 14 direct insurers (including Switzerland General Insurance Company, Zurich, the Vereinigte Insurance Group and the Magdeburger Insurance Group, both in Germany). In 1980, as a result of an international expansion programme, it took a 50% interest in the Fidelity and Deposit Company of Maryland, Baltimore, USA, one of the leading companies in the United States in the field of surety and fidelity insurance (the other 50% holding was taken by the Zurich Insurance Company). In 1983 the gross premium income of the group rose by 0.9% to SFr 10.15 billion. The breakdown by segment and class of insurance was:

Reinsurance 65%: fire 17%, accident and health 6%, liability and motor 13%, transport 3%, life 17%, other lines 9%.
Direct insurance 35%: fire 4%, accident and health 17%, liability and motor 7%, transport 1%, life 5%, other lines 1%.

Gross premium income broken down by continents is as follows: Europe 61%, America 23%, Asia 8%, Africa 6% and Australia/New Zealand 2%.
  At the end of 1983 there were 13,699 people employed worldwide.

Outlook

The company's leading marketing position and its broad diversification form a solid base for a consistent growth rate. However, stiff competition has dampened somewhat the expansion of the group in the last few years. Substantial efforts are made to improve the quality of the reinsurance portfolio. Premium adjustments expected in the foreseeable future should contribute to a higher profit margin, while the still relatively high underwriting loss should be offset by the rise in investment income. In some markets there are signs of improvement, and the reinsurance cycle is tending upwards. A clear profit advance may be expected for the medium term. The stocks can be bought for the medium and long term.

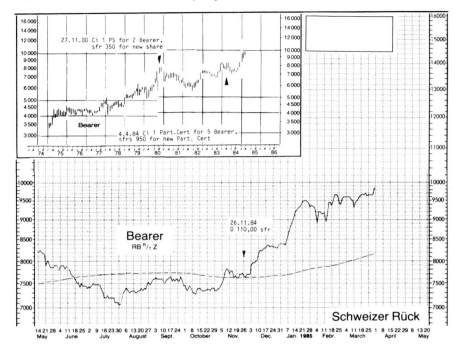

Price range (adjusted) and dividend (actual) of bearer shares and registered shares in SFr

		1984	1983	1982	1981	1980
Bearer shares	H	8,350	8,201	7,061	7,358	7,680
	L	7,050	6,640	5,451	6,045	4,788
Dividend		110	110	105	105	100
Registered	H	3,800	3,394	3,110	3,326	3,460
shares	L	3,435	3,129	2,502	2,609	2,441
Dividend		110	110	105	105	100

Stock exchange listings: Zurich, Basle, Geneva

Stockholders' equity at 31 December 1983: SFr 936 million

	SFr par.	SFr mill.
44,000 bearer shares	250	11
400,000 registered shares	250	100
240,000 participation certificates	50	12
Open reserves incl. profit carry-forward		813

Stock market value at 28 December 1984: SFr 2,400 million

Selected consolidated balance sheet data in million SFr	1983	1982	1981	1980	1979
Investments	16,030	14,778	12,556	11,506	10,111
Underwriting reserves	17,543	16,636	14,492	13,234	11,322
Share and PC capital	123	123	123	123	111

Selected profit and loss statement data in million SFr					
Premium income: gross	10,151	10,058	9,334	8,390	7,221
net	8,894	8,740	8,137	7,551	6,492
Underwriting results	−299	−246	−80	−25	19
Net earnings	105	97	82	95	105

Board of Directors: Dr W. Diehl, Chairman*; H. B. Vischer, Vice-Chairman*; Prof. Dr H. Bühlmann; Dr E. L. Keller; F. Luterbacher; H. R. Lüthy*; Dr M. Odier; Dr H. F. Rudolf; Dr Dr h.c. E. Stopper*; Prof. Dr Dr h.c. H. Ulrich
* Member of Board of Directors' Committee

Zurich Insurance

Activity

The Zurich insurance group, whose origins go back to 1872, is the largest casualty/property underwriter in Switzerland and, together with its domestic and foreign subsidiaries and affiliates, one of the leading European multi-line insurers operating worldwide. The group, which reported a gross premium income of SFr 9.6 billion in 1984 is, through the parent company and 34 subsidiaries, active in 27 countries. Of the group's total gross premium income, 76.4% was attributable to casualty/property lines and reinsurance, and 23.6% to life insurance. The group's major markets in the general insurance sector are the United States/Canada 33% (previous year 31%); Switzerland 18% (20%); West Germany 16% (17%); other countries 33% (32%). In the life insurance sector the main markets have traditionally been Switzerland and West Germany, which contributed 42% and 24% respectively in the fiscal year 1984. The most important of the group companies located in Switzerland are Vita Life Insurance Co. Ltd (SFr 1.43 billion gross premium income), Alpina Insurance Co. Ltd (SFr 311.3 million) and Turegum Insurance Co. (reinsurance, SFr 160.2 million). The group also holds a strong position in the West German market-place, primarily through its 99% participation in the Agrippina Group (gross premiums DM 1.12 billion). During recent years, the group has strengthened its position in the United States. Following its acquisition of 50% of the share capital of the Fidelity and Deposit Company of Maryland in 1980 (the other half being acquired by Swiss Re), the Zurich group further strengthened its position in the US market by its takeover early in 1982 of the Universal Underwriters Group of Kansas City. The latter is engaged primarily in the casualty and damage insurance business, and for 1983 had a gross premium income of US$ 188.9 million. In 1980 a co-operation agreement was concluded with the well-known Malayan Group of Insurance Companies. This collaboration enables Zurich to gain access to the South-east Asian insurance markets. At the end of 1983 the group had about 23,000 employees, of whom 5,270 were based in Switzerland.

Outlook

Prospects for the medium term are improving. In the recent past management has put more emphasis on rentability in the insurance portfolio, and efforts have been made to diversify more efficiently in order to limit the risk factor, while in the United States rate increases in the different sectors are expected to be passed. The sharp competition is receding somewhat. Moreover, the still rather low inflation internationally and the favourable profit from capital investments should contribute to an earnings increase in the longer term, while the 1984 profit advance was relatively moderate. Underwriting results should tend to be more favourable for 1985. The stocks are of top quality and can be bought for the conservative investor.

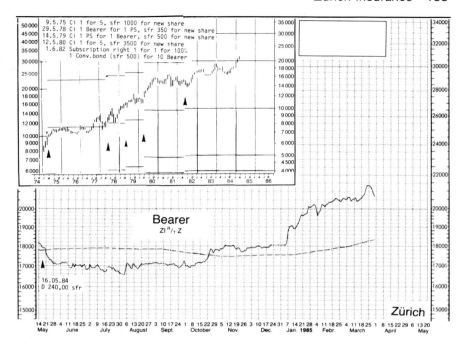

Price range (adjusted) and dividend (actual) of bearer shares and registered shares in SFr

		1984	1983	1982	1981	1980
Bearer shares	H	19,100	19,250	16,900	16,464	15,729
	L	16,500	16,200	13,900	13,916	10,865
Dividend		240	240	240	220	220
Registered	H	10,950	10,900	9,250	9,839	9,863
shares	L	9,800	9,250	8,225	6,962	8,339
Dividend		240	240	240	220	220

Stock exchange listings: Zurich, Basle, Geneva

Stockholders' equity at 31 December 1984: SFr 1,427.8 million

	SFr par.	SFr mill.
50,000 bearer shares	500	25
158,400 registered shares	500	79
600,000 participation certificates	50	30
Open reserves incl. profit carry-forward		1,294

Market value at 28 December 1984: SFr 3,638 million

Parent company

Selected balance sheet data in million SFr	1984	1983	1982	1981	1980
Investments	9,073	8,036	7,368	6,587	6,332
Technical reserves	8,357	7,177	6,645	5,979	5,724
Capital stock	134	134	128	121	121

Selected profit and loss statement data in million SFr

	1984	1983	1982	1981	1980
Premium income (incl. policy fees): gross	4,565	3,882	3,732	3,325	3,225
net	4,185	3,559	3,412	3,083	2,983
Net claims paid	2,821	2,289	2,155	1,859	1,775
Investment income: before depreciation	692	571	525	446	
after depreciation	687	540	483	356	345
Net earnings	112	101	90	80	71
Zurich Group in million SFr					
Gross premium income	9,612	8,337	7,829	6,669	6,467
Net premium income	8,439	7,300	6,868	5,858	5,711
Investment income	1,790	1,558	1,398	1,145	1,025
Investments	23,935	21,014	19,209	16,968	16,229
Underwriting reserves	22,712	19,699	18,128	15,854	15,109

Board of Directors: F. Gerber, Chairman; E. von Schulthess, Vice-Chairman; E. Meyer; Dr P. Hefti; H. C. M. Bodmer; Prof. Dr P. Böckli; B. de Kalbermatten; F. Luterbacher; M. Kündig

Swiss Aluminium Ltd

Activity

Originally founded as Aluminium-Industrie AG in 1888, the company has been operating since 1963 under the name of Swiss Aluminium Ltd (Alusuisse). The company is the sixth-largest aluminium producer in the Western world, and with sales of SFr 8.3 billion in 1984 is Switzerland's eighth largest industrial concern. The breakdown of 1984 group sales shows that the production of aluminium accounts for the largest portion, namely 61.7% (previous year 61.6%) (bauxite and alumina 5.6%, primary metal 22.4%, processed aluminium 33.7%); second in importance are chemical products with 17.9% (17.4%), followed by automotive parts, accessories (including shock absorbers, exhaust systems, etc.) and services with 20.4% (20%). The company's chemicals sector, which, since the takeover of Lonza in 1974, has become the principal sector of diversification, was expanded in 1979 and 1980 by several additional acquisitions in the United States (including Bio-Lab Inc.) and in Italy (Distillerie Italiana SpA). With the aim of further reducing its dependence on the aluminium sector, the company took over the US firm Maremont Corp. in 1979 and thereby acquired a stake in the automotive parts and accessory business. By contrast, Alusuisse sold the Brazilian company Aisa (São Paulo) to Alcoa on 1 July 1983. The services division, with its various engineering companies in Zurich and New York, is another diversification *vis-à-vis* the group's other activities. The production of electrical energy holds an important position since the mining of bauxite and production of primary aluminium, semi-finished goods and chemical substances requires considerable amounts of electricity. In 1984 Alusuisse's power requirement was 12.7 billion kWh (11.4 billion kWh), 27.6% (33%) of which was produced by the group itself. At the end of 1984 the group had 35,329 employees, up 2.6% from the 1983 level.

Outlook

The group's restructuring programme – more diversification in value added products – should improve rentability, reduce the cyclical element, and build a solid basis for long-term growth potential. In view of a relatively favourable economic growth and a further increase in investments in the Western world, internal growth should continue. The profit margin should increase in the near future; prospects appear favourable in the majority of the divisions. For the fiscal year 1985, satisfactory results are expected.

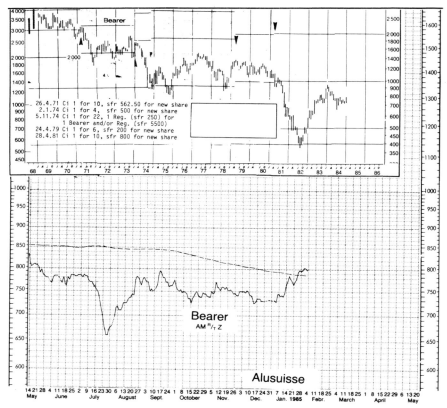

Price range (adjusted) and dividend (actual) of bearer shares and registered shares in SFr

		1984	1983	1982	1981	1980
Bearer shares	H	935	900	680	1,164	1,340
	L	660	500	380	590	1,075
Dividend		30	–	–	25.00	50.00
Registered	H	310	307	268	441	495
shares	L	235	170	120	245	431
Dividend		15	–	–	12.50	25.00

Stock exchange listings: Zurich, Basle, Geneva, Frankfurt

Stockholders' equity at 31 December 1984: SFr 2,637 million

	SFr par.	SFr mill.
934,000 bearer shares	500	467
1,492,000 registered shares	250	373
624,401 participation certificates	50	31
Open reserves incl. profit carry-forward		1,766

Market value at 28 December 1984: SFr 1,116 million

Consolidated balance sheet data in million SFr	1984	1983	1982	1981	1980
Current assets: liquid assets	544	508	557	683	767
other	3,593	3,416	3,412	3,590	3,234
Fixed assets	4,912	5,135	5,207	4,728	4,502
Liabilities: short-term	2,688	2,640	2,571	2,529	2,383
long-term	3,367	3,419	3,391	3,287	2,898
Shareholders' equity and minority interests	2,740	2,751	2,995	2,989	3,058
Consolidated profit and loss data statement					
Sales	8,344	7,222	6,588	6,888	6,903
Net income from production and services	1,831	1,371	1,258	1,333	1,629
Earnings from investments and long-term loans	24	13	13	16	92
Net interest expenses	281	263	346	385	336
General and administrative expenses and taxes	966	825	829	823	836
Depreciation	418	414	414	412	413
Net extraordinary income	−21	36	139	218	–
Net profit	169	−82	−179	−52	135

BBC Brown, Boveri & Co. Ltd

Activity

Brown, Boveri & Co. Ltd, Baden, founded in 1891 ranks among the largest electrical engineering groups in the world. The manufacturing programme includes virtually all sectors of electrical equipment, ranging from the generation to the utilisation of electrical energy. Of 1984 sales totalling SFr 11.2 billion, machinery for power generation accounted for 20.3% (previous year 25.1%), products for power conversion, transmission and distribution for 29.5% (31.6%), industrial equipment and transport for 18.9% (17.1%), standard engineering products for 15.1% (13%), electronics, measurement and control for 5.2% (8.6%), services and other products for 4.1% (4.6%). Group sales in 1984 centred on Europe 55% (55%), Africa 9.1% (5.6%), North America 8.7% (9.4%), Latin America 7.3% (6.8%), Asia and Oceania 20% (21.4%). The company is structured into four corporate groups:
- The Swiss Group, comprising the parent company in Baden, BBC-Sécheron SA in Geneva, Micafil Ltd in Zurich, and Brown Boveri Rollar AG in Schlieren.
- The German Group, composed of Brown, Boveri & Cie AG in Mannheim and numerous holdings.
- The Mediums Manufacturing Companies Group, to which belong holdings in Brazil, Canada, France, Italy, Norway, Austria and Spain.
- The Brown Boveri International Group, comprising various companies in Europe, America, Africa, Asia and Oceania.

The North American Group is directly responsible to the chairman of BBC's Managing Committee.

In 1984 the total number of employees amounted to 100,100 (previous year 90,600).

Outlook

Prospects for the medium term have improved markedly. Rationalisation, restructuring and cost-cutting measures are beginning to bear fruit. More emphasis is being placed on sectors with consistent growth rates, such as industrial electronics and telecommunications, and promising product lines. In view of further economic growth, it may be assumed that cash flow should improve considerably during fiscal 1985, while earnings should also increase noticeably. The stocks can be bought for longer-term investors in particular.

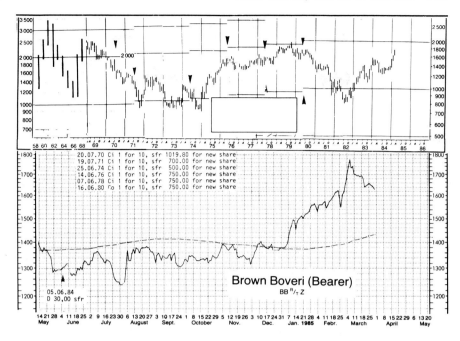

20.07.70 Ci 1 for 10, sfr 1019.80 for new share
19.07.71 Ci 1 for 10, sfr 700.00 for new share
25.06.74 Ci 1 for 10, sfr 500.00 for new share
14.06.76 Ci 1 for 10, sfr 750.00 for new share
07.06.78 Ci 1 for 10, sfr 750.00 for new share
16.06.80 Co 1 for 10, sfr 750.00 for new share

Brown Boveri (Bearer)
BB R/T Z

05.06.84
D 30,00 sfr

Price range and dividend of bearer shares (adjusted) in SFr

		1984	1983	1982	1981	1980
Bearer shares	H	1,580	1,430	1,150	1,510	1,800
	L	1,240	960	810	900	1,420
Dividend		30	30	30	50	50

Stock exchange listings: Zurich, Basle, Geneva

Stockholders' equity at 31 December 1984: SFr 1,018 million

	SFr par.	SFr mill.
732,550 bearer shares 'A'	500	366
732,550 restricted registered shares 'B'	100	73
1,138,720 PCs	100	114

In addition, 450,000 PCs had been reserved for the 4% warrant issue 1983–94 (option until 30/9/1988) and had not been issued.

Open reserves incl. profit carry-forward	465

Market value at 28 December 1984: SFr 1,456 million

Parent company balance sheet data in million SFr	1984	1983	1982	1981	1980
Current assets: liquid funds	662	537	420	355	576
other	1,880	2,311	2,584	2,219	2,130
Fixed assets	1,468	1,383	1,289	1,224	1,110
Liabilities: advance payments	588	800	878	662	656
others, excl. provisions	1,903	1,975	2,206	1,694	1,669
Provisions and value adjustments	501	508	442	495	544
Shareholders' equity	1,046	978	975	992	991
Selected group and income statement data in million SFr					
Sales	11,214	10,658	9,701	9,897	10,059
Incoming orders	12,431	10,501	10,243	11,643	10,484
Cash flow	650	464	390	355	412
Investments in plant and equipment	382	364	452	520	544
Expenditure for research and development	984	998	1,006	917	898
Parent company					
Sales	2,776	3,375	2,760	2,552	2,759
Depreciation on plant and equipment	66.7	52.9	45.3	84.5	82.2
Net income	28.4	29.5	27.9	44.3	44.3

Board of Directors: F. Luterbacher, Chairman*; Dr Dr h.c. L. von Planta, Vice-Chairman*; P. Hummel, Managing Director*; Dr O. Aeppli; Dr U. Albers; Prof. Dr A. Cerletti; Dr W. Diehl*; Dr P. Eisenring; Dr F. Galliker; Dr R. Holzach; R. Koch; Prof. Dr H. Letsch; Prof. Dr Dr E.h. R. Sammet; Dr S Schmidheiny; Dr H. R. Schwarzenbach; Dr R. Sontheim; H. Strasser; Prof. Dr H. Uyterhoeven; P. de Weck*
* Member of Board Committee

Grands Magasins Jelmoli SA

Activity

Grands Magasins Jelmoli SA, founded in Zurich in 1896, reported consolidated sales for 1984 of SFr 1,333 million, with the parent company, Jelmoli SA, Zurich, contributing over 50% of revenues. It is one of the three leading department store chains in the Swiss retail trade. The Jelmoli Group operates 15 general merchandise stores in major shopping centres and 47 other city and suburban department stores. The company's range of services includes, in addition, travel agencies, restaurants and dry-cleaning establishments, not to mention its considerable mail-order volume. Through the acquisition of the Regina department store chain with six branches from Oskar Weber in 1980, Jelmoli was able to expand its market position in the Zurich area. In French-speaking Switzerland, Jelmoli is represented by Innovation SA, Lausanne (holding 52.4%), and Au Grand Passage SA, Geneva (holding 51.2%). Innovation runs 20 department stores with total revenues of SFr 234 million, while Au Grand Passage, with four department stores, achieved revenues of SFr 220 million (1984).

The group's first store abroad was opened in Lyons, France, in 1975 – a joint venture with Karstadt of West Germany (each with a 50% holding).

The minority holding in the Gerngross Group, acquired in 1978, was sold in 1983. The controlling interest in Jelmoli is held by UTC International Ltd, a subsidiary of the Basel Trading Company Ltd. Jelmoli in its turn holds a 51% interest in the UTC subsidiary Union Trading Company, Basle, which operates on an international scale. In 1984 the company employed 5,191 people. A breakdown of sales by product categories and services for 1983 appears as follows: food products 15% (previous year 15.5%); clothing and textiles 34.2% (34.4%); durable goods 36% (37.2%) and services 14.8% (12.9%).

Outlook

Prospects for the medium term are favourable. After some restructuring in the product line – introduction of more promising products and rationalisation – earnings should edge up. Moreover, in view of continued economic growth, a further advance in consumer spending and the leading marketing position in Switzerland, the group should offer a relatively consistent growth rate and contribute to favourable operating results in the longer term as well. Because of the strong financial position, further expansion can be made through internal financing alone. This quality stock can be bought for the longer term.

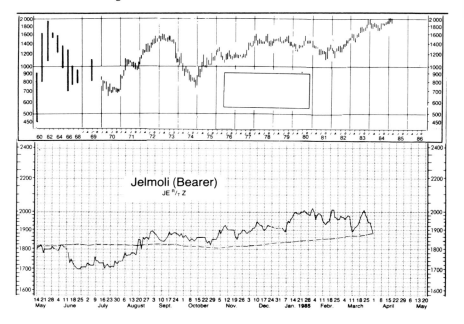

Price range and dividend of bearer shares in SFr

		1984	1983	1982	1981	1980
Bearer shares	H	2,005	2,000	1,530	1,485	1,490
	L	1,700	1,450	1,150	1,140	1,230
Dividend		32	32	30*	27	25

*incl. anniversary bonus of SFr 3

Stock exchange listings: Zurich, Basle, Geneva

Stockholders' equity at 31 December 1984: SFr 528.5 million

	SFr par.	SFr mill.
315,000 bearer shares	100	31.5
Open reserves incl. profit carry-forward		497.0

Market value at 28 December 1984: SFr 602 million

Consolidated balance sheet data in million SFr	1984	1983	1982	1981	1980
Current assets: liquid funds	198.0	203.2	174.7	159.0	143.6
other	218.5	199.2	178.4	169.2	158.0
Fixed assets	428.3	421.3	437.9	442.8	462.9
Liabilities: short-term	144.6	151.4	138.7	135.4	131.0
long-term	84.0	79.4	105.4	116.7	147.4
Minority interests	87.7	86.5	82.2	79.0	75.0
Shareholders' equity	528.5	506.4	464.7	439.9	411.1
Consolidated profit and loss statement data/investments					
Sales	1,333.0	1,278.0	1,236.0	1,211.0	1,137.0
Revenue from sale of goods	389.0	379.0	369.0	359.0	333.0
Operating income	66.0	69.1	65.2	65.9	65.3
Depreciation	38.7	39.1	36.8	41.3	40.8
Net earnings*	31.8	33.3	30.8	28.5	27.0
Capital expenditure	20.3	0.2	21.4	11.2	29.5

*after deduction of minority stockholders' earnings

Board of Directors: A. E. Sarasin*, Chairman; Dr P. Gloor, Vice-Chairman; Dr Dr h.c. M. Bohren-Hoerni; F. Peyrot; Prof. Dr H. Tschirky; E. Wamister; J. Zumstein*
* Member of Board of Directors' Committee

Ciba-Geigy Ltd

Activity

Ciba-Geigy Ltd, Basle, which was formed in 1970 by the merger of the two Basle firms Ciba Ltd (founded in 1884) and J. R. Geigy Ltd (founded in 1758), is, with sales of SFr 17.5 billion, Switzerland's largest pharmaceutical–chemical company. The company is also a leading producer worldwide in the sector of chemical specialities. Ciba-Geigy's well-balanced production programme consists of the following sectors:

– *Pharmaceuticals Division* (29%): Close to 75% of pharmaceutical sales can be attributed to around 300 compounds of cardiovascular products, antirheumatics and other inflammation-impeding compounds, psychopharmaceuticals and neurotropic drugs, as well as anti-infective agents.
– *Agricultural Division* (26.2%): By far the largest part of this division's sales is in plant protection agents such as herbicides, pesticides and fungicides. Ciba-Geigy's corn herbicides have a leading position on the American market.
– *Plastics and Additives Division* (20.6%): The product range encompasses a broad assortment of epoxy resins, pigments, special plastics, as well as a variety of additional materials. The most important customers are the construction industry, automobile sector, electrical equipment and electronics industries.
– *Dyestuffs and Chemicals Division* (13.8%): Inputs for the textile industry as well as for the detergent, cosmetics, leather and paper industries.
– *Airwich Group* (4.2%): This division is responsible for various categories of household products, hygiene and body care items (e.g. sold at retail level).
– *Electronic Equipment Group* (3.3%): Products of Gretag and the Mettler Group: the latter was acquired only in 1980.
– *Ilford* (2.9%): Concentrates on the manufacture of photographic films and papers.

Ciba-Geigy operates over 120 companies in more than 60 countries. A geographical breakdown of 1984 sales gives the following picture: Europe 39% (previous year 42%); North America 34% (30%); Asia 12% (12%); Latin America 10% (10%); remaining 6% (6%). Its most important markets are the United States, West Germany, Great Britain and France, together roughly 50% of total sales. At the end of 1984 the group had 81,423 people on its payroll, of which 27.4% were employed in Switzerland.

Outlook

During the first half of 1984 sales advanced considerably. This was due primarily to the favourable economic climate. Earnings for the year 1985 are expected to increase by over 30%. During the years 1982–83 the company implemented a restructuring programme (cost cutting and improvement of efficiency in research operations) which has now increased productivity considerably. This will also bear fruit in the longer term. Furthermore, several new products in the drug sector have been introduced into the market during the last few years; and due to high research and development expenditure, Ciba-Geigy has promising research activities for the longer term, particularly in the agricultural and drug divisions,

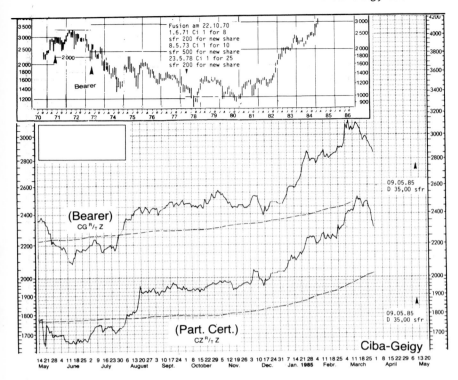

which will enhance the earning power of the group. For 1985 and 1986 a relatively stable profit growth is expected. The stocks are recommended for a longer-term investment.

Price range and dividend of bearer shares and participation certificates in SFr

		1984	1983	1982	1981	1980
Bearer shares	H	2,560	2,475	1,645	1,320	1,285
	L	2,080	1,600	1,160	970	920
Participation	H	1,985	1,970	1,310	995	1,000
certificates	L	1,640	1,290	910	750	740
Dividend		35	31	28	25	22

Stock exchange listings: Zurich, Basle, Berne, Geneva, Lausanne, St Gall

Stockholders' equity (parent company) at 31 December 1984:
SFr 2,848 million

	SFr par.	SFr mill.
3,512,030 registered shares	100	351
749,034 bearer shares	100	75
1,102,981 participation certificates	100	110
Open reserves incl. profit carry-forward		2,312

Market value at 28 December 1984: SFr 7,988 million

Consolidated balance sheet data, current values in million SFr	1984	1983	1982	1981	1980
Current assets: liquid assets	3,470	2,767	2,381	1,978	1,700
other	8,296	6,928	6,724	6,306	6,585
Fixed assets	10,709	10,035	9,737	9,289	9,372
Liabilities: short-term	4,919	4,216	3,943	3,557	3,739
long-term	3,469	3,289	3,220	2,998	3,070
Shareholders' equity and minority interests	14,087	12,225	11,679	11,018	10,848
Value adjustments	+709	+167	+382	−58	+1,064
Consolidated profit and loss data statement					
Consolidated sales	17,474	14,741	13,808	13,599	11,914
Material expenditure	5,447	4,675	4,360	4,450	4,030
Personnel	4,893	4,390	4,206	4,095	3,719
Other expenditure	5,410	4,346	4,037	3,952	3,302
Depreciation	863	804	836	818	727
Net profit	1,187	776	622	521	305
Investment in plant and equipment	1,007	830	868	875	853

Board of Directors: Dr R. Käppeli, Honorary Chairman; Dr L. v. Planta, Chairman and Managing Director*; Dr E. Vischer, Vice-Chairman*; Dr O. Aeppli; Prof. Dr M. M. Burger; Dr h.c. E. Mettler; Prof. Dr A. F. Müller; Prof. Dr F. Schaller; Dr H. Schramek*; Dr H. Sihler; Dipl. Ing. R. Staubli; H. Strasser; Dr V. H. Umbricht; Prof. Dr H. E. R. Uyterhoeven; Prof. Dr F. Vischer; Dipl. Ing. J. J. Vischer; Prof. Dr S. P. Jacot, Secretary
* Member of Committee of the Board

F. Hoffmann-La Roche & Co. Ltd

Activity

With consolidated sales of SFr 8.3 billion in 1984, Hoffmann-La Roche & Co. (Roche) is the second largest Swiss pharmaceutical–chemical group. The company, founded in 1896, consists legally (but not from the business point of view) of two corporate entities: Hoffmann-La Roche & Co. Ltd, Basle, and SAPAC Corp. Ltd, incorporated in New Brunswick, Canada, with headquarters in Montevideo. Roche is one of the leading companies in several fields of the industry. It is, for example, the world's largest producer of vitamins and the world's second-largest producer of perfumes and flavourings. Further, Roche, as one of the biggest drug manufacturers, holds an important position in hypnotics and psychopharmaceuticals as well as anti-infectives. The group's activities are divided as follows:

- *Pharmaceuticals* (42% of sales). Primarily psychopharmaceuticals and sleep-inducing agents; also anti-infectives, vitamin specialities and preparations for the treatment of tropical diseases, skin disorders and certain forms of cancer.
- *Vitamins and fine chemicals* (28%). The leading product group consists of vitamin additives for feeds as well as for the food and pharmaceutical industries. Natural food dyes, citric acid and sugar substitutes are gaining strongly in importance.
- *Perfumes and flavourings* (11%) Perfume components and food flavourings manufactured by subsidiaries Givaudan and Roure Bertrand, both of which belong to the world's largest enterprises in this industry.
- *Other products* (19%). This sector includes diagnostics (strongly expanded in 1982 through the acquisition of two firms in the United States), instruments (Kontron AG, Zurich) and herbicides (Dr R. Maag AG). Roche-Maag Ltd (Australia) and Burdick & Jackson Laboratories Inc. (USA) were sold in 1983. Also sold in 1983 was the cosmetics division (2%).

Geographically, 1984 sales broke down as follows: Switzerland 3%; rest of Europe 35%; North America 40%; Latin America 9%; Asia 9%; other regions 4%. At the end of 1984 the total number of employees was 46,199, up 0.8% from the previous year.

Outlook

The company, with its strong marketing position, primarily in the health care sector, has a good basis for stable growth, while it should be able to enlarge its product range in the longer term. Several new drugs are in different stages of development. It has expanded its biotechnological research markedly during the last few years, and the large research expenditure in relation to sales raises the possibilities of new product innovations. Moreover, prospects for improved rentability appear more favourable at this stage, after cost-cutting measures have been passed. The group has a strong financial structure, so that further expansion should be possible through internally generated financing. The shares offer good capital appreciation potential for the longer term.

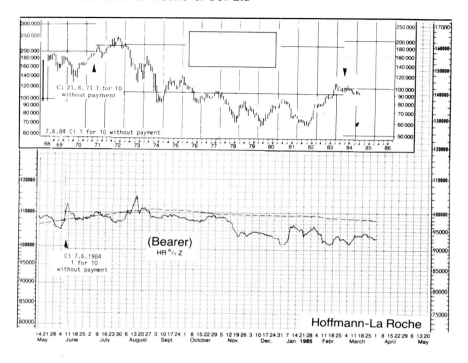

Hoffmann-La Roche

Price range and dividend of bearer shares (adjusted) in SFr

		1984	1983	1982	1981	1980
Bearer shares	H	106,015	106,938	79,518	84,088	77,690
	L	93,750	75,177	57,582	63,523	54,383
Dividend		1,200	1,175	1,150	1,125	1,100

Stock exchange listings: Over-the-counter Basle, Zurich, Geneva

Stockholders' equity at 31 December 1984: SFr 7,599 million

	SFr par.	SFr mill.
16,000 bearer shares	3⅛	0.1
61,440 bearer dividend rights cert.	p.m.*	
Open reserves incl. profit carry-forward		7,599

* p.m. = per memorial

Market value at 28 December 1984: SFr 6,886 million

Principal balance sheet items in million SFr

Assets	1984	1983	1982	1981	1980
Liquid funds and securities	2,721	2,237	1,689	1,400	1,477
Other current assets	4,107	3,567	3,457	3,298	3,169
Fixed assets	5,630	5,639	5,695	5,248	5,043
Liabilities: short-term	2,127	2,108	2,032	1,676	1,830
long-term	1,568	930	848	787	540
	1,149	1,087	889	611	621
Shareholders' equity and minority holdings	7,613	7,318	7,073	6,873	6,698
Provisions					
Consolidated profit and loss data statement	8,267	7,510	7,103	6,775	5,856
Sales	3,062	2,797	2,723	2,551	2,265
Costs of goods and materials	2,844	2,581	2,463	2,316	1,986
Personnel expenditure	1,437	1,199	1,083	1,137	913
Other operating expenses	5	87	67	71	+2
Currency losses	495	454	393	395	402
Depreciation	380	328	281	253	232
Net earnings	456	454	704	605	516
Investment in plant and equipment					

Board of Directors: F. Gerber, Chairman; Dr R. Probst, Vice-Chairman; Dr A. F. Leuenberger, Managing Director; Dr L. Hoffmann; Prof. Dr A. Labhart; Dr J. Oeri; Dr h.c. P. Sacher; Dr B. A. Sarasin; Dr J.-J. Fuchs, Secretary

Sandoz Ltd

Activity

Sandoz Ltd, founded in 1886 in Basle, is the parent company of the internationally operative Sandoz Group. With sales of SFr 7.4 billion in 1984, the company ranks third among Swiss chemical and pharmaceutical companies. By international standards, Sandoz is a medium-sized concern in the industry. Originally engaged primarily in the manufacture of dyes, Sandoz has extended its production range over the years to include industry-related divisions, with the pharmaceuticals sector developing into a focal point. Today the firm's activities cover the following areas:

- *Pharmaceuticals* (46% of 1984 sales). With the manufacture of pharmaceuticals of both natural and synthetic origin, Sandoz has acquired a fine reputation on the world market. The product range includes cardio-vascular preparations, painkillers, migraine drugs and others. Through Sopamed AG, a joint venture with the major French chemical concern Rhône-Poulenc, Sandoz is also represented on the market for medical equipment.
- *Dyes* (23%). This division manufactures industrial chemicals such as soap powder additives, textile processing agents, leather and paper processing chemicals. The most important customers are the textile, leather, paper and plastics industries.
- *Food* (14%). Products of the Wander (Ovaltine, dietetics, special formulations for athletes, baby foods) and Leofarin Groups, of three food processing companies in the United States, and of the Swedish group Wasa, the world's largest producer of crisp-bread. The Wasa Group was acquired in 1982.
- *Seeds* (9%). With products of the US firms Northrop King Co. and Rogers Brothers Seed Co., and of the Dutch enterprise Zoadumie B.V. Sandoz is the world's foremost seed producer.
- *Agriculture* (8%). The activities of this division centre primarily on insecticides, herbicides and other plant-protection agents.

By market territories, sales in 1984 were divided as follows: Europe 41%; USA/Canada 32%; Asia 15%; Latin America 8%; Africa/Australia 4%. At the end of 1984 the Group's payroll numbered 38,036 persons, of whom 6,843 (18%) were employed in Switzerland.

Outlook

After the reorganisation of the group and the introduction of a cost-cutting programme, prospects for growth potential have improved considerably. In the drug division a number of products have good profit margins, whereas other products are in development. Moreover, the marketing position is expanding in the agro and seed divisions by the integration of Zoecon, while in chemicals a continued growth rate is expected as long as the economy is tending upward. In the longer term the company should be able to enhance its productivity and further improve the research innovation – Sandoz ranks among the leading firms in biotechnological research. Its strong financial position offers substantial

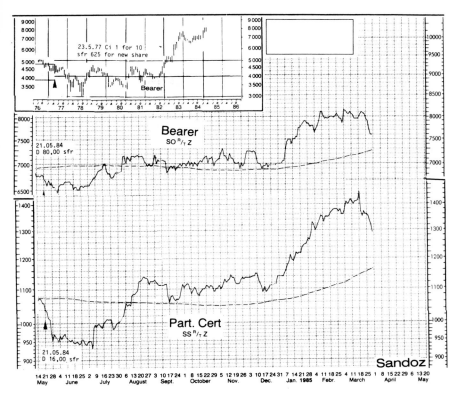

possibilities for further expansion. The shares are considered of top quality and can be bought for the medium and long term.

Price range and dividend of bearer shares and participation certificates in SFr

		1984	1983	1982	1981	1980
Bearer shares	H	7,600	7,650	4,600	4,625	4,250
	L	6,450	4,475	3,825	3,350	3,350
Dividend		80.00	80.00	72.50	65.00	65.00
PC	H	1,230	1,200	675	590	530
	L	940	661	495	429	425
Dividend		16.00	16.00	14.50	13.00	13.00

Stock exchange listings: Zurich, Basle, Berne, Geneva, Lausanne

Stockholders' equity at 31 December 1984: SFr 4,182 million

	SFr par.	SFr mill.
50,286 bearer shares	250	12.6
930,286 restr. registered shares	250	232.6
734,359 participation certificates	50	36.7
Open reserves incl. profit carry-forward		3,900.1

Market value at 28 December 1984: SFr 3,543 million

Principal balance sheet items in million SFr

Assets	1984	1983	1982	1981	1980
Liquid funds and securities	1,734	1,358	1,315	1,127	1,049
Other current assets	3,577	3,257	3,063	2,774	2,631
Fixed assets	2,279	2,307	2,243	2,158	2,101
Liabilities: short-term	1,607	1,533	1,435	1,281	1,125
long-term	695	627	662	601	632
Provisions	1,083	924	872	741	690
Shareholders' equity and minority holdings	4,205	3,838	3,652	3,436	3,334
Consolidated profit and loss data statement					
Consolidated sales	7,434	6,546	6,053	5,766	4,900
Cost of goods and materials	1,959	1,759	1,652	1,642	1,433
Personnel expenditure	2,128	1,931	1,905	1,770	1,521
Other operating expenses	2,645	2,261	1,999	1,841	1,603
Currency losses	61	85	65	128	0
Depreciation	364	357	337	316	286
Net earnings	411	320	273	227	202
Investment in plant and equipment	304	270	253	305	257

Board of Directors: Dr Y. Dunant, Chairman; Dr M. Moret, Vice-Chairman and Managing Director; Prof. Dr D. Arigoni, Vice-Chairman; Prof. Dr P. Böckli; Dr Dr h.c. R. Burkard; F.-H. Firmenich; Dr N. Gossweiler; Dr h.c. K. Hess; Dr J. Landolt; Prof. Dr H. Letsch; L. Dominique de Meuron; Dr J. Wander

Nestlé SA

Activity

With sales of SFr 31 billion (1984), Nestlé is the leading food producer of the world and Switzerland's biggest industrial enterprise. Nestlé was formed in 1905 through the merger of Anglo-Swiss Condensed Milk Co. (Cham, founded 1866) and the firm of Henri Nestlé (Vevey, founded 1867). In 1936 the holding company Unilac Inc., Panama City, was founded to attend to Nestlé's interests, primarily in the Western hemisphere. Nestlé holds, through the intermediary of a Canadian subsidiary company, all the Unilac founders' shares with voting rights, whereas the ordinary bearer non-voting shares have been issued to Nestlé shareholders. Originally concentrated on condensed milk, baby cereals and other infant foods, the product range has grown steadily over the years. Through a policy of selective acquisition and purchase of direct interests in existing concerns, Nestlé has diversified its activities into a number of sectors of rapid growth and high earnings potential (frozen foods, catering, mineral waters, cosmetics, pharmaceuticals). A breakdown of 1984 group sales by product categories shows the following: instant drinks, 28.8% (previous year 27.7%); dairy products, 20.1% (20.4%); culinary products and miscellaneous, 13% (13.9%); deep frozen foods and ice-cream, 10.8% (10.3%); dietetic products and infant foods, 7.9% (8.4%); chocolate and confectionery, 8.8% (8.1%); catering and hotel operations, 1.8% (3%); other beverages, 3.1% (2.9%); refrigerated foods, 3.1% (3%); pharmaceuticals, dermatological products and cosmetics, 2.6% (2.4%).

Geographically, the company's sales were divided as follows: Europe, 37.3% (previous year 40.2%); North America, 24.1% (20.9%); Asia, 15% (15%); Latin America and Caribbean, 16.9% (15%); Africa, 4.3% (5.7%); Oceania, 2.4% (2.2%).

At the end of 1984 the group employed 137,950 people (140,400 in the previous year), 6,849 or 5% of them in Switzerland.

Outlook

The programme of reorganisation of the last few years and considerable investments are now bearing fruit: the profit margin is increasing markedly. The strong international position, after a phase of acquisitory expansion, should now consolidate. In this period of internal growth, rentability will develop favourably. Nestlé will market new products of high quality, which should have a positive impact on earnings growth and produce a stable sales increase in the coming years. For 1985 it may be assumed that an increase in net profit of about 14% p.a. will be maintained. The dynamic management will also follow a flexible dividend policy, and further dividend increases are therefore expected. This high-quality stock (bearer and registered) should be bought for the medium and long term.

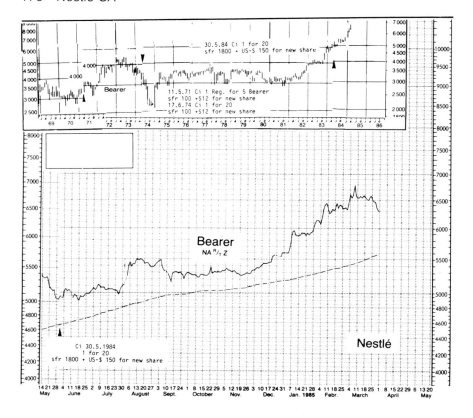

Price range and dividend of bearer shares (adjusted) in SFr

		1984	1983	1982	1981	1980
Bearer shares	H	5,505	1,884	3,752	3,178	3,449
	L	4,520	3,694	2,965	2,741	2,910
Dividend: Nestlé	(SFr)	115.00	109.00	96.00	85.00	75.00
Unilac	($)	8.00	8.00	8.00	8.00	7.00
Total	(SFr)	135.00	127.00	112.50	100.66	89.23

Stock exchange listings: paired Nestlé/Unilac bearer and registered shares: Zurich, Geneva, Basle,
Berne, Lausanne, St Gall; bearer shares only: Amsterdam, Düsseldorf, Frankfurt, Paris and Vienna

Stockholders' equity at 31 December 1984: SFr 12,989 million

	SFr par.	SFr mill.
1,073,000 bearer shares	100	107.3
2,227,000 registered shares with restricted transferability	100	222.7
150,000 participation certificates	20	3.0

Each Nestlé share has one share of
Unilac, inc. common stock of the same
number attached. The two shares may not
be legally separated
Unilac, Inc: $40 million

3,300,000 shares of common stock	$ 12 ⎫	
5,400 founders' shares	$100 ⎬	100.0
Open reserves incl. profit carry-forward		12,555

Market value at 28 December 1984: SFr 13,494 million

Consolidated balance sheet data in million SFr	1984	1983	1982	1981	1980
Current assets: liquid funds	6,168	5,238	4,073	3,519	2,982
others	10,296	8,630	8,758	8,554	9,400
Fixed assets	8,010	6,621	6,127	5,707	5,719
Liabilities: short-term	7,651	6,092	5,802	6,127	6,821
medium and long-term	583	608	495	526	642
Long-term provisions	2,893	2,331	2,235	1,950	1,728
Shareholders' equity	12,989	11,120	10,081	8,962	8,660
Selected group data in million SFr					
Sales	31,141	27,943	27,664	27,734	24,479
Sales per employee (SFr)	225,741	199,024	195,490	190,193	160,350
New capital expenditure	1,339	1,122	1,062	1,111	1,208
Cash flow	2,491	2,171	1,984	1,875	1,446
Depreciation on plant and equipment	1,004	910	886	911	763
Net earnings	1,487	1,261	1,098	964	683

Board of Directors: Dr Dr h.c. P. R. Jolles, Chairman*; Dr H. R. Schwarzenbach, Vice-Chairman*; H. Maucher, Managing Director*; Dr C. L. Angst; A. Baltensweiler; A. Bettencourt; F. Dalle*; Prof. Dr J. Freymond; Dr Dr h.c. A. Fürer; F. Gerber; E. A. Giorgis; R. E. Gut; B. de Kalbermatten; Prof. Dr P. Lalive; Dr V. Mortes Alfonso; Dr Dr h.c. E. Stopper; H. Strasser; Dr A. E. Sulzer; Ph. de Weck*
* Member of Committee of the Board

Appendix 2 Agreement on the observance of care by the banks in accepting funds and on the practice of banking secrecy (ACB)

Agreement

on the observance of care by the banks in accepting funds and on the practice of banking secrecy (ACB)

with executive regulations
of the Swiss National Bank, Zurich,
and the Swiss Bankers' Association, Basle,

of 1st July, 1982

(Translation)

Introduction

Art. 1 Preamble

- In their endeavour, by careful examination of the bank customer's identity, to prevent assets being invested in the Swiss banking system anonymously,

- in their effort to maintain Switzerland's good reputation as a financial centre and to combat economic criminality,

- with the intent of confirming, defining and laying down in a binding way the established rules of good conduct in bank management,

the signatory banks and the Swiss Bankers' Association conclude the present agreement with the Swiss National Bank.

1 The agreement is valid for all the signatory banks and their branches domiciled in Switzerland, but not their foreign branches, representative offices and subsidiary companies (but see point 13).

2 The agreement in no way changes the banks' obligation to observe banking secrecy. It cannot and is not intended to

- incorporate foreign currency, fiscal or other economic regulations into Swiss law and declare them to be applicable to the Swiss banks (unless this is already the case under existing international treaties and Swiss law);

- affect the current legal practice in the field of international law;

- change existing civil law relationship between the bank and the customer.

Swiss legislation and judicial practice as well as the treaties Switzerland has concluded with other countries continue to represent the guiding principle for the banks in Switzerland.

3 The agreement lays down in a binding way the valid rules of good conduct in bank management according to the code of professional ethics; it is not intended to impede normal banking business.

3

Art. 2   Forbidden acts

Acts contrary to this agreement are:

a)   the opening and maintaining of accounts and deposits without having ascertained the identity of the entitled party (Art. 3–6);

b)   the renting of safe-deposit boxes without having observed the necessary care (Art. 7);

c)   the active aiding and abetting of capital flight, tax evasion and so forth (Art. 8 and 9).

4   The agreement is intended to ensure the careful clarification of a bank customer's identity and to permit thereby the efficient accomplishment of the bank's obligation to testify and furnish information, as provided for in federal and cantonal stipulations.

5   Acts contrary to the agreement are subject to the sanctions in Art. 13.

6   The enumeration of acts contrary to this agreement is exhaustive. The definition of such acts is solely given in the articles mentioned between brackets in Art. 2 subsections a–c. Art. 2 cannot be interpreted independently.

4

A   Observance of care in accepting funds

Art. 3   Ascertaining of the entitled party

[1] **The banks undertake not to open bank accounts or securities deposits nor to effect fiduciary investments unless they have ascertained with such care as can be reasonably expected in the circumstances the identity of the person entitled to the funds to be credited or to be invested.**

[2] **When opening an account or deposit as by concluding a fiduciary operation the identity of the contracting party as well as of the beneficial owner is to be established in accordance with the executive regulations (points 10–27).**

[3] **In the case of transactions for large amounts at bank counters, the identity of the contracting party is to be examined.**

I. Scope of application

7   The obligation to check identity is valid, under reserve of point 18, for the opening of accounts, savings books and deposits of any kind whatsoever, irrespective of whether they are maintained under the name of the customer or under a number.

8   Nor are bearer savings books to be opened without the checking of identity. In the case of the savings book not being entrusted to the bank for safekeeping, the bank is not in a position and consequently not under obligation to trace the changes in the book's bearer so as to know the entitled party.

9   In the case of cash transactions at bank counters (exchange, purchase and sale of precious metals, cash subscriptions to bank issued medium-term notes and bonds, cashing cheques, etc.), the obligation to check the identity of the contracting party applies to transactions exceeding Sfr. 500,000.

5

II. Identification of the contracting party

A. Individuals

a) domiciled in Switzerland

10 In the case of personal appearance of the customer, the bank checks the identity of the contracting party when domiciled in Switzerland by means of an official document (passport, identity card, driving licence, etc.). Residents of Switzerland who are personally known to the bank are not required to furnish an identity document.

11 In the case of the customer relationship being initiated by correspondence, the bank checks the identity of the contracting party residing in Switzerland by obtaining confirmation as to the address of the domicile by way of postal delivery or by some other equally valid method.

b) not domiciled in Switzerland

12 In the case of personal appearance of the customer, the bank checks the identity of the contracting party having no fixed domicile or being domiciled abroad by means of an official identity document. The identity can also be ascertained by the customer's furnishing a written recommendation:

– from a foreign branch, representative office or subsidiary company of the bank,

– from a trustworthy customer personally well-known to the bank,

– from a bank listed in a recognized publication of banks (Banker's Almanac and Year Book, The Banker's World Directory, Polk's World Bank Directory).

13 The bank may accept recommendations from its foreign branches, representative offices and subsidiary companies provided it has instructed them to check the identity of persons they recommend in accordance with the present agreement.

14 Where the customer relationship is initiated by correspondence, the bank requests certification of the foreign contracting party's signature from a bank, in accordance with point 12, or from a

6

trustworthy customer personally well-known to it. Confirmation of the address of domicile is to be obtained by postal delivery or by some other equally valid method.

B. Legal entities and companies

a)   registered in Switzerland

15   The bank ascertains whether the firm name of the contracting party is published in the bulletin of the Registry of Commerce ('Schweizerisches Handelsamtblatt/Feuille officielle suisse du commerce') or listed in the Swiss Commercial Directory ('Schweizerisches Ragionenbuch/Annuaire suisse du Registre du commerce'); otherwise identity must be ascertained by means of an extract from the Commercial Register ('Handelsregister/Registre du commerce').

16   The identity of legal entities not listed in the Commercial Register (associations, foundations) is to be examined by obtaining confirmation of the address indicated by the entity by way of postal delivery or some other equally valid method.

b)   registered abroad

17   Identity checking of such a contracting party is to be effected by way of an extract from a commercial register or from some other equally valid document (e.g. certificate of incorporation).

C. Exceptions applicable to customers domiciled in Switzerland

18   The identity of a contracting party domiciled or registered in Switzerland need not to be checked when the customer wishes to open

a)   a salary account,

b)   a savings book or savings account, a deposit book or deposit account, an investment book or investment account, designated by name and with an initial sum of less than Sfr. 50,000,

c)   an account for paying in share capital at a cantonal consignment office with a view to founding or increasing the capital of a joint stock company.

7

The exception under point a) is also valid for staff resident abroad of an employer domiciled or registered in Switzerland, provided the latter requests the opening of accounts for his employees collectively.

III. Ascertaining the identity of the beneficial owner

19   The identity of the beneficial owner of the assets to be deposited is to be ascertained at the time of opening the account or deposit.

20   All care which can be reasonably expected under the circumstances must be exercised in identifying the beneficial owner. The bank may assume that the contracting party and the beneficial owner are identical. This can no longer be assumed, however, if unusual observations are made (see points 23 and 28–32).

A. Individuals

21   If the contracting party declares himself to be acting on behalf of a third party, the bank has to obtain the third party's full name, domicile and country of domicile.

B. Legal entities and companies

22   If the contracting party acts for the account of a legal entity or company, the bank registers the firm name, the domicile and country of domicile.

IV. Cases of doubt

23   If any doubts arise, the procedure according to Art. 4 is to be followed, particularly when the details as to identity appear to be doubtful or when there are indications which give doubt as to the contracting party's being identical with the beneficial owner (see points 28–32).

24   Reserve is made for the special stipulations as to domiciliary companies and persons sworn to professional secrecy (Art. 5 and 6, points 33–39 and 40–47).

8

V. Surveillance

25   The bank has to ensure that its internal control department and the auditing firm required by the Federal Law on Banks and Savings Banks can check as to the identification procedure being carried out.

26   Appropriate record is to be kept of the name, christian name, address and country of domicile of the contracting party as well as of the means used to establish identitiy. Any documents obtained in the case of legal entities are to be preserved.

27   The details specified in points 21 and 22 as to the identity of the beneficial owner or of the individuals controlling a domiciliary company must be available.

Art. 4   **Procedure in cases of doubt**

[1] In cases of doubt, when opening accounts or deposits, the banks require a written declaration from the customer as to whether he is acting for his own account or for account of a third party and in the latter case, for whose account.

[2] For this purpose the banks use form A, which is an integral part of this agreement.

28   In the case of doubts arising as to whether the contracting party is identical with the beneficial owner, form A 'Declaration on opening an account or deposit' is to be presented for signature.

29   For example, doubt is justified in the following cases:

a)   The opening of an account or deposit is requested by a person domiciled in Switzerland. At the same time a power of attorney is given to a person not recognizable as being closely enough related to the account holder (e.g. to a foreigner), or if any other unusual aspects arise.

b)   The opening of an account or a deposit is requested by a person domiciled in Switzerland whose financial situation is known to the bank. The assets handed over or to be remitted are beyond the limits of the customer's financial situation.

9

c)   The opening of an account or a deposit is requested by a person domiciled abroad, who has been introduced to the bank (see points 12 and 13). At the same time a power of attorney is given to a person who is not recognizable as being in a sufficiently close relationship to the account holder.

d)   The opening of an account or a deposit is requested by a person domiciled abroad, who has been introduced to the bank (see points 12 and 13) and whose financial situation is known to the bank. The assets handed over or to be remitted are beyond his financial situation.

e)   The opening of an account or a deposit is requested by a person domiciled abroad who has not been recommended to the bank. The discussion the bank must have with the customer at the time of opening the account or deposit brings to light unusual aspects.

f)   The opening of an account or a deposit is requested by a person domiciled abroad by way of correspondence, accompanied by an attestation of the signature (see point 14), but who is not personally known to the bank.

30   Where serious doubt remains as to the accuracy of the customer's written declaration, which cannot be eliminated by further clarification, the bank declines the request for the opening of the account or deposit.

31   Form A, which is to be utilized in accordance with Art. 4, para. 2, is annexed to this agreement and can be obtained from the Swiss Bankers' Association in Basle. It is available in German, French, Italian and English.

32   The banks are at liberty to produce their own forms, adapted for their own particular needs. However, such forms must contain the full text of the sample form and in particular, the indication as to the importance of banking secrecy and the bank's obligation to furnish information is not to be given in smaller or weaker print than the rest of the text.

Art. 5   Procedure in the case of domiciliary companies

¹ The following documents are to be requested from domestic and foreign domiciliary companies:

10

a)   an extract from the Commercial Register or a similarly valid credential,

b)   the declaration of the competent organ on form A as to the controlling individuals.

² Considered as domiciliary companies within the meaning of this agreement are all companies, establishments, foundations, trusts etc., which do not exercise activity in Switzerland by trading, manufacturing or in any other form of commercially managed business.

³ The utilization of form A can be waived where the affiliation of a domiciliary company to a group or where the controlling interests and the identity of the controlling individuals are known to the bank.

I. Domiciliary company

33   Domestic and foreign enterprises are considered as domiciliary companies, irrespective of their purpose, function and registered office, when

a)   no business premises of their own exist (domiciled with a solicitor, with a fiduciary company, with a bank, etc.) or

b)   no staff of their own, employed exclusively by them or when such own staff is employed solely in administrative work (book-keeping, correspondence on instructions from the persons or companies controlling the domiciliary company).

34   Domestic companies with an operation of their own, where the Board of Directors and Management are identical (e.g. companies managed by a sole person), are not considered as domiciliary companies within the meaning of this agreement.

II. Controlling interests

35   A company is controlled by that person or group of persons who disposes directly or indirectly of more than half of the company's capital or the voting rights or who exercises decisive influence on it in some other recognizable way.

36   In the case of companies which are controlled by legal entities, the bank must ascertain the identity of the individuals controlling

11

the legal entity by having form A completed by the contracting party. Point 30 is applicable.

37 In cases where, in accordance with Art. 5, para. 3, form A need not be to presented, points 21, 22, 25 and 26 are to be applied accordingly.

III. Ascertaining the identity of the controlling individuals

38 The identity of individuals controlling domiciliary companies is to be ascertained and recorded in accordance with point 21.

39 Where changes in the authorized signatures for domiciliary companies occur in business with the bank, the latter has to repeat the procedure laid down in Art. 5, para. 1. Where clarification as to the controlling individuals is not obtainable, Art. 11 is applicable.

Art. 6   Persons bound by professional secrecy

¹ Where a customer acts through a person domiciled or with registered office in Switzerland, who is bound by a legally protected professional secrecy, or who is a member of an association affiliated to the 'Schweizerische Treuhand- und Revisionskammer/Chambre suisse des Sociétés fiduciaires et des Experts-comptables', the bank must obtain from such a person on form B a written declaration to the effect that the beneficial owner is known to him and that no forbidden transaction within the meaning of this agreement is being concluded.

² A written declaration is waived in the case of accounts and deposits of domestic and foreign banks.

I. Privileged professions

40 Particularly lawyers and notaries are bound in Switzerland by professional secrecy which is protected by law (Art. 321, point 1 of the Swiss Criminal Code).

12

41 Analogously treated are trustees and portfolio managers who are members of an association affiliated to the 'Schweizerische Treuhand- und Revisionskammer/Chambre suisse des Sociétés fiduciaires et des Experts-comptables'.

42 The Swiss Bankers' Association places at the banks' disposal periodically lists of these members. The banks must check as to whether the trustee or portfolio manager is a member.

43 In the case of lawyers, notaries, trustees and portfolio managers with domicile or registered office abroad form A is to be used with a view to ascertaining the beneficial owner.

II. Signing the declaration

44 Form B, which is to be utilized in accordance with Art. 6, para. 1, constitutes an integral part of the agreement and can be obtained from the Swiss Bankers' Association in Basle. It is available in German, French, Italian and English.

Any form produced by the banks for their special needs must contain the full text of the sample form (see Annex) and must not show the confirmation of the person bound by professional secrecy in smaller or weaker print than the rest of the text.

45 Where the party bound by professional secrecy is a legal entity or a company, form B is to be signed in the name of the entity or company.

46 The party bound by professional secrecy in accordance with Art. 6, para. 1 can avail himself of the exception ruling irrespective of whether he is acting in the capacity of mandatary or as organ of a legal entity or company.

Where the party bound by professional secrecy is an employee or member of a managing organ of a bank, he cannot avail himself of the exception ruling under Art. 6, para. 1 vis-à-vis the bank, but has to confirm in each case on form A on whose behalf he is acting; in the case of domiciliary companies, he has also to indicate the controlling individuals.

13

III. Exception for banks

47   No declaration is to be remitted for accounts and deposits belonging to banks. Domestic banks are those subject to the Federal Law on Banks and Savings Banks of 8th November, 1934/11th March, 1971. Institutions whose registered office is abroad are to be considered as banks if they qualify as such under the laws of their country of domicile.

IV. Identification of the person bound by professional secrecy

48   The identity of persons who claim to be bound by professional secrecy is to be ascertained in accordance with points 10–18; points 25 and 26 are to be applied accordingly.

14

B   Observance of care in renting safe-deposit boxes

Art. 7   Identity checking and trustworthiness

¹ When a safe-deposit box is rented, the identity of the renter is to be ascertained. The procedure is in accordance with points 10–18.

² The banks undertake to rent safe-deposit boxes only to persons whose trustworthiness gives no cause for doubt after having observed all care which can be reasonably expected under the circumstances.

49   Art. 7 is applicable to persons and companies in Switzerland and abroad.

50   The trustworthiness of the renter can be considered as proved, e.g. when:

a) he already maintains a business relationship with the bank;

b) he is known personally to an employee or a member of a managing organ of the bank;

c) he is introduced by a customer or another bank;

d) no firm indication exists of the safe-deposit box being rented for illegal purposes.

15

C   Prohibition of actively aiding and abetting capital flight, tax evasion and similar acts

Art. 8   Capital flight

[1] **The banks undertake not to actively assist in the transfer of capital from countries whose legislation restricts the investment of funds abroad.**

[2] **The following are considered as active assistance:**

a)   arrangements to receive customers abroad outside the offices of the bank with a view to accepting funds;

b)   participation in the organisation of compensation transactions abroad when it is known to the bank or when it should know from the circumstances in general that the compensation serves the purpose of capital flight;

c)   active cooperation with persons and companies organizing capital flight or giving assistance for such, by

–   remitting orders,

–   promising commission,

–   maintaining their accounts, when such persons and companies are domiciled or have registered office in Switzerland and when it is known to the bank that they use their accounts professionally for the purpose of assisting capital flight;

d)   referring customers to the persons and companies indicated under c).

51   Capital flight is a not authorized transfer of capital in the form of foreign currency, banknotes or securities from a country prohibiting or restricting such transfers abroad by its residents.

52   Art. 8 is not applicable to transfers of capital from Switzerland abroad.

16

53 Visiting customers abroad is permitted provided the bank's representative neither accepts funds, the transfer of which is forbidden, nor gives advice as to the illegal transfer of capital nor participates in compensation transactions.

54 Otherwise, assets may be accepted from foreign customers in Switzerland.

Art. 9   Tax evasion and similar acts

The banks do not support attempts of their customers to deceive authorities in Switzerland or abroad, in particular tax authorities, either by way of incomplete or in any other way misleading attestations.

55 It is forbidden to remit incomplete or in any other way misleading attestations to customers themselves or on their request directly to authorities in Switzerland or abroad.

Particularly the following are considered as authorities: tax authorities, custom offices, monetary and bank supervisory authorities.

56 The prohibition covers primarily special attestations to authorities at the customer's request.

The bank is not permitted to alter routine advices such as account and deposit statements, credit and debit advices, settlement notes for foreign exchange transactions, coupon and stock exchange transactions for the purpose of deception.

57 Attestations are incomplete when relevant facts are omitted with a view to deceiving authorities, such as the bank's omitting on the customer's request certain items from a special confirmation or from a statement of account or deposit.

It is not necessary to indicate on statements of account or deposit that other accounts or deposits are maintained for the same customer.

58 Attestations are misleading when, with a view to deceiving authorities, facts are presented contrary to the truth, e.g. by

17

a)   false dating, false amounts, fictive rates or by establishing credit or debit advices bearing false indications about the titulary of the account;

b)   attestation as to fictive claims or debts (irrespective of whether the attestation corresponds to the ledgers of the bank or not).

18

D Other provisions

Art. 10 **Numbered accounts and numbered deposits**

The prescriptions of the present agreement apply without restriction to accounts and deposits maintained under numbers or passwords.

59 Confirmations as to the total business relationship with a customer are to include accounts and deposits maintained under numbers or passwords, also fiduciary accounts and deposits.

Art. 11 **Dissolution of business relations**

The banks undertake to break off a relationship with a customer when in the course of business with him suspicion arises as to the details on the beneficial owner of the funds credited or invested or on the renter of a safe-deposit box being inexact.

60 The current relationship is to be terminated as quickly as is possible without violating the contract with the customer, if the bank discovers that the customer on opening the account or deposit intentionally made false statements as to the beneficial owner.

61 If the bank is prevented from reaching the customer owing to mailing instructions, it can postpone, in the case of point 60, the dissolution of the relationship to the next visit of the customer or to the next occasion of mailing correspondence.

Art. 12 **Control by the auditing firms**

[1] In signing this agreement the banks instruct and authorize their auditing firms required by the Federal Law on Banks and Savings Banks to check as to the observance of the agreement at the time of their regular auditing by way of random tests and to report offences or justified suspicion of offences to the Arbitration Committee as laid down in Art. 13, as well as to the Federal Banking Commission.

19

² The National Bank will make known to the authorized auditing firms the text of this agreement as well as a list of the signatories and thus their mandate.

Art. 13 Arbitration Committee, sanctions

¹ An Arbitration Committee is set up, with seat in Berne, for the enquiry and punishment of violations to this agreement. The National Bank and the Swiss Bankers' Association delegate two members each to the Arbitration Committee which is chaired by a federal judge, nominated unanimously by the members. The Committee nominates a secretary.

² The National Bank and the Swiss Bankers' Association designate jointly a person entrusted with the investigation. This investigator proposes to the Arbitration Committee either to open proceedings and to impose a conventional fine or to suspend the enquiry. When requesting information from a bank, he informs the latter of the capacity in which it is being implicated in the investigation.

³ The Arbitration Committee can sentence a bank convicted of an offence against the agreement to a conventional fine of up to ten million Swiss francs. In fixing the conventional fine due regard is to be paid to the gravity of the breach of the agreement, the degree of the bank's fault and its financial situation. The Arbitration Committee donates the conventional fine to a charitable institution.

⁴ The Arbitration Committee arranges the procedure; Art. 36–65 of the Federal Law of 4th December, 1947 on the Federal Rules of Civil Procedure and Art. 22–26 of the Federal Law of 16th December, 1943 on the Organisation of the Federal Administration of Justice are to be applied accordingly.

⁵ As mandataries of the bank in the sense of Art. 47, para. 1 of the Federal Banking Law, the members of the Arbitration Committee, the secretary as well as the person charged with the investigation are to observe strict secrecy as to the facts which become known to them in

20

the course of the proceedings. **In signing the agreement the banks waive the possibility of invoking banking secrecy as regards their customers vis-à-vis the Arbitration Committee or the person entrusted with the investigation.**

⁶ The Arbitration Committee informs the Federal Banking Commission of its decisions to enable them to examine the question as to whether the persons entrusted with the administration and management of the bank concerned still give 'warranty for an irreproachable conduct of business' in the sense of Art. 3, para. 2, lit. c of the Banking Law.

62   The representatives of the Swiss National Bank in the Arbitration Committee must be members of the Governing Board or their deputies, those of the Swiss Bankers' Association members of the Board of Directors or the Management.

63   Periodically the Arbitration Committee gives the banks an insight into its jurisprudence under due observance of banking and business secrecy.

Art. 14   Entry into force

¹ This agreement enters into force on 1st October, 1982 and is valid for a fixed period of five years.

² Subsequently it is valid for further periods of one year unless denounced by the Swiss Bankers' Association or the National Bank under observance of three months' notice.

³ Each signatory bank has the right to denounce the agreement under observance of three months' notice as per the end of the contract year, for the first time as per 30th September, 1987.

⁴The signatory banks authorize the Board of Directors of the Swiss Bankers' Association, in cooperation with the National Bank, to make any modifications and definitions to the agreement which may prove necessary in the light of experience gained.

21

64   The authorization in Art. 14, para. 4 does not include the competence of the Swiss Bankers' Association to alter the substance of the agreement to the disadvantage of the signatory banks.

65   Neither the Swiss Bankers' Association nor the National Bank is to give an authentic interpretation of the agreement. The Swiss National Bank and the Swiss Bankers' Association are jointly competent for the interpretation.

22

Annex

Declaration on opening an account or deposit

(Form A according to Art. 4 and 5 ACB)

The undersigned hereby declares:

☐ that he is acting for his own account,

☐ that he is acting for the account of the following person(s):

Name/Company   Domicile, Country

_____

☐ that the domiciliary company he is representing is controlled by the following individual(s):

Name(s)   Christian name(s)   Place of residence, Country

_____

(cross where applicable)

The undersigned is aware of the fact that banking secrecy, protected in accordance with Art. 47 of the Federal Law on Banks and Savings Banks of 8th November, 1934/11th March, 1971, is not unrestricted: The organs, employees and mandataries of the bank are liable to give evidence and information vis-a-vis the authorities where federal and cantonal stipulations require their so doing (e.g. in criminal proceedings). This obligation also exists vis-à-vis foreign authorities insofar as the Swiss Confederation grants judicial assistance to the country in question.
The undersigned is also aware of the fact that the establishment of accounts and deposits maintained under numbers or passwords is a purely internal measure of the bank affecting in no way its obligation vis-à-vis the authorities to testify or to furnish information.

_____
Name   Christian name

_____
Address of residence

_____
Place, date   Signature

**Declaration on the opening of an account or a deposit
by a Swiss national bound by professional secrecy**

(Form B according to Art. 6 ACB)

The undersigned hereby declares:

☐ that he is bound by a legally protected professional secrecy (Art. 321, point 1 of the Swiss Criminal Code),

☐ that he is a member of an association affiliated to the 'Schweizerische Treuhand- und Revisionskammer/Chambre suisse des Sociétés fiduciaires et des Experts-comptables'.

(cross where applicable)

In this capacity he confirms that the beneficial owner of the assets to be deposited with the bank is known to him personally and that by observing all the care which can be reasonably expected under the circumstances, no fact is known to him which gives indication of banking secrecy being availed of abusively by the entitled party and in particular of criminal acquisition of the assets in question.

_____   _____
Name   Christian name

_____
Address of residence or business address

_____   _____
Place, date   Signature

Bibliography

Bauer, H.   *Die Basler Börse 1876–1976*, Basle, 1976.

Bodmer, D., Kernen, J-P. and Schönle, H.   *Le secret bancaire suisse*, 1982.

Bodmer, D., Kleiner, B. and Lutz, B.   *Kommentar zum Schweizerischen Bankengesetzt*, 1976/82.

Boemle, M.   *Wertpapiere des Zahlungs- und Kreditverkehrs sowie der Kapitalanlage*, Zurich, 1983.

Esslen, G.   *How to Buy Foreign Stocks*, London 1972.

Fama, E. F.   'Stock Returns, Real Activity, Inflation, and Money', *The American Economic Review*, September 1981.

Feldstein, M.   'Inflation and the Stock Market', *The American Economic Review*, December 1980.

Firth, M.   *The Valuation of Shares and the Efficient-Markets Theory*, London, 1977.

Flannery, M. J. and James, Chr. M.   'The Effects of Interest Rate Changes on the Common Stock Returns of Financial Institutions', *The Journal of Finance*, September 1984.

Forstmoser, P. and Meier-Hayoz, A.   *Einführung in das schweizerische Aktienrecht*, 1980.

Galli, A.   'Switzerland: Equity Markets', in: George, A. M. and Giddy, I. H. (eds.), *International Financial Handbook*, New York, 1983.

Gultekin, N. B.   'Stock Market Returns and Inflation Forecasts', *The Journal of Finance*, June 1983.

Hausmann, A.   *Vom Aktienwesen und vom Aktienrecht*.

Iklé, M.   *Die Schweiz als internationaler Bank- und Finanzplatz*, Zurich, 1970.

Lehmann, C.   *Die geschichtliche Entwicklung des Aktienrechts bis zum Code de Commerce*, Berlin, 1895.

Lerch, H.   *Aktienkursindizes und Konjunkturverlauf*, Berne, 1971.

Meier, H. B.   *Swiss Capital Markets*, Euromoney Publ., London, 1983.

Nobel, P.   *Einführung in das Schweizerische Aktienrecht*, Berne, 1980.

Pearce, D. K.   'Stock Prices and the Economy', *Federal Reserve Bank of Kansas City Economic Review*, November 1983.

Pearce, D. K.   'An Empirical Analysis of Expected Stock Price Movements', *Journal of Money, Credit and Banking*, August 1984.

Rutz, A.   'Der Kurs schweizerischer Aktien im letzten Jahrzehnt: Regressions-technische Bestimmung möglicher Einflussgrössen', *Schweiz. Zeitschrift für Volkswirtschaft und Statistik*, Juli 1973.

Rutz, A. and Zehnder, R.   'Eine spektraltechnische Schätzung zum Kursverlauf der Schweizer Aktien', University of Basle, Discussion Paper 14, 1977.

Santoni, G. J.   'Interest Rate Risk and the Stock Prices of Financial Institutions', *Federal Reserve Bank of St. Louis Review*, August/September 1984.

Schiltknecht, K.   *Beurteilung der Gentlemen's Agreements und Konjunkturbeschlüsse der Jahre 1954–1966*, Zurich, 1970.

Shiller, R. J.   'Theories of aggregate stock price movements', *The Journal of Portfolio Management*, 1984.

Von Steiger, F.   *Das Recht der Aktiengesellschaft in der Schweiz*, 1970.

Institutional publications

Crédit Suisse   *Schweizer Börsenplätze*.

HandelsBank NW   *Swiss Banking Secrecy, Science and Fiction*, Zurich, 1982.

Periodical publications of the Swiss stock exchanges   (Basle, Berne, Geneva, Lausanne, Lucerne, Neuchâtel, St Gall, Zurich).

Union Bank of Switzerland   *Swiss Stock Guide 1983*.

Swiss National Bank   Monthly Bulletin.

Botschaft des Schweiz. Bundesrates über die Revision des Aktienrechts, vom 23. Februar 1983.

European Stock Exchange Handbook, London, 1973.

Handbuch des Geld-, Bank- und Börsenwesens der Schweiz, Thun, 1977.

Index